Best
Of The Best
1995
A Celebration of
the Finest In Dog Writing

Edited by
September B. Morn

Pawprince Press
Marblemount, WA U.S.A.

Dedicated To

The Dogs We Love To Write About

With Many Thanks To

The Winning Writers, Photographers and Artists

Whose Work Fills These Pages

and

Their Editors and Publishers

For Graciously Allowing
The Dog Writers Association of America
Permission to Preserve and Publish These Collected Works

Best Of The Best 1995

A Celebraton of the Finest In Dog Writing

ISBN 0-9633884-9-5

Published by
Pawprince Press
815 Clark Road
Marblemount, WA 98267

Printed by Gorham Printing — Rochester, WA 98579

From the President of
Dog Writers Association of America

As the communication arts become a major factor in our various nations' progress and the wide involvement with dogs continues to grow, membership in the Dog Writers becomes more and more significant. Over the years this organization has brought together almost all of those who write, publish, or present news, information, and literature about dogs.

DWAA encourages its members to strive for accuracy and integrity in their writing efforts; to exchange views and information; and to develop good fellowship. The very existence of DWAA has established dog writing as a respected genre. Since its formation in 1935, the dog writers have been everywhere, telling the dog story. The century is getting ready to turn and bring with it an exciting period for everyone in dogs. In the decades ahead we have the potential for becoming an even greater force than we are now.

This book, *The Best of the Best*, is a splendid representation of who we are, what we do, and where we are heading. It is more than a sampling of our work, it is more than a sampling of our *best* work. This book is tangible evidence of our existence as an important body of writers and communicators of all things canine.

We have been brought together in a community of interests. As you turn these pages you will discover the best work of the year and how it offers the greater world around us much that is valuable and enjoyable. Our annual writing competition is the jewel in the crown of DWAA because it reaches out to everyone with something to say about dogs whether they are members or not. Here is what they accomplished in 1995. *The Best of the Best* is our offering to anyone interested in just how well it can be done.

It is to be hoped that this volume will bring pleasure and knowledge to its readers and, most important of all, will inspire all those who take on the assignment.

Mordecai Siegal
July 1996

It is my great pleasure to commend our hard-working, caring members who have made this book possible. To wit: September Morn, Ed and Toni Eames, and Jan Mahood.

Report from the Writing Competition Chair

As I come to the end of my first year as the DWAA Writing Competition Chair, I am pleased to say that it has been quite a pleasure for me, as well as an honor, to commandeer the competition. How else could I feel when heading up a competition that in celebrating the writing on one of my favorite subjects, has proven to be a testament both to the organization and to the craft of dog writing at large?

The numbers and the enthusiasm that marked the 1995 competition speak for themselves. When all was said and done, we received almost 700 entries, and hundreds more for the corporate-sponsored special awards. The few that emerged the winners are proudly represented in this volume.

In celebrating these winning entries, a special note of recognition must also be offered to the judges who made those victories happen. The fruits of their diligent efforts are found on these pages, each representing a great deal of voluntary time and effort on the part of its category's judges. In reviewing the material for writing excellence as well as accuracy, and, where appropriate, emotional appeal, the judges exhibited their own fine evaluation skills that lend this competition so much credibility. Each winner may thus revel in his or her victory, knowing that to be nominated, let alone to win, is indeed a profound accomplishment.

From watching the entries pour in and reveling in what wonderful work was produced this year; to speaking with hundreds of writers, editors, photographers, artists and publishers during the past months, chairing this competition has shown me even more clearly what a grand accomplishment it is to be published for writing on a subject about which one is so passionate. All participants, those whose works appear on the pages of this anthology, and those who will continue to strive for that, are to be congratulated.

Betsy Sikora Siino
DWAA Writing Competition Chair

A Word from the Editor...

It has been my distinct pleasure to compile this anthology of the winning entries in each category of the Dog Writers Association of America annual writing competition. I love dogs and also good writing, so this opportunity to read and savor all the winners has been a delight and a dream come true. The breadth, depth, and diversity of views expressed in these works tells so much about the world of dogs today. In years to come we'll look back at these writings as a slice of the history of our civilization.

My thanks to the contest winners and the Dog Writers Association of America for allowing this opportunity to place together these fine works, representing so much talent and energy. May all who hold this book enjoy reading it as much as I have enjoyed compiling it.

September B. Morn
Editor of *Best Of The Best - 1995*

1995 DWAA COMPETITION AWARD WINNERS

Category I

NEWSPAPERS

Category I-A-1 — Column (more than 150,000 circulation)

YOUR PET
by Gina Spadafori

(THE SACRAMENTO BEE)

Room Enough for All We Love

When I was a schoolgirl, I was troubled by a question of a theological bent. I decided to take it up with someone I figured was better connected, the stone-faced and particularly humorless nun who served as my teacher.

I stayed a few minutes into recess, so pressing was the matter, hovering over her desk as she organized papers and no doubt thought of new ways to torture us with multiplication tables.

"Sister?" I said at last, and she glanced up, slightly annoyed.

"Yes?" she said. "What is it?"

"Sister," I said. "I have a question."

She nodded, waiting, secure in her ability to impart absolute knowledge on all things in heaven and earth. "Let's have it, then."

"Sister," I said. "Do pets go to heaven?"

"Of course not!" she sputtered. "Animals don't have souls." And she turned back to her work, considering the subject closed.

I have thought about

> "Sister," I said.
> "Do pets go to
> heaven?"
> "Of course not!"
> she sputtered.
> "Animals don't
> have souls."

her answer off and on for close to two decades, and although I am far from a theologian, I think she was wrong. And I think my grandmother would agree with me.

My grandmother died a few days ago, and my last conversation with her, in her hospital room, was no different than so many others. We talked about my parents and my brothers. We talked about my job. And then,

as always, we talked about my dogs, Toni in particular.

Toni was always her favorite.

I was living with my grandmother, a short respite from college roommate hassles, when I brought Toni home, a leggy and awkward puppy, a little too shy for her own good. It is a measure of my grandmother's love for me that she not only took in me and my other dog, Lance, with hardly a moment's hesitation, but that she also allowed me to double the canine presence in her neat, quiet home.

I'm sure she regretted it in the early going. While Lance was well-nigh perfect, Toni and I were not. I was a little too messy, too noisy, too busy.

Toni was a normal puppy, putting puddles on the carpet and holes in the linoleum. But Gram let us stay.

And young Toni, who spent more time with my grandmother than with me in those days, became the company for her that I was not.

Toni was barely grown when I moved again, but the special

bond stayed between the two. I had only to say the word "Grandma" to have Toni dancing, ears up and ready to jump in the car for a visit. "The boys," first Lance, then Andy, loved Gram; for the fresh smells in her massive yard, for the

I have thought about her answer off and on for close to two decades, and although I am far from a theologian, I think she was wrong.

box of dog treats she always kept in the cupboard, but Toni never forgot who raised her, and was always as much Gram's dog as mine.

In a strange, sad way, the two started feeling the strains of old age at the same time, Gram after her 80th birthday, Toni after her 10th. Arthritis plagued and frustrated them; things that once were simple —like climbing stairs—became impossible without help.

After she moved to a place where she could be better cared for, Gram never saw Toni, but she never stopped asking about her. Last winter, when I almost lost Toni, I had decided the kind thing to do would have been to answer as always, "she's fine," rather than add another pain to my grandmother's life.

I never had to put that kind little charade into play. The night Gram died, I spoke to Toni in the way that pet lovers understand and others believe is proof of questionable sanity. I told her, and although she can no longer jump up, her big deer ears leapt every time I said "Grandma."

She got up then and struggled over to me, resting her head on my knee as I stroked her muzzle, nowadays as much white as golden.

I felt better, right away.

It won't be that much longer before Toni is gone, too, to be with my grandmother in that proverbial better place. I've been thinking these days about that, and that nun. And although I'm no closer now to being a theologian, I still think

she was wrong.

Heaven it could not be if all the beings and things we love aren't there.

It's often strange the thoughts that get us through difficult times.

Collar Your Dog, But Do It Right

When you consider that last year four of the nation's top five breeds were big dogs, it's no surprise that there are a lot of dog owners out there with sore arms and shoulders from trying to control their great beasties.

And no surprise, either, that in recent years more and more of these dogs—Labs and Rottweilers, German shepherds and goldens, more than 350,000 registered with the AKC in 1994 alone—have been spotted with strange-looking contraptions around their necks or on their muzzles, as these same owners try to shift the balance of power to their side.

While most owners will still opt for the more familiar buckled collar or slip collar— the latter better known as a "choke" collar— an increasing number are choosing pinch collars or head halters.

Of the two, the pinch collar—also called a prong collar—is probably the more controversial, based mostly on its appearance. The collar is made of metal links, with blunt prongs evenly spaced along its length. With a pull of the leash, the collar tightens, pressing the prongs into the dogs skin and getting his attention in a hurry.

There's no doubt the collar is effective when used correctly, especially on dogs such as Rotties, or others with well-muscled necks. But because of its appearance, the pinch collar often draws nasty looks and comments on its apparent cruelty.

In a way, this is unfortunate. For despite its looks, the pinch collar can be less cruel than the more popular choke collar, especially in the hands of ordinary pet lovers. That's because a properly fitted pinch collar cannot be tightened beyond the point of pushing the prongs against the skin, unlike the choke collar, which has no limits—the harder you or the dog pulls, the tighter it gets.

While trainers know the correct way to use the choke collar is to snap quickly and release, a trip to any public park will prove that most dog owners never grasp this concept. Their leashes are kept taut behind pulling dogs, and the collars are tight, so much so that their dogs are constantly gasping for air.

In time, both owner and dog come to believe this is the normal way of walking, and with the most powerful dogs, the choke collar—which is put on wrong half the time anyway—loses almost all its effectiveness as a tool for training and control.

The pinch collar is easier to put on properly, will not tighten beyond a predetermined point and gets the message across efficiently to even the strongest dog. All of which makes it a good choice for some dogs and some owners, as well as a more humane choice in the end than an incorrectly used choke collar.

The other choice for large dogs—a head halter—also has its image problems, because it looks to many people like a muzzle. And when someone sees a 90-pound German shepherd wearing what looks like a muzzle, all the discussion in the world isn't likely to convince that person the dog's not a vicious killer.

Which is certainly not good public relations at a time when many communities are considering ordinances banning "dangerous" breeds.

But, again, appearance can be deceiving. Head halters are touted by many as the humane alternative to pinch or choke collars, and rightfully so. They work on the principle of "where the head goes, the body follows" and may make handling a large dog possible for small adults or even children.

With a halter, a tug on the leash puts pressure around the muzzle, and the dog has no choice but to follow his head—which is following you.

Is a pinch collar or head halter—or for that matter, the more commonplace choke or buckle collar—right for your out-of-control dog? The best way to find out is to talk to a trainer or behaviorist, who can not only help you make the right choice but also show you the right way to use what you buy and train your dog to make outings the pleasant experience they should be.

Category I-A-2 — Column (less than 150,000 circ.)

YOUR ANIMAL COMPANIONS
by Mary Johnson
(WILSON NEWSPAPERS)

Help end animal overpopulation: don't breed and visit local shelters

When my favorite animal actor, Beau, died in August many people grieved. Bill Berloni, who rescued Beau from the New York City AS-PCA, and I were joined in our sorrow by hundreds of actors who had performed alongside Beau over the years.

Beau, in my humble opinion, was the best dog in the whole world. He was friendly, obedient, funny, and he had a great smile. He loved everyone and everything. Well, everything except horses; for some unaccountable reason, this quiet dog who had to be coaxed and cajoled into barking, yapped incessantly at horses. But that's another story. Dozens of little girls fell in love with Beau, and all of them

wanted a dog just like him to call their own. We always urged them to visit the animal shelters in their hometown. Shelters are teeming with dogs like Beau -- if you look long enough, you'll find one.

If we'd had Beau puppies, we never would have found Zappa, Cosmo, Cindy Lou, and Sparky.

Many people Beau and I met during our travels considered it a shame that Beau had been neutered. While I've wished for a Beau clone many times myself over the years, I'm not sorry we had him fixed. If we'd had Beau puppies, we never would have found

Zappa, Cosmo, Cindy Lou, and Sparky. We found the four of them in shelters, too. All four are wonderful, sweet, and happy dogs who have gone on to have respectable careers of their own.

I'm sure you, too, own the best, sweetest, smartest, most loving dog in the world. And you, too, are probably approached from time to time by people who would love to have a dog just like yours. But before you rush out to breed him or her please think twice, Your dog may be very cool, but unless he is a purebred of high quality, with an excellent temperament, good looks and superior genetic history, then chances are there really isn't much of a market for your dog's puppies.

In Rhode Island alone, nearly 45,000 animals are destroyed each year. Chances are, the people who want a dog just like yours could adopt one just like yours, or perhaps just like Beau, Zappa, Cosmo, Cindy, and Sparky, at their local shelter.

The pet overpopulation problem is beginning to ease thanks to the tremendous educational efforts of shelters and rescue leagues across the country. But there is still work to be done, for far too many dogs with great potential to be wonderful family pets are euthanized each year.

You can do your part by spaying or neutering your pet now. It's not cheap ($80 $120 depending on the veterinarian you see and the size and

> Far too
> many dogs
> with great
> potential to
> be wonderful
> family pets
> are euthanized
> each year.

sex of your dog). However, when compared to the cost of whelping a litter of puppies, stocking up on puppy chow, vaccinating the little ones, and advertising to find them good homes, it's a bargain. And there are other benefits, too. Fixed pets are healthier and live longer than those which are left intact. Male dogs who have not been neutered run a much higher

risk of contracting prostate cancer while unspayed females stand a greater chance of developing ovarian cancer and mammary tumors.

If it's money which is your primary worry, consider the cost of treating any of these cancers. An added bonus of spaying or neutering is that fixed dogs are less likely to get into fights, roam or bite.

Please consider taking your pet to the veterinarian to be spayed or neutered in the next few weeks. February is National Pet Health month, and getting your dog fixed is the best thing you can do for your pet's health. If you think you can't afford it, contact the Rhode Island Veterinary Medical Association (RIVMA). You may qualify for their assistance program. If you qualify, you will receive a certificate for a discount when you have your pet sterilized. Call 254-1052 for details.

If you still feel you cannot afford the surgery, speak with your veterinarian privately. Many will offer to either reduce their fees or set up a payment plan.

Your dog, like Beau,

is certainly the coolest dog in history. But trust me when I tell you that the shelters are full of neat dogs who deserve the chance to find a home. Spay or neuter your pet, and direct all those people who are looking for a dog just like yours to the shelter. I know they'll find one.

NE Assistance Dog Service Offers Hope for the Disabled

Robert Tamborelli was robbed at gunpoint and shot on June 21, 1990, but this isn't an article about the horrors of street crime in the city; not is it a story about a "victim" who is "confined" to a wheelchair. This is a story about a friendship.

Two years ago, Bob learned about an organization called the New England Assistance Dog Service (NEADS) from a physical therapist at Rhode Island Hospital. NEADS, one of several organizations nationwide devoted to training service dogs for people who are in wheelchairs or who are hearing impaired, placed between 25 to 40 service dogs a year.

The demand is much greater; Bob's two-year wait was not unusual, some wait as long as five years.

Bob called NEADS and was asked to fill out an application and come up to their West Boylston, Mass. office for an interview. NEADS decided that Bob was a good candidate for an assistance dog, and he was placed on a waiting list until NEADS could find the right dog for him.

Sundance was a stray who landed matted and covered with fleas, at the Auburn, Mass. Municipal Shelter in the spring of 1994. When no one claimed him, the shelter called NEADS. About 75 percent of NEADS' service dogs are found at shelters or through purebreed rescue organizations. (The rest are puppies donated by breeders and placed with loving foster homes until they begin their formal training.)

Under the tutelage of trainers at NEADS, Sundance started basic obedience training and then learned the special commands he would need to serve someone in a wheelchair.

During that six-month training period, the trainers evaluate the dog's personality and temperament. Then they compare the dog's profile with the applications on hand and play matchmaker.

Bob received a call from NEADS earlier this year, asking him to clear his schedule for two weeks. NEADS had found him a dog, and it was time for training to begin.

The minute Bob entered NEADS be hoped Sundance would be his dog. For starters, the

About 75 percent of NEADS' service dogs are found at shelters or purebreed rescue organizations.

dog is gorgeous. After six months at NEADS, he was no longer skinny and straggly. He had filled out. His coat was glossy, his eyes shone. But it was more than his looks; Sundance exuded the confidence of a dog who understands and loves his job.

The trainers at NEADS, who have an 88 percent success rate at this special kind of matchmaking, hedge their bets a bit by having a backup dog available in case the chemistry isn't right.

But Bob never doubted for a moment that everything would work out. Sundance was special. He was the right dog.

Together the pair began an intensive 50-hour training program at the NEADS site in West Boylston. Mike St. Louis and Brian Jennings, the NEADS trainers, patiently taught Bob what he needed to know about being a responsible pet owner and a good dog trainer.

Sundance already knew the behaviors he needed — retrieving dropped items, turning lights on and off, carrying books or papers, getting a soda out of the fridge, among others.

Now it was time for the two of them to learn to work as a team. Sundance had to learn that he would look to Bob for leadership from this day forward; Bob had to figure out how to communicate with Sundance so that the dog would respond.

Maintaining a high level of training requires a skilled owner who is consistent, kind and patient, that Bob learned quickly. (If Sundance fails to respond properly, Bob takes him through that particular command three times in a row, so that he won't forget it again.)

During their 10 days at NEADS, Bob and Sundance and their trainers headed out to pet supply stores, malls and grocery stores. Every day brought a new challenge as the team grew accustomed to working together.

The duo is allowed, by law, to go anywhere Bob could go on his own.

Bob and Sundance passed their exam with flying colors and are now a certified service team. Sundance wears his red working dog backpack, and Bob carried his identification; the duo is allowed, by law, to go anywhere Bob could go on his own.

Sundance came home with Bob two months ago. Their bond has grown stronger as they face life together. Bob's mom has been in and out of the hospital, so there have been some trying times in the past few months, but Sundance has made life easier. They go out for long walks together often. When Bob's feeling blue, Sundance will cheer him up with a silly look or by wagging his tail so hard against the garbage can that the lid flies off. During quiet time, Sundance will curl up with Indy, Bob's cat, and quietly wait to be of service.

Bob and Sundance are looking forward to the warm weather. Bob recently purchased all-terrain wheels for his chair and is headed offroad. Bob's always enjoyed hiking, but has been afraid to try it on his own for fear that he'll take a bump too hard and tip his chair.

Sundance can help Bob in situations like these. By bracing himself on Sundance's back for support, Bob can right himself, if that fails, Sundance is trained to bark until help arrives.

With Sundance at his side, Bob feels confident about returning to hobbies he enjoyed.

Security isn't the only benefit of having a partner like Sundance. Bob says he had grown accustomed to answering questions about the

With Sundance at his side, Bob feels confident about returning to hobbies he enjoyed.

wheelchair and being shot, but that it's never been his favorite subject. Nobody thinks to ask those questions any more, they're too busy asking about the beautiful, obedient and helpful dog at his side. And that's just fine with Bob.

(For more information about NEADS, call 508-835-3304, or write to P.O. Box 213, West Boylston, MA 01583.)

Category I-B-1 — Feature/News Story (150,000+ circ.)

DINNER'S GONE TO THE DOGS

by Kathie Jenkins

(LOS ANGELES TIMES)

It's Dining Cats and Dogs

Every week Genora Hall makes a kettle of vegetable soup, meatloaf and a big pot of pasta or rice. Her husband, Rick, especially loves the carrot-studded meatloaf. He says it makes a great sandwich.

Hall occasionally has a bowl of the soup but she tries not to eat too much of it. Otherwise, she says, "I just have to make more."

She means she'll just have to make more soup for the intended recipients—her dogs.

Although her four big chow hounds get a daily ration of kibble, she supplements their diet with vitamins and home cooked meals. "I call it preventive... holistic," says Hall, after groping for a better term. "I hate using that word because then people think you are a screwball. And I'm not."

Hall runs Adopt-A-Pooch, a volunteer group dedicated to finding homes for orphan dogs, and doesn't really have time to cook elaborate meals for herself, much less her pets. "I

> Just as owners have become more health conscious about their own diets, they're worrying about what their pets are eating too.

know someone who roasts a turkey once a week for her dog," she says. "I'm much too busy for that."

Certain pets have always enjoyed home-cooked meals—think of the French and their pampered lapdogs. But these days, even middle-class dogs and cats are getting especially cooked chow and it's more than just a few table scraps or the bone from the Sunday roast. Just as owners have become more health conscious about their own diets, they're worrying about what their pets are eating too. They read pet food labels and are more selective in choosing products. The old supermarket kibble just won't do anymore.

Certainly pet food manufacturers know they've got an attentive audience. Just check out the pet food aisle at your local supermarket. Only cereal and soft drinks occupy more shelf space. And then there's the fastest growing division—premium pet food, sold at pet stores, grooming shops and veterinary clinics where kibble can really run up a big chunk of change.

But despite all the beefy dinners, butcher blends, kibble and chicken nuggets to choose from, some feel it's dog-gone impossible to find a completely wholesome pet food. Only homecooked will do for these choosy owners.

"How would you like it if all you had to eat every day was Grapenuts?" says Dr. Richard Pitcairn, the Euell Gibbons of pet food, when asked about commercial kibble. "Well, the high point of a dog's day is getting fed and look what you're giving her."

Pitcairn thinks he knows what constitutes a good pet diet. But there are almost as many different feeding philosophies as there are experts. Many claim that fourfooted creatures can live perfectly well on a scientifically formulated diet of meat and poultry byproducts as long as the necessary nutrients have been added. Others, like Pitcairn, are "seriously concerned about the nutritional quality of animal convenience foods, and advise preparing a good

homecooked meal every day." Some are adamant about feeding a dog or cat as it would feed itself if it were living in the wild. There are those who advise a varied diet, while others believe the

---

GENORA HALL'S SOUP FOR DOGS

3 tablespoons olive oil
3 cloves garlic, minced
6 cups chopped vegetables
1 cup cooked rice

Genora Hall uses whatever vegetables she has on hand— cabbage, carrots, cauliflower, broccoli and peas, for instance—to make this flavorful soup. Hall recommends ladling a cup of the soup over a bowl of kibble just before serving.

Heat oil in soup pot. Add garlic and cook over low heat until garlic is tender, about 5 minutes. Add vegetables and cook until just beginning to brown, about 10 to 15 minutes.

Add cooked rice and water. Bring to boil. Reduce heat, cover and simmer 10 minutes.

Makes about 3 quarts, or 12 servings. Each serving contains about: 64 calories; 22 mg. sodium; 0 cholesterol; 4 grams fat; 8 grams carbohydrates; 1 gram protein; 0.46 gram fiber.

---

opposite, that pets are better off if they're fed the same diet every day as long as it's completely balanced. One faction feeds their pets only raw foods, another cooks everything thoroughly.

"Most people want to feed their pets something

that looks good," says Pitcairn. "But just because it looks good, does not necessarily mean it's good for them. Being carnivores, dogs and cats need a lot more protein and more calcium than we do."

In 1982, Pitcairn and his wife, Susan, published "Dr. Pitcairn's Complete Guide to Natural Health for Dogs & Cats," one of the first books to focus on animal nutrition, now considered the bible of homeopathic pet health. At a time when most people were feeding their animals cans of stinky, purple dreck, the Pitcairns advised owners to feed pets the best whole, fresh food they could afford.

"We see a big difference in animals that go on a good diet," says Pitcairn. "A lot of chronic health problems are nutritional, either from food contamination or deficiencies. There are rules about what can't go into human food—although I'm-sure things slip in now or then— but most of them don't, apply to pet food."

Julie Zimmerman, a feed control officer for the State of Colorado and vice chair of the American Assn. of Feed Control Officials, a non-regulatory organization that formulates uniform regulations and nutritional guidelines pertaining to pet food, has a more positive view of commercial pet food, and even of that scary sounding kibble staple, byproducts.

"We may think [byproducts] are not real pleasant, but they contain good nutrition and are safe," Zimmerman says. "One of the things we do on a state level is randomly pull feed samples and have our own lab do

---

Go Ask Alice -- The Making of a Doggy Foodie

Meet Alice (my Bouvier des Flandres). She was born in Covina four years ago, but her parents are from Belgium, just like Bernard Erpicum, the former Spago maitre d' who now owns the celebrity hot spot Eclipse on Melrose. Alice doesn't own a tuxedo, but her bangs were trimmed for this picture, and she weighs almost as much as Bernard. These days just like Bernard, Alice is into food too.

Alice had her first home-cooked meal last month. As I researched pet food trends and tested pet recipes, she was my willing guinea pig. Except for celery and bananas, which she likes—but only as objects to roll on—there is practically nothing she won't put in her mouth. Still, until she became a Times taste tester, she'd never gotten excited about food before—that was because she'd never had anything but kibble.

Then one day I fed Alice doggie oats from a recipe by Dr. Richard Pitcairn, a well-known animal nutrition expert. When I set the oats in front of her, she smelled the plate, her ears perked up, and she gobbled up every bit as if it were rare aged meat. The next day she came over and stood right beside me as I prepared her food, staring into my eyes until I set down her bowl. Alice is now a foodie.

Alice also likes La Brea Bakery dog biscuits with fresh mint (I like them because they make her breath smell sweet). Genora's vegetable soup and rice spooned over delicious-smelling Flint Ranch kibble makes her happy, even though the vegetables might have been cut a little smaller and maybe some chicken thrown in.

But Thirsty Dog sparkling water? Uh uh. Not a taste she was willing to acquire.

One night I stayed up past midnight slow-roasting bones because someone said they were excellent for cleaning canine teeth and a lot easier on a dog than being put under anesthesia, which most veterinarians recommend. Alice quickly polished off the entire bone, but her diarrhea lasted several days. Later I realized I was supposed to buy beef bones, not pork.

I'm still cooking for Alice, feeding her a varied diet—meat, fish, grains, pasta, vegetables, and kibble—and she's never looked better. Her wiry coat glistens she seldom scratches and her teeth are white as chalk. I've toyed with the idea of trying more exotic recipes, but I don't think Alice would approve. Her tastes, though elegant, are quite simple. Maybe that's a Belgian thing too.

an analysis. And we see a very low violation rate."

Pat McKay, author of the animal nutrition book, "Reigning Cats and Dogs," isn't convinced. She stopped feeding her pets commercial food 25 years ago. Now her animals' menu consists only of fresh, raw foods. McKay believes that heat destroys nutrients and the enzymes necessary for digestion.

" 'Cook' is four-letter word as far as carnivores are concerned," she says. "There isn't an animal in the wild that eats anything that comes anywhere close to kibble. Mother Nature did a swell job. But people always think they know more."

If it were up to her, McKay would encourage people to feed mice, birds, lizards and insects to their pets because that's what they ate in the wild. "But if I did that," she says, "I'd have a whole other animal activist group come after me — 'Oh, how cruel!'"

"If you knew what dogs ate in the wild, it would be totally disgusting to you, but they think it's the best thing on Earth," says David Dzanis, a veterinary nutritionist with the FDA's Center for Veterinary

Medicine, adding that his dog's favorite meal "is the cat's litter box." He wouldn't go as far as McKay, however, in advocating a wild-food pet diet. Neither would many other pet nutrition experts.

"I would not feed raw meat to any animal," says Dr. Leland Shapiro, a licensed animal nutritionist and reproductive physiologist at Pierce

I wouldn't feed my kids bad food and I feel the same way about my animals.

College in Woodland Hills. "They say it's more natural, but it's also more natural for people to eat raw meat too, if you go back far enough." And when humans eat raw meat, Shapiro points out, they run the risk of infection from salmonella and E. Coli.

McKay, who sells frozen pet food and vitamins, is the first to admit that a lot of veterinarians are against feeding raw

meat. Still, she won't be swayed. "It's just shocking," she says. "Lots of animals that go on my fresh food program get well right away. I'm not a veterinarian and all these other people are. I think sometimes there's an ego problem."

"Pat McKay is a groomer," says Dr. John Limehouse, who practices holistic medicine at his North Hollywood veterinary clinic. "She has no background in nutrition. Her expertise is putting other people down and selling her book and her food. She got her information from a study that was done in 1930 where they fed raw foods to cats. The cats did do a lot better, but in 1930 processed cat food was extremely terrible."

"Why go to school when what they teach is absolutely worthless to me," responds McKay. "I'm telling people how to re-create a mouse, to get close to what animals were eating in the wild."

Although Limehouse highly recommends a home-cooked diet and has even devised his own ideal pet diet (50% pasta, brown rice or millet, 25% diced turkey or chicken breasts, 25% vegetables),

Limehouse believes there are some fairly decent commercial pet foods on the market, especially the premium lines. "Even though they do have questionable or even harmful things in them, they are really lots better than some of the cheap junk food that is out there. And oddly enough," he adds, "some animals do OK on even the cheapest of these."

"Commercial food may be to high in salt and too high in fat says Shapiro, "but pet food is still regulated to the point it's considered safe for humans to consume and there are many people who do. I wouldn't, but there is nothing in it that would poison you."

Shapiro, who has been teaching animal nutrition at Pierce College for 10 years, cautions against falling for fad pet foods. To really know that a certain diet causes longer life involves years of blind studies on multiple animals. "There are a lot of people who say 'I'm successful because this is what I've been feeding my animal and they've lived a long time,' " says Shapiro. "Well, there are people who smoke three or four packs of cigarettes a day and live to be 98. That doesn't mean that smoking is not bad for you." :

> There are people who smoke three or four packs of cigarettes a day and live to be 98. That doesn't mean that smoking is not bad for you.

Hanna Quinn-Bleicher doesn't need a study to prove to her that home-cooked meals make a difference. 'My animals aren't fat and' blubbery like animals get on commercial foods," she says. "And they do major zooms every day!"

For Quinn-Bleicher, the hardest part about cooking dinner for her pets is explaining it to other people. "Friends of ours roll their eyes up at us, but I wouldn't feed my kids bad food and I feel the same way about my animals. It isn't horribly time consuming, and what extra time it does take I include in what I call care-giving."

Even so, the Sherman Oaks acupuncturist and doctor of Oriental medicine knows her regimen is not for everybody. "As a health professional, I know how some people get really fixed on a certain way of doing something. But there isn't one way to do anything. Like that "Fit for Life" diet that has everybody eating fruit for breakfast, it works for some people and it makes some really sick. It's the same thing with our animals. Whether you feed them raw or cooked food depends on them and also how much you are willing to do. It has to be an individual choice."

Quinn-Bleicher read about a woman in England who used to feed her dogs raw meat that she had buried in her backyard for weeks. "I thought about it for a minute," says Quinn-Bleicher, "but so far I don't have any plans."

Category I-B-2 — Feature/News Story (under 150,000)

FINNIGAN IS MORE THAN A COMPANION FOR ST. PAT'S DAY

by Nona Kilgore Bauer

(THE INDEPENDENCE)

Brent Gallina has been a dog man all his life. Brent hunted with Labrador Retrievers before he was old enough to shave, and for eight years he trained an 80-pound Lab lamed Trapper for Retriever field trials. He also admits he used to snicker a bit at the mention of those furry blond "rugs" called Golden Retrievers.

Not any more. Today Brent's best friend and constant companion is big, rangy "rug" named Finnigan. Brent and Finnigan met in March, 1992, at the training center for Support Dogs, Inc. in St. Louis. You see, Brent has multiple sclerosis, and Finnigan is his service dog.

Finnigan has been at Brent's side 24 hours a day since the two graduated from the Support Dog team training program in April, 1992. This Golden Retriever has restored the freedom Brent lost after contracting MS in 1990. At 95 pounds, the dog retrieves, carries, pushes, and pulls, often when Brent's wife and daughter would have been physically unable to assist him. "I don't know what I'd do without this guy," Brent said. "Finn has improved the quality of my life by 150 %. He's the perfect dog for me."

Perfect was apparent from the first time Finnigan was introduced to Brent. "We bonded almost instantly ," he said with a huge grin. "On the second day of training when my group came into the training room, Finn was already looking for me."

During their 4-week team-training program at the SD training center, Brent and Finnigan worked together on tasks the dog had mastered as part of SD's customized training for the individual client-dog team. Finn already was pulling 170 pounds and opening heavy doors with ease when he was three-fourths through his formal training. To prepare for Brent, he was taught to pull a wheelchair and other strenuous tasks.

On a more intricate level, when the dog picked up a coin, he learned to place it in the front of his mouth and drop it into the side of his jowl where Brent could easily remove it. He was also trained to operate an emergency switch by pulling on a lever to call the paramedics in case Brent fell or needed help.

Finn also had the stability to ignore the extraneous movement due to intention tremors... the shaking and wobbling typical of someone affected with MS... as well as the ability to continue his working skills during the physical deterioration associated with MS. Brent uses a wheelchair and occasionally walks, and it is difficult for most dogs to adapt to both, but Finnigan demonstrated his adaptability as well.

A large and strong-willed dog, Finnigan needed an assertive individual handling the business end of his leash. With his field trial experience and understanding of dog training; Brent easily convinced the dog he was in charge. Brent was the first person in his training group to gain his dog's confidence, respect and love.

Brent credits his success with Finnigan to SD's strict training and prematch program. And he's quick to applaud the Kirkbrides, SD Executive Director Mitzi Kirkbride and husband Jerry, Director of Training, for their roles in developing the SD program and their continued interest in Finnigan's progress.

"A while back Finn developed a little problem with mall doors,". Brent explained, "I called Jerry, and he drove up to Wisconsin that weekend. He cured the problem with one simple maneuver at the local mall."

Finnigan can open and close mall doors entirely on his own now without any help from Brent. From a lengthy process that involved five separate commands... "Take door," (grab the pull strap in his mouth) "Back," (Move backwards while pulling on the cord) "Over," (Move over to make room for the wheelchair) "Sit" and "Stay," (followed of course by lots of praise!)

Brent was the first person in his training group to gain his dog's confidence.

Finn now opens mall doors with one simple command, "Take door," without assistance or another word from Brent. The two of them still go to malls three times a week so practice and keep Finnigan's skills at peak performance level.

Together the two also have learned and mastered other new tasks since their March graduation. "Finn is so smart and always ready for something new," Brent said. "He's a very trac-

table dog."

That high level of trainability is an essential part of the SD breeding program. The Missouri-based, not-for-profit agency breeds and trains its own service dogs, mostly Golden Retrievers, Labradors and German Shepherds. Support Dogs, Inc., annually produces 12 to 15 fully trained service dogs, each one matched to a client according to the dog's personality and abilities.

Mitzi emphasized that the successful placement of these Support Dogs hinges on the SD prematch program. Due to stringent prematch requirements, they have a very high success rate with their dogs.

And their highest success rate is with Goldens. Mitzi explained that the Golden has a more highly developed capacity for understanding precise detail, an ability most apparent in the Golden bloodlines she uses in the SD breeding program.

"For example, some individuals in a wheelchair may use a lap tray, and there may be a one-to-two inch area on the tray where they are able to accept objects that are

21

retrieved. A service dog must not only retrieve an object that is very small, awkward or heavy, pick it up with the correct grip and return it to the person, but they must also be able to do it in a specific manner to a specific spot," Mitzi explained. "Many

> A service dog must retrieve an object that is very small, awkward or heavy, pick it up with the correct grip and return it to the person.

of our Labs are unable to grasp such concepts and are what we call 'broad-based' in these concepts and are better suited to bigger challenges."

Brent considers himself one of Finnigan's "bigger challenges." He and the 95-pound Golden were matched to accommodate Brent's 6-foot 2-inch frame, his range of motion, as well as his aptitude and preference for

a big dog with a strong personality. "I didn't want a soft, wimpy dog," Brent said. "And Finn is not a marshmallow."

Finnigan demonstrated his back bone recently during a trip to the Brookfield Mall where Brent meets his wife for lunch each week. A half-dozen 16-to-17-year-old boys followed Brent and Finn around the mall, taunting the dog and throwing small objects at him. When Brent retreated into the men's room, two of the youths came in after him. Finnigan instantly stood guard. He filled the room with a deep growl, and his body posture seemed to double his 95 pounds. Brent warned the boys, "At the count of five I'm going to take off his leash." They immediately turned and fled.

(Support Dogs, Inc., stressed that, even though Brent felt in need of protection, by SD standards the dog was out of line for growling at a human being. Many clients may suddenly need human assistance, and SD cannot risk having a Support Dog protect" its person from getting help

from another human.)

Encounters such as these are rare, however, and Brent usually has the opposite problem of people trying to pet Finnigan while he's working. The main disadvantage with a Golden Retriever service dog is their soft, appealing look, he

> It's a constant battle trying to educate the public on the role of a service dog and how to treat it properly.

said. "People are always trying to sneak in pets when he walks by." Public petting distracts a service dog and adds to its stress while it's working. "It's a constant battle trying to educate the public on the role of a service dog and how to treat it properly," he observed.

Brent makes a point of including the proper treatment of a service dog in his speeches to MS support groups and civic organizations. He is a frequent spokesperson for the National Multiple Sclerosis Society Wisconsin Chapter. He talks to schools and self-help groups, as well as to parent groups to encourage other MS parents to continue their involvement with their children's activities.

In the summer of 1992, he was the guest speaker at the Wisconsin Chapter's "Best Damn Bike Tour" fund-raiser, with 2,000 cyclists, at their halfway tour point on the University of Wisconsin Whitewater campus. As usual, Brent downplayed his own role as guest speaker and preferred to brag about his dog.

The MS Chapter had built a special ramp up the steep hill to the speaker's platform to accommodate Brent's wheelchair. "Finn leaned into his harness and took off pulling my chair, and my wife had to actually run to keep up with him. At the top he wasn't even breathing hard, and just stood there asking... okay, which way do we go now?"

Colleen Kalt, director of the MS Wisconsin Chapter, watched Brent and Finnigan climb that hill. "It had a very powerful impact on the cyclists," she recalled. "They saw a man who was determined to press on despite his disability. His ingenuity in coping with his illness has a positive effect on every audience he speaks to.

> Each dog will ultimately retrieve objects up to 50 pounds, then back up with that weight and pull on it by dragging the heavy object.

In April, Brent was named the 1992 National Multiple Sclerosis Society Wisconsin Chapter Father of the Year. Kalt said candidates are screened and selected for their dedication to enriching their child's life, and their ability to encourage and motivate other parents with MS to remain involved with their child's life, and convince them of the quality of life despite their disease.

Brent accepted the award at a ceremony at the Sheraton Inn in Milwaukee. Brent claims, however, that his wife and daughter are the real winners of this award and deserve it more than he does. And who else will accompany Brent, who will be the real hero of the festivities? You guessed it ... Finnigan. He wouldn't let Brent go without him.

The Support Dog Story

Support Dogs. Inc. has been growing since 1981. The second oldest service dog organization in the United States, SD provides service dogs for people with disabilities, such as multiple sclerosis, muscular dystrophy, polio, spinal injuries and other functional disorders, thereby enabling them to lead more self-sufficient lives. Now training 12 to 15 service dogs a year, at approximately $8,000 per dog, there is a two-year waiting list for dogs.

Donated puppies and those bred by Support Dogs are raised in approved foster homes for the first 15-18 months of life. In foster homes the dogs are socialized within the family and taught basic control and several specific commands. From 7 weeks of age the puppies and their foster parents attend weekly training classes to build the basic instincts Kirkbride has bred them for: retrieving desire, work drive and pulling.

The pups are taught inducively to sit, and must sit and wait before being fed, going in or outdoors, and before entering a car. They also learn to "kennel" into a crate, a bathtub and a car.

"Our puppies will pick up and carry anything," Mitzi said. 'They are never discouraged. Our foster families teach a structured hold process, and the puppies are taught to pick up wooden dowels, soft objects like gloves, wallets or hats, spoons. Frisbees, a variety of textures and materials, but nothing awkward or heavy. We are building on success in very small increments." SD also has a similarly structured pulling program.

At 15 to 18 months of age the dogs are screened and selected for service work. Dogs who fail the initial screening or are unable to complete formal training are released and offered to the foster family before placement in a permanent pet home

Training dogs for these tasks requires exceptional canine communication skills and a thorough understanding of dog psychology.

Formal training takes six to eight months in a customized program to develop the dog's agility, endurance and strength.

All dogs are started on the same program to learn about their potential for retrieving and pulling and determine each dog's drive for those tasks. They first

learn to position themselves on both sides of the body... left, right and front, for the sit and all position commands (stand and down), and then learn to back ups from these positions as well. They are taught to retrieve, first a thrown object, then a placed object, finally a variety of things... coats, towels, shoes, coins, etc., and to retrieve them from an area "seeded" with up to 25 different items. The dogs first retrieve off carpet, and then a tile floor.

Each dog will ultimately retrieve objects up to 50 pounds, then back up with that weight and pull on it by dragging the heavy object. These weight-pulling exercises are the foundation for opening mall doors, cupboards, refrigerator doors and other similar tasks.

Dogs in formal training also learn to stand on their hind legs, then position themselves on counters and walls, which leads to accepting packages from store clerks, taking objects from counter tops, and other like areas.

All dogs are taught to operate a switch box,

built and donated by the Telephone Pioneers of America, which is later customized to suit each clients needs. The dogs learn to pull a handle, then let go when a beep sounds, which teaches them to pull and release immediately. The box is later installed in the client's home for turning on light switches, automatic dialers and other electrical devices.

About 90 days before training is complete, each dog is evaluated to determine its best skills, and then paired with an appropriate person so the dog can be custom trained for that individual. The dogs are matched according to the client's needs, not only on physical abilities and range of motion, but on lifestyle, goals, personality, attitudes and many other factors.

In team training, during four weeks of close supervision, the dog and client learn to work as a team. It's a critical time for both. The dog learns to transfer its skills to a new working partner, the client learns to manage the dog, give commands

and function with the dog in public.

Training dogs for these out-of-the-ordinary tasks requires exceptional canine communication skills and a thorough understanding of dog psychology. The Kirkbrides were experienced obedience trainers when they joined the Support Dog staff in 1981. Their expertise in training and breeding a

In team training, during four weeks of close supervision, the dog and client learn to work as a team.

superior service dog has earned national recognition within the service dog industry.

In 1990 SD was selected as a model program by the California State Guide Dog Board. It was also rated as the best program in this country by the Executive

Director of the South African Guide Dog Association for the Blind. After a tour of several U.S. assistance dog programs, S.A.G.D.A,'s Ken Lord wrote, "...for pure professionalism and quality of training, Support Dogs is way ahead of the other organizations I visited in the U.S. This program, in terms of pure training of dogs and disabled clients, was superb."

More recently the Missouri Veterinary Medical Association voted at its 1992 convention to endorse and assist SD. The MVMA is encouraging its members to provide free or discounted veterinary care to Support Dog puppies in foster care as well as those in service. The MVMA is only the second veterinary association in the U.S. to endorse and support an assistance dog program.

(For more information about Support Dogs, Inc., contact Support Dogs, 301 Sovereign Court, Suite 311, St. Louis, MO 63011.)

Category I-C — Best Editorial, Opinion Piece, Essay

*This essay was also winner of The President's Award

OUR TEACHER, OUR DOG
by Joseph Cerquone
(THE WASHINGTON POST)

As we waited for our veterinarian's injection to take hold on our dog, Opie, we tried to say our piece — our final good-bye. "Love you, boy," we chorused as a family. "Thanks so much. We won't forget you."

Probably such things are said by many who stay with their pets to the end. But in Opie's case, the words had special meaning. For as I watched Opie's brown eyes slowly close, I also saw my foster children, two kids who know much human rejection, bidding farewell to the most dependable creature in their lives.

"He always kissed me three times!" one of them likes to say emphatically.

Experts concur on what the children know. "Many times, kids at risk have experienced a lot of sadness. They haven't been around people they trust," explains Earl Strimple, a veterinarian and president of People, Animals, Love, a Washington-based group that works with District youth. "But animals are responsive," Strimple points out. "They're something to have faith in."

Opie, though, was unique. He had natural "animal magnetism," but he also knew what it was like to be an outcast. When we adopted him, he had spent five years in a shelter for homeless dogs and cats; his history of living among the unwanted bonded him with the kids like nothing else could have.

Naturally, we would have preferred that Opie never suffered

Opie

that treatment, but we tried to use it as a positive lesson. For example, during family talks, with Opie lying by serenely, adult counsel often went like this: "Keep your chin up. You see what a great dog Opie is—he's a fine animal no matter what the world thought of

> Try not to
> be bitter.
> Look at Opie...
> He was
> rejected
> constantly,
> yet he found
> a way to
> remain gentle.

him. So don't let anyone tell you you're not good enough."

Or: "Try not to be bitter. Look at Opie. He was rejected constantly, yet he found a way to remain gentle."

Indeed, thinking about life in the mix of Opie and our foster kids, I find it hard to easily summarize the important connections that were made—there were so many. In fact, one child might not have moved in at all had Opie not been with us. The dog put him at ease and got him to trust humans again, a prospect that can be scary and seem impossible to a foster child.

Bonding was everywhere with Opie in the house. It was symbolized by the dog statuettes in the children's rooms, and the pictures of our pooch that littered the pages of the kids' photo albums. Also, there were family times watching movies like "Homeward Bound," where a character reminds us of Opie, or laughing over the get-ups loving owners put on their hounds for Alexandria's annual St. Patrick's Day parade. Opie even helped the kids with their schooling. He served as a subject for more than one writing assignment, homework that otherwise might have been neglected. Meanwhile, lessons about responsibility came in the form of animal care, chores willingly done because Opie was such a popular family member.

Even having a great dog can't erase all the rough spots. At

> The dog put
> him at ease
> and got him
> to trust
> humans
> again,
> a prospect
> that can be
> scary and seem
> impossible
> to a
> foster child.

my house, disagreements are unique, because there is no built-in biological basis for getting along; everyone must work a bit harder at forgiveness. Sometimes when there was a problem, the kids got through being upset because of Opie. "If he likes it here, I guess it can't be so bad after all" seemed to be their feeling.

Everyone wanted to be present when Opie was put to sleep. He was still well enough to display his charm: Though lame and cancer-stricken, on his last day he pushed himself to roll over and face us as we all sat at the kitchen table, sad-eyed. It was as though he heard duty calling him to be central to another family discussion. At a deeper level, choosing to euthanize Opie was tough because we knew it would mean losing the warm neutral core to our makeshift family.

"No!" is what I heard when the kids were told Opie's time had come. But they understood eventually, after they felt the lumps in his throat and heard his constant panting.

Often putting an animal to Sleep is "much harder on the owner," according to

> "No!" is what I heard when the kids were told Opie's time had come. But they understood eventually, after they felt the lumps in his throat and heard his constant panting.

Millie Bobbitt of the Alexandria Animal Welfare League. But Bobbitt stresses that "the important thing to

do what is best for the pet."

In the months since Opie's death we've wept and ached. But we now have a new family member, a Washington Humane Society hound.

Part of us worried whether were being disloyal getting another dog so quickly. But in the end, we chose to act on Opie's legacy: After all, he had opened our hearts to the worth of unwanted animals.

Opie, you would have been happy to hear what one of the children said when we brought the new dog home: "Look, Dad," he exclaimed, excited by the steady wag in the animal's tail, "he likes me!"

CATEGORY II

MAGAZINES

AND

CANINE

NEWSPAPERS

A TASTE OF *SHIBA JOURNAL...*
RANDOM NOTES
by GRETCHEN HASKETT

Will you be surprised at receiving this issue early or wondering why it was so late? I wonder myself! My due date has been moved up so that the baby may possibly arrive as early as September 28! I usually mail the fall Shiba Journal out around the first week of October, so we are going to try to cut things a little short in the hopes that we can get it printed and out of here a little earlier.

The new due date means that I am definitely not going to risk a trip to the National in Minneapolis, even though one friend suggested that since she and other breeders making the trip had delivered so many litters over the years that they could probably deliver a human baby (echoing my husband's comments). No thanks folks, I prefer a hospital and as much pain killer as my body will take! Take a look in this issue for the California girl that wowed the obedience crowd with a 196 her first time out in the Novice ring. The rumor is that she might make the trip to Minneapolis! By the time this issue is out, the '95 National will be history.

Don't know how the heat is in your part of the country, but I, for one, am anxious for fall weather. The Chicago area has been steaming with an unusually long run of high heat and humidity. The dogs are tired of the house, but it is too hot to be anywhere but inside. Tim has been to several conformation shows this summer, almost all over 90 degrees and a couple over 100. Few of our summer shows are indoors so everyone is miserable. It is in this weather that the professional handlers really earn their pay!

More about allergies. We are still getting calls about itchy Shibas, especially from California and Texas. Did you know that there is an allergy test for dogs that your vet can give? All that is needed is a blood sample. If your Shiba is not crazy about having blood drawn, ask your vet for a mild sedative to give him or her about an hour or two beforehand. The manufacturer of the test is Im-Vet and the address is 460 Park Ave. S., Suite 1100, New York, NY 10016. If your Shiba's allergies are severe, the dog can receive allergy treatments just as people do. If you have had this test run, I would like to hear the details of the results.

Along with the info that Jeri Braviroff mailed in on her latest pet store rescues (see "Our Readers Write") came a copy of a brochure from one of the breeders. Apparently the breeder, Sharon Munk of Terry Kennels & BJ's & Guys is a member of APPDI or American Professional Pet Distributors, Inc. The brochure also states that Ms. Monk is one of the nine members of the Companion Animal Advisory Board, along with "veterinarians, former state senators and representatives, lawyers and the humane society." This group "is working with the Governor, the Attorney General, and the Animal Health Commissioner of the state of Kansas, to assure you of receiving healthy quality companion animals from their state."

There is even a picture of a group of people standing on the state seal and another photo of a puppy on the Governor's desk. There are also some partial shots of what looks to be a very large and slick kennel operation. Now if you were a novice pet buyer wouldn't you like to purchase your puppy from a kennel that is involved so closely with the state government? This brochure would make the average hobby/show kennel look pretty pitiful.

Category II-A — Single Breed Magazine

SHIBA JOURNAL
Gretchen Haskett, Editor

Features

Departments

Subscriptions (4 issues):
$30 per year (U.S.);
$34 (Canada/Mexico); $42 (foreign)
The Shiba Journal
1988 Madison Ave.
Gurnee, IL 60031

A TASTE OF *DOG FANCY*...

VIEWPOINT

by KIM THORNTON

When most people hear the words dog show, they think one of two things: beauty contest or trick demonstrations. It's not quite that simple, though. Not only should a dog show be much more than a beauty contest, it can take many forms.

Dog shows originated as a way of evaluating breeding stock. Hunters, herders and others who worked their dogs came together to test their dogs' skills against one another. The best dogs would be bred to carry on their working ability.

Today, dog shows are still used to evaluate breeding stock — although in many breeds working ability has gone by the wayside—but they are a hobby, too. Camaraderie and competition go hand in hand each weekend as breeders meet to see whose dogs most closely resemble the breed standard. For diehard competitors with money and drive — and champion dogs — the Westminster Kennel Club show is the culmination of their efforts. Each February, dogs that have already earned championships fill Madison Square Garden in New York City, their owners all hoping against hope that their dog will win Best in Show at this prestigious event. Dog lovers across the country watch the Group competitions on cable television, trying to read the judges' minds and choosing their own winners from among all the gorgeous specimens.

But conformation shows like Westminster are just the beginning when it comes to dog showing. Dog owners may train and compete with their dogs in herding, tracking, field trials, lure coursing, agility, flyball, scent hurdles, Frisbee and more. For people who prize their relationships with their dogs, such activities offer an opportunity to develop a bond through training, quality time through competition, friendships with others. They are far more than "trick demonstrations"; in many cases they are a living tableau of canine history.

Whether your interests lie in conformation or performance events, there is something for you in this issue. Those who are planning to attend Westminster this year, perhaps for the first time, will find a guide to the show by longtime denizen Marion Lane, a member of the Dog Writers Association of America and former editor of the AKC Gazette, and Cairn Terrier fancier Denny Vinson shares his experiences when he and his wife decided their dog Aggie deserved a shot at the big time. Dog trainer Liz Palika outlines the variety of activities available to dog owners and how to get started, while Beardie breeder Chris Walkowicz tells the tales of three dogs that made it to the top in the obedience ring: an obedience trial championship. Poodles have been known for their beauty and for their brains for years, so they fit right in this issue. (Last month, I promised you two breed profiles in each issue, but we are cheating with the Poodles: Since they come in three sizes and are members of both the Non-Sporting and Toy Groups, they are the only breed profile this month.)

Last but not least, it is my pleasure this month to congratulate the Dog Writers Association of America on its sixtieth anniversary. Its members not only publicize the doings of dogs, they also contribute to canine welfare and to the education of young dog lovers who will be the next generation of writers, editors, veterinarians, breeders and trainers. Long may they write!

Category II-B — All Breed Magazine

DOG FANCY
Kim Thornton, Editor

Subscriptions (12 issues):
$25.97 per year (U.S.); $33.97 (Canada)
Dog Fancy Magazine
P.O. Box 53264
Boulder, CO 80322

A TASTE OF
POINTING DOG JOURNAL...
OUR POINT

by *DAVID G. MEISNER*

In the Summer issue of Pheasants Forever magazine, Jim Wooley writes, "In the next few weeks, you have the opportunity to influence the largest wildlife habitat enterprise in your lifetime. Today, its benefits extend to all of society. If allowed to continue and evolve, it could be providing value to your children's children."

Of course, Wooley is talking about the Conservation Reserve Program (CRP). Without any doubt whatsoever, the CRP has been the biggest boon to wildlife habitat in history, and as Wooley points out later in his article, "Its reauthorization and full funding are of monumental consequence." Each of us, individually, needs to do all we can to encourage Congress to continue the program.

Listed below are the phone and fax numbers of the Chairman of the House Agricultural Committee and of the Senate Agricultural Committee. Drop each of them a brief letter or fax letting them know that you support the continuation of the CRP at its current level of 36.4 million acres.

House Agricultural Committee
Representative Pat Roberts
(202) 225-2715; fax (202) 225-5375
Senate Agricultural Committee
Senator Richard Lugar
(202) 224-4814; fax (202) 228-0360

In addition, please take the time to write your own Senator and Congressman.

Letters really do make a difference, and now, while the 1995 Farm Bill is being discussed in Congress, is the time to write.

Another personal and positive step each of us can take in the battle to preserve wildlife habitat is to join Pheasants Forever. These guys have been in the front lines of the battle to protect and preserve our future afield. They deserve our support. Send your $20 membership fee to: Pheasants Forever, P.O. Box 75473, St. Paul, Minnesota 55175. You'll receive a membership card, window decal, and a year's subscription to Pheasants Forever magazine.

Make special note of this issue's front cover. It's the Bird Dog Foundation's 1995 Annual Art Print, "Autumn Majesty," by Robert K. Abbett. If you purchase one, not only will you have a beautiful print that's bound to appreciate in value, but you will also be helping out a very worthwhile organization. One hundred percent of the proceeds from the sale of prints goes directly to the Bird Dog Foundation. I've ordered mine.

Gilly and I endured a pretty fair dose of humility during our first NSTRA trial season this past spring. I tried to keep it in perspective and view our defeats as learning experiences - paying dues, if you know what I mean. There were times I could have killed the little monster, like when temporary deafness set in which happened frequently. But then, he probably felt the same way about me while I was in the process of committing innumerable handling errors.

Anyway, I am happy to report that in our very last trial of the spring season, late in May, we did get our first placement -- a first yet -- in a trial in northern Iowa. On the drive back home, I was on Cloud 9, and Gilly got a Whopper Junior and some fries.

Walking trials and tests -- NSTRA, NBHA, NAVHDA, and AKC Hunt Tests - are great ways for hunters to extend their season and spend high-quality time with their dogs. If you've not yet become involved, I would urge you to do so.

God bless, Dave

Category II-C — Multi-Breed or Hunting Magazine

THE **POINTING DOG JOURNAL**
David G. Meisner, Editor

Subscriptions (6 issues):
$21.95 per year (U.S.); $31.95 (Canada)
The Pointing Dog Journal
P.O. Box 968
Traverse City, MI 49685

A TASTE OF *YOUR DOG...*
CHEWING IT OVER

HAIR, THERE, EVERYWHERE

"Lady, my 6-year-old shepherd-husky, sheds excessively at certain times of the year, but she sheds only her white undercoat. Is something missing from her diet? (I feed her top-quality food.) Or does the change of seasons cause the shedding? I've had several shepherds, and they never shed as much as Lady does!"

George Schafer, Roselle, NJ

"Hair, hair, everywhere," is a common seasonal lament of dog owners. To a greater or lesser degree, most dogs undergo a normal, cyclical shedding of their hair coat. Dogs shed when their hair follicles (the cavities that hold hair) release old hairs to make way for new ones. It may seem like there's more hair on your carpets and furniture than could possibly be on your dog—yet your dog looks fully coated because new hair is replacing shed hair.

Numerous factors — including environmental temperature, nutrition, hormones, general health, and genetic makeup—affect a dog's shedding cycle, but recent studies indicate that length of daylight (photoperiod) is the predominant factor. So, as George observes, certain seasons—namely spring (increasing daylight) and fall (decreasing daylight) trigger increased shedding in the average dog and mean about 5 weeks of "bad hair days" for the owner.

The amount of hair a dog sheds depends on its breed and individual genetic makeup. (Poodles and some terriers, for example, shed minimally, while north-ern breeds such as huskies shed prodigiously.) The genetics of shedding remain one of dogdom's unsolved mysteries. We know, for example, that two dogs of the same breed and lineage, kept in identical environments and fed similar diets, may vary tremendously in their shedding "habits.

Although George notices the abundance of hairs from Lady's white, fluffy undercoat, his dog almost certainly sheds her stiffer outercoat as well. George is more aware of the undercoat hairs because they far outnumber the outercoat hairs.

George is obviously very concerned about Lady's diet. But if he is already feeding Lady a brand-name commercial food proven to be 100-percent nutritionally complete through feeding trials on dogs, he probably will not reduce Lady's shedding by changing her diet.

Most shedding, as we've said, is perfectly normal. But if Lady's shedding is accompanied by bald spots (alopecia) or crusty, scaly, or inflamed skin, George and Lady should pay a visit to their veterinarian. Such signs indicate that a hormonal, allergic, infectious, or even immune mediated disorder may be involved.

If George and his veterinarian rule out disease and nutritional deficiency as causes of Lady's shedding, George's next move is to get out the 30-gallon trash bag and groom Lady daily during shedding season. (Carefully vacuuming Lady's coat may also help, as long as Lady doesn't mind.) In addition to removing loose hair, regular grooming promotes healthy skin and a shiny coat and gives owners opportunities to spot injury or signs of illness early on.

Category II-D — Canine Newspaper or Newsletter

YOUR DOG
Lloyd D. Resnick, Editor
(Published by Tufts University School of Veterinary Medicine)

Contents

Subscriptions: (12 issues)
$30 per year (U.S.), $42 per year (Canada)
Your Dog
P.O. Box 420272
Palm Coast, FL 32142

A TASTE OF
*SOUTHERN
CALIFORNIA DOG...*

BEHIND
THE LINES

by SHIRLEY THAYER

I have loved dogs all my life and have almost always had at least one. But I didn't understand much about dogs and didn't do much with them. They were just sort of "there." Sometimes things worked out well; sometimes they didn't. I thought it was the luck of the draw.

With more experience in journalism and publishing than with dogs, I have been learning along with many of you. When I read Marjorie Hudson's "Socialization: Getting the Dog of Your Dreams," (page 40), I was struck by what an important article this is.

How simple it is, I thought — not easy, mind you, but simple. If only I had known this 20 years ago. How different things would have been — for me and for the dogs who shared my life along the way (especially Maggie).

Suddenly, I wanted to grab each of you by the sleeve, tug it and say, "Hey, don't miss this article. This has the potential to change your life with dogs. Do more than read it. Watch your dogs and think about what they do, what you do, what you say, how they act."

Consider your sleeve tugged.

Shirley Thayer
Managing Editor

Category II-E — Special Interest Animal Magazine

SOUTHERN CALIFORNIA DOG
Shirley Thayer, Managing Editor

Contents

Subscriptions (12 issues):
$18.95 per year (U.S.)
Southern California Dog Magazine
P.O. Box 900069
San Diego, CA 92190

Cat. II-F-1 — Individ. Feature In A Single Breed Magazine

GENTLEMAN COLE: SERVICE DOG
by Jean Levitt
(COLLIE EXPRESSIONS)

As an Assistance Dog Team our work together includes a great deal of travel, including flying. We have completed twenty-two in-cabin airplane flights in the two years we have worked together, visiting 18 states. We have flown so many miles, we have free frequent flyer tickets for flights this winter and spring.

Recently while waiting in an airport lounge during a change of planes, Cole and I were the objects of much discussion by a very distressed older woman. She was clearly very upset to see a dog in the airport lounge. Her worst fears were confirmed when she and the gentleman traveling with her inquired of the ground personnel whether or not the offending dog was going to actually board the plane.

As usual, Cole rested quietly at my feet, interested in the sights, sounds, and especially smells of the airport. On a recent trip changing planes in Detroit, traveling with my son, Barry, Cole and I visited some bushes outside the airport terminal while Barry waited in the gate lounge for our flight. A last minute gate change was announced, so Barry went to the new gate, assuming I would check the information screen when I didn't see anyone at our gate. Upon arriving at the empty lounge, I said, "Where's Barry?" aloud. Lifting his nose to scent the air where Barry had been waiting, Cole picked up the fresh track, fouled by at least a hundred passengers, and purposefully led me out in the main hall and down a completely different corridor to a lounge where Barry was waiting! On this particular trip, Cole as usual remained politely aloof when enthusiastic travelers who did not know they should not pet or feed an Assistance Dog in harness, fondled him and offered him food. When a pair of restless children began crawling on him and in general creating a disturbance, he tolerated the inconvenience until I was able to explain the hands-off guidelines to the harassed parent and all of the people gathered around us, softening my request by offering Cole's brochure to each interested person.

From time to time as I politely accepted compliments and chatted with fellow travelers about Cole's appearance, manners, and professionalism, (thanks to his breeders and trainers, Eva and Leslie Rappaport of Kings Valley Collies in Oregon; Peggy Beattie of Welwyn Collies, in Millbrook, NY, who grooms him and Rene Bayha, DVM of Pound Ridge, NY Veterinary Clinic, his veterinarian), I caught a glimpse of the unhappy woman who by now was worked up into such a state the gentleman tried to calm her by walking her to an empty lounge nearby. They were joined by an airline supervisor, and I observed much gesturing, arguing, pleading, and finally, tears. Normally, we board first, but I decided to board last in order to allow her to get settled on the plane.

As sometimes happens when I'm very tired - I had been traveling since 5:00 AM, and it was now nearly 6:00 PM, my left side was completely numb. Cole senses when I need extra support, and he braced himself so I could balance against him to get out of my chair. He carefully walked to the boarding ramp, leaning into me to provide balance. His backpack was bulging with essentials for me, and Nutro Max and a bottle of water for him. (Although it's never happened, I'm always prepared for our luggage to be lost by packing at least two days' food for him in his backpack.)

Cole patiently stopped and braced me when I needed to rest, and automatically slowed his pace as we went down a slight slope on the boarding ramp.

I was concentrating so hard on

Jean Levitt & Cole - *photo Barry Levitt*

walking that I didn't notice the man standing in the elbow of the boarding ramp was the same man accompanying the distraught woman. As we approached, the man stepped forward. I saw he was shielding the woman with his body. She edged behind him and away from Cole.

The gentleman, speaking in a foreign accent, looked somewhat embarrassed as he explained that his wife, at the age of twelve, had witnessed her mother and father torn to pieces by attack dogs in Nazi Germany during World War II.

As the cockpit crew and the cabin crew of our plane patiently observed us from a few feet away in the waiting plane, he further explained she had boarded the plane, but panicked when she was strapped into her seat. She couldn't face flying in a plane with a big dog in the cabin. The ground personnel had explained Cole's job to them, and the Americans with Disabilities Act, Title III which permits Assistance Dogs in any place open to the public when assisting their person. The

41

couple had decided to leave the plane and forfeit over a thousand dollars in ticket fees... until she saw Cole so carefully, so professionally, assisting me into the plane.

The waiting cabin crew escorted the couple back into the plane, and seated them in the tail section again. Cole and I sat forward in the bulkhead seats. He scrunched down on the floor at my feet with his nose pointing toward the aisle so he could watch comings and goings. Once his backpack was removed he took a little nap. Several times during the flight, the woman chose to visit the forward bathroom rather than the one nearest her seat in the rear of the plane.

Each time, her husband accompanied her past Cole and waited the few seconds she was inside to escort her past us again. When we landed, I decided to get off last rather than hold everyone up. The couple chose to get off last also. When I got up to leave, assisted by Cole, they approached from the rear. In tears the woman sat on the arm of the seat across the aisle and told me how Cole had changed her life. She explained the terror she had felt every time she saw a big dog, how she relived the thing that happened to her parents every night as she slept. Now she was going to be all right. She was sure of it.

I invited her to touch Cole. Very cautiously she half extended her arm, and elevating her fingers just above the tips of the hair of his frill, she slowly lowered her fingers into his fur. Leaving her hand resting on Cole's neck, she looked toward her husband who had crouched down in the aisle beside Cole, and she put her head on his coat lapel, sobbing out aloud. She hid her face with her other hand. He comforted her as Cole stood perfectly still in place, tolerating the hand on his neck, understanding the significance of the moment.

The sympathetic cabin crew, watching our little group from first class, detained maintenance staff that had boarded to clean the plane.

The woman got off her seat, and crouched down on the floor beside her husband. She whispered something to Cole in a foreign language, thanked me in English, and got up to leave the plane. The gentleman stroked Cole under the chin. In return Cole gave him a little lick on the face, and the man stood up to join his wife.

As Cole assisted me up the aisle and off of the plane, the cabin crew walked with us on the boarding ramp, then into the airport. As we said our good-byes, one of the pilots who had watched us talk with the couple earlier on the ramp, came to attention and saluted Cole as we passed by.

To date, over 11,000 "Cole" brochures have been distributed to school children, seminar audiences, interested strangers, who stop us in restaurants, airports, on the street, patients in hospitals and nursing homes, health care professionals, television audiences, a little boy on the Staten Island Ferry, and "dog people".

For your free copy of the "Cole" brochure, send a SASE to: "Cole" brochure c/o Jean Levitt 208 Harris Road, Fa-1 Bedford Hills, NY 10507

Cat. II-F-2 — Individual Feature in All Breed Magazine

* This article was also winner of the ALPINE/DENLINGER AWARD as most outstanding individual article in a magazine or canine newspaper.

A BOND OF TRUST
by Jan Mahood
(THE AKC GAZETTE)

When Caroline Hebard's husband Arthur comes home from work and sees a pile of duffel bags by the door, he knows somewhere in the world a disaster has just occurred and his wife and her dog are on the move again. He knows there is no stopping them. They will drive, trek, fly and hitchhike to wherever disaster strikes. Once there, they may find themselves sleeping on floors, crawling through collapsed buildings or rappeling down cliffs.

Currently at home, Hebard— Whippet-trim and dressed for action in

Hebard & Pascha - Ed Murray

jeans, working shoes and fleece anorak, her blonde hair in a ponytail—is relating spine-tingling adventures in measured tones. Pascha, a handsome German Shepherd Dog is napping on the kitchen floor of the white clapboard home in Bernardsville, N.J. The pair might be any suburban housewife and her faithful family dog.

Once called to work, however, the duo transforms into a search and rescue (SAR) precision team, focusing on finding and—if possible—saving disaster victims. After January's quake in Japan,

Pascha's bark alerted searchers among the crumpled remains of Kobe (see the March AKC GAZETTE). In April the pair sifted through the Oklahoma City Federal Building after the bombing. They've assisted police and fire department teams in dozens of regional searches over water, through wooded areas and in urban crack alleys. Hebard and Pascha participate in approximately 60 searches a year.

Hebard is the only person prominent in SAR to have worked the five worst earthquakes in modern history — Kobe; the Philippines in 1990; Armenia in 1988; El Salvador in 1986; and Mexico City in 1985. "It was in Mexico City that I first truly knew, I love doing this!" says Hebard. "It was that total partnership with my dog and the joy of watching a well-trained working dog do exactly what he was meant to do. You really know you're helping people. We rescued two women ten days after the quake."

"She's the bravest woman I've ever met," says Doug Copp, a California demolitions expert who, like Hebard, is one of a handful of experienced SAR workers who have defined the discipline since its inception in the U.S.

It was William Syrotuck who brought the practice of search and rescue dogs to this country. While living in Seattle, he adapted avalanche rescue dog techniques he learned in Switzerland to help locate people lost in the northwestern wilderness. (Syrotuck's book, "Scent and the Scenting Dog," is required reading for Hebard's trainees.) Hebard has been training her dogs and working tornado sites and floods since the early 1970s. She cites the Mexico quake of 1985 as a watershed event: "Things really got more organized, there was more awareness of SAR as a distinct discipline after that disaster."

Between searches, Hebard and Pascha teach SAR at the FBI Academy, Lackland Air Force Base and various law enforcement, military and civilian canine units around the U.S., as well as in Finland, Australia, Iceland, Germany, France and Czechoslovakia. They also conduct programs in schools, rehab centers and nursing homes. "I teach, and he's the dog and pony show," she laughs.

FATE TAKES A HAND

Hebard developed her penchant for a peripatetic lifestyle as the child of a British diplomat whose career required the family to move every few years. Her first dog was an Airedale. However, family pets were not the norm because of the difficulties presented by various countries' quarantine regulations.

"In Turkey," she says, recalling one of her family's relocations, "I tried to adopt an Anatolian Sheepdog puppy. I hid him in the attic for two weeks, until the cook ratted on me. There was food missing from the kitchen."

Hebard first experienced the human-canine bond as a Stanford University graduate student in applied linguistics. "An Australian Shepherd-Border Collie mix—Pickles, from the Palo Alto Animal Shelter—became my constant companion," she recalls. "She went everywhere with me. She'd wait outside my classes. As a teaching assistant, I'd sneak her into class with me."

In 1968, she married Arthur Hebard, a renowned research physicist, and started a family—two children born within 10 months of each other and, of course, a dog. "Art wanted a German Shorthaired Pointer, which I think are wonderful dogs, but I had always wanted a GSD." She brought home Yaeger, U.S. born of a German line, and presented Arthur with a fait accompli rather than a GSP.

Before long, Hebard found herself enjoying "basic AKC-type obedience training" with Yaeger. From there, she got involved with Schutzhund training. When her next GSD, German-born Zibo, joined the family, he already had his SchH 1, the first level of three in this discipline. (Her current partner, Pascha, is SchH 3.)

"I joined an all-male group in the California Peninsula Police Canine Corps, one of the first Schutzhund clubs in this country. There, I trained under Gernot Liedel, a leading advocate of Schutzhund," says Hebard.

In an effort that exemplifies Hebard's uncompromising demands on herself as well as on her dogs, she put Zibo through SchH I a second time in order to make herself proficient in the discipline. Then, just as she and Zibo were approaching certification in SchH 2, Arthur Hebard took a position with Bell Laboratories in New Jersey.

No novice at pulling up stakes and moving on, Hebard drove cross-country with husband, children and dogs to their new home in the wooded countryside of central New Jersey. When she got settled and looked around, she discovered there was no Schutzhund group in the area. "I wasn't the type to join women's clubs," she says with a blue-eyed twinkle. "I needed something to get me out of the house, though." At that point, fate stepped in.

Hebard

"Barbara Ward, a prominent GSD person in California, had given me the name of Margot Roehling DeHope, and she's the culprit who got me into this!" says Hebard. "I joined the Ramapo SAR organization in Ramsey, N.J. But I saw that we were losing people because the Ramapo group works only with GSDs." Although Hebard prefers working with GSDs, she acknowledges that a number of breeds can succeed at SAR. She likes GSDs because they are faithful and can withstand extreme heat and cold. They also have a presence that commands respect. "When I go unarmed into an urban search situation, or after a disaster when there may be looting, I feel very safe traveling with these dogs."

Lt. Dan Kluge of the Baltimore County, MD., fire department works with Golden Retrievers and Labrador Retrievers. Their birding instinct, he says, keeps their heads up and searching the air for human scent. He also praises their ability to charm youngsters during SAR programs at schools. Hebard trained Kluge and his Golden, Barney, and helped set up the department's canine unit in 1989.

"Caroline is an excellent teacher," Kluge says. "She has more field experience than anyone else in the world. That's the kind of knowledge you don't get from books." It was all worth it when Barney saved a 10-year-old boy's life. When he found the boy huddled under a bush in the woods, his temperature had dropped to 88 degrees. He would not have survived the night.

Hebard eventually left the Ramapo unit and formed her own group. Her first actual rescue work was during the Johnstown floods in the 1970s. "I was pregnant," she recalls. "We were working a devastated trailer park. There were bloated animals floating everywhere. The stench was horrible. I'd work with Zibo for awhile, then go behind a tree and puke, then go back to work." Undeterred, she went on to the Schoharie Creek Bridge collapse in New York State and the Ambiance Plaza collapse in Bridgeport, Conn. She also organized the first biennial International Disaster Dog Conference, in Orlando, Fla. That was followed by conferences in Mexico, Italy, Germany and Sweden, as well as the U.S.

Hebard's son Alastair, now 20, arrived shortly after Johnstown, apparently influenced in utero by his mother's activities. "He's my SAR buddy," she says. An avid scuba diver, Alastair is majoring in marine biology at the University of Miami. Her other children are Joanne, 25, who works in hotel management in Florida; Andrew, 24, a Ph.D. candidate in comparative literature at the University of Chicago and Heather, 17, who aspires to a writing career.

TRUST YOUR DOG

Hebard notes that GSD breeders

45

who want to work their dogs are breeding for size, temperament and keen play-prey instinct — "good, even-keel, solid type working dogs." She points out Pascha's physical attributes, including strong hips and a straight back rather than the overly sloped top line that was fashionable for a while: "The straighter the back, the better the hips."

Other breeds in SAR work today are Belgian Malinois, Border Collies, Newfoundlands and Labrador, Golden and Flat-Coated Retrievers. "And I'm seeing more Airedales and Schnauzers, even Mini Schnauzers. One of the best in Czechoslovakia is a Miniature Schnauzer!"

In Australia, Hebard's GSD Aly, which she selected in Germany, worked SAR with a 40-pound Blue Heeler, or Australian Cattle Dog, named Merlin. One of Hebard's objectives is to work large dog-small dog teams. "The large dog with the greater scenting ability gives the alert, and the smaller dog can go into holes in rubble where a larger dog won't fit."

Hebard gets a distant look as she reminisces about Aly, "a big shepherd, a classic in search." The dog's talents saved his partner's life. Searching through the devastation of the 1988 El Salvador quake, Aly started acting strangely, but Hebard, thinking they were close to a find, put him off. Suddenly, an aftershock hit, "the biggest danger in SAR work." The rubble shifted. Hebard was trapped, and couldn't see Aly through the blinding dust. "Adding to my panic, I thought my dog had been injured or killed," she says.

But Aly wasn't about to give up. He found a way out of the building, then came back, tail wagging, to get his partner. Hebard, trusting her dog completely, followed

him to safety. "When we got out I was hugging him and laughing and crying."

"That's what I mean when I tell handlers, 'You have to read your dog. When he tells you it's time to get out, you get out!' That's the bond between dog and handler. It's the difference between total control over the dog and a real partnership."

Aly died last year. He is widely recognized as one of the best SAR dogs ever.

LESSONS FROM OKLAHOMA CITY

Not all of Hebard's GSDs have been top-notch SAR workers. There was Sasquatch, an all-American grandson of John DeHope's well-known U.S. Champion Reno, "good with kids, but not exactly what I was looking for." When Hebard took him on a search in Maine, he chased a moose, right in front of the game warden. "That was his last search!"

Then there was Marko, an American show dog who needed a home and joined the Hebards as an older dog. And Hebard adopted Max, a German import, when his owners moved to an apartment in Manhattan.

"We've always had three or four GSDs at a time," Hebard says. "I always keep my SAR dogs after they retire. And when *I* retire. I'm 50 now and I'll be doing this for quite a while yet, but at the same time I'd like to get the new generation properly trained, with properly trained dogs."

She's looking forward to working with the Tokyo Fire Department. "After the Kobe disaster, they realized that they should have their own SAR teams in Japan, especially because of the quarantine." (Incoming dogs must wait 48 hours before being released from quarantine. Japan is rigid in this policy and boasts of being rabies-free.)

"I'll also be working more with law enforcement and military units. They bond with their dogs. I don't like to work with people who keep their dogs in an installation. A dog needs to live with its handler."

Closer to home is Hebard's newest training project, her 50th birthday present, Aranka, an exuberant 14-month-old GSD bitch who shows promise as an SAR worker. "Great nose! The other day I dropped my glasses somewhere in the woods. The next morning, Aranka came out of the woods with my glasses in her mouth!"

The basic curriculum for developing effective SAR teams includes classroom work and outdoor training, but the best education takes place on the job; that is, at actual disaster sites. Recruits Joyce Pugh and her GSD, Leda, of Langhorne, Pa., received a proper introduction to SAR work when they accompanied Hebard and Pascha to Oklahoma City.

"She's dynamite!" Pugh says of Hebard. "She's a teacher. She's a friend. I've never seen her lose her temper, and she's always fair in her criticism. Leda's come a long way. Caroline had more confidence in Leda than I did!"

Hebard says Pugh came a long way, too, through the Oklahoma City experience. "She saw some really fine workers, and she also saw what shouldn't be done."

Hebard's eyes harden a bit when she speaks of less than professional handler conduct. "Booties!" she scoffs with a derisive laugh. "Some of the handlers put booties on their dogs! " Bad idea, she says, because a dog's feet need to breathe. They need to have traction to feel the way through rubble. "I saw dogs' pads swell to enormous size because they were injured by wearing the booties too long."

According to Hebard, some other lessons of Oklahoma City are: "Let dogs limber up before putting them to work. Cover their crates if they are outside in the rain. In Oklahoma, there were lots of muscle problems because these things were not done.

"Work dogs only 30 minutes in rubble. Then give them a rest. Clean out their eyes. Give them water. Make sure their noses are clean and moist to optimize their sense of smell. Don't work dogs on leash—no collar, no vest, no leash, so they can find their way over mounds of sharp metal and broken glass.

"Handlers must realize that their dogs get stressed. They need frequent breaks. Feed them the same food they get at home. They usually adjust to the water unless, of course, it's polluted, in which case they drink bottled water."

Dogs get depressed after finding only dead victims. In Oklahoma City, to lift their dogs' spirits, some of the handlers staged live finds by taking turns hiding among the ruins. Also, like human rescue workers, the dogs need critical incident stress debriefing. When Hebard and Pascha return from a search, she allows him to sleep in the master bedroom for a few nights.

Hebard praises most of the workers

Aly

at the bombing scene—the Oklahoma City Police Department, university volunteers, fire departments, Red Cross, clergy, Salvation Army and others who worked tirelessly to save the living and find the dead. She was not as impressed, however, with FEMA—Federal Emergency Management Agency.

"They have some very good people and some very good handlers, but there were mistakes at Oklahoma City, and there will be fallout because of it over the next year," she predicts. In her opinion, the Department of Defense does a better job. "DOD has the capabilities and the resources—top handlers, a couple of hundred dogs. They have a disciplined approach to their training.

"I warned Oklahoma City personnel that FEMA would try to close down the search eight days after the explosion, and I was right. I will not stop as long as I feel there is hope. Even after there is none, people need to bury their dead. They shouldn't have to leave them under a collapsed building."

She decries the lack of coordination in general in the U.S. "In most European nations you have to go through national rescue dog certification." This involves training in avalanche search, tracking/trailing, two levels of disaster and water search. No such certification exists here.

A PROUD MOMENT

At rest after completing his most recent mission, Pascha is a big, friendly, well mannered dog. His noble bearing is marred only by fresh scars on his head—no doubt injuries caused by glass shards or jagged metal during the Oklahoma City search.

"When we got back," Hebard says, "Iago was jealous of Pascha, the alpha dog who got to go with me and be a hero while he had to stay at home. As soon as he saw Pascha, he attacked him and went for his head." Iago is a younger GSD Hebard has been evaluating for SAR work. Shortly after his challenge to Pascha, Iago joined the Southampton, N.Y., police canine unit, where he may realize his dream of being top dog.

Not many would argue that Hebard herself is a top dog in the world of SAR. Her achievements as an international trainer, handler and teacher have brought Hebard recognition by world leaders as well as by her peers. One of her proudest moments was when she was invited to the Russian Embassy in Washington, D.C., to accept the Soviet Medal of Supreme Courage from General Secretary Mikhail Gorbachev for her heroic service in Albania alter the earthquake.

"I phoned and said I wouldn't feel right being there without my partner," Hebard relates. "Well, they agreed and, oh, it was a great moment to see my dog right up there at the podium with me." Other awards have come from former President Ronald Reagan, U.S. Senator Bill Bradley and New Jersey Governor Thomas H. Kean. Recently, she received a letter of thanks from the governor of Kobe, Japan, for her part in that city's search.

But when a Japanese Broadcasting Company television crew arrived recently to interview her and asked to see her "awards room," they were surprised to see that all her medals and certificates are tucked away in boxes. A small detail perhaps, but a telling one. For Hebard, it's yet another way she keeps the focus on her work.

Cat. II-F-3 — Indiv. Feat. in Multi-Breed or Hunting Mag.

TOTALLY POSITIVE WHAT?
by James B. Spencer
(GUN DOG)

The latest catch phrase in the bird-dog world, especially among obedience specialists and self-anointed canine psychologists, is Totally Positive Reinforcement, or TPR. Without ever precisely defining the term (definitions are so confining!), TPR apostles preach that trainers should religiously reward proper behavior but should never correct misconduct. Clearly, TPR mimics the permissive child-rearing theories that sprouted and grew like bindweed after World War II, theories which explain, at least in part, why sociopaths abound today and why prison construction has become a growth industry. Thus, I wonder how much TPR has contributed to the alarming rise in serious canine temperament problems that we are experiencing.

TPR, gratifying as it may be to the human ego, simply does not adequately address canine nature. In fact, it ignores everything except the reward half of the conditioning process. But no amount of praise, or cookies, will incline a retriever to take a straight line when he thinks he has a better idea. Ignoring his bad lines, hoping for an eventual good one to "reinforce positively," is sillier than giving a roomful of monkeys typewriters and waiting for one of them to type a Shakespearean sonnet.

The dog just won't do it—at least not as long as he thinks he has a better idea—until the trainer convinces him otherwise with appropriate corrections.

CANINE NATURE

To train any animal, you must understand that animal's nature. Training theories, approaches, and techniques derive any validity they may have from their relevance to the nature of the animal being trained, not from the preconceived notion or self-esteem aspirations of the trainer. If I wanted to train a horse (a laughable thought, really), I would first have to learn what horses are like, then how they are trained. Winging it with dog training techniques wouldn't work; in fact, that might get me killed.

THE CANINE MIND

For the trainer, the most significant element in canine nature is the sub-human, nonintellectual mind. Dogs cannot reason abstractly or grasp abstract concepts, such as nation, mind, or tomorrow. We cannot motivate them with long-delayed rewards ("don't bark and you'll earn a cookie in four hours") as we can a human ("study hard and you'll earn a college degree in four years"). And we cannot teach them, as we do people, with verbal explanations, discussions, reading assignments, term papers, and so on. Instead, we breed them to do certain things instinctively and, beyond that, we condition them to behave in certain ways. But conditioning, by any reasonable definition, involves both rewards and punishments.

*Nota Bene: The chasm between human nature and the natures of all lower animals, clearly demonstrable from mental differences, is the linchpin of every rational argument against the demands of the animal rights looneys.

PACK INSTINCT

Another significant element of canine nature is that they are pack animals. Each dog needs a known place in his pack's pecking order. In every litter, the puppies work out their places, sometimes not too politely, while the dam asserts overall control, sometimes not too politely. TPR, being totally polite, encourages the dog to believe he has dominance over his trainer. Should the "subordinate" trainer slip up and try to correct the dog, or should he inadvertently act in a manner the dog perceives as dominant (for example, stare absentmindedly at the dog's eyes), the dog will react as a dominant pack animal. He will put the upstart human in his place, and not too politely. Thus, through human folly, a perfectly normal dog can behave as if afflicted with hereditary rage syndrome.

HUNTING INSTINCT

A final significant element in canine nature is the set of specialized hunting instincts we have selectively bred into the various breeds: birdiness, pointing, retrieving, love of water, marking, and so on. These provide "positive reinforcement" in and of themselves.

TRAINING IMPLICATIONS

From the trainer's perspective, a dog is a conditionable pack animal with specialized instincts. Understanding that and building your training program on it will make you a more effective trainer. What's more, it will make you a more devoted dog lover, for you will love them as is, not according to some unrealistic fantasy.

Therefore, to train a dog, you must establish yourself as the pack leader, bring out his specialized instincts, and condition him to behave as you wish. All effective training techniques assist you to do one or more of those three things.

> You are the boss; the pup's job is to please you; and, in exchange for this, you will take care of all his needs.

ASSERTING YOURSELF

If you start with a well-bred pup from a responsible breeder, establishing yourself as the pack leader is almost trivial. Start off recognizing the realities of the situation: You are the boss; the pup's job is to please you; and, in exchange for this, you will take care of all his needs. Actually, the pup drew the long straw, for most of your expectations involve the work for which he was bred, the work he loves, the work for which you must provide even the opportunities.

Unless you convince him otherwise, the pup will assume that you are the pack leader. After all, you are bigger than he is; you carry him around, you feed and water him; and so on. Because of his pack animal nature, he will try to please you. Great! Give him plenty of opportunities to do so and show your appreciation when he does. Earned appreciation is your most powerful tool. Similarly, he will try to avoid displeasing you.

Again, great! When he misbehaves, show your displeasure appropriately. Justified displeasure is your second most powerful tool.

If, ignoring our current abundance of canine psycho-babble, you take this common-sense approach to puppy raising—set the rules, appreciate compliance, correct disobedience, and take proper care of the pup's needs—a normal pup will never question your position as pack leader.

DEVELOPING INSTINCTS

Selective breeding inclines a dog

> Selective
> breeding
> inclines a dog
> to hunt in
> certain ways.

to hunt in certain ways. Even so, the trainer must provide opportunities for these instincts to assert themselves. All sporting dogs should love birds, but each one requires a nonthreatening introduction to them. Retrievers love to carry things, but we must convert this into retrieving. Retrievers can mark and remember falls quite well—provided they have enough opportunities in the field to develop this instinct. And so on.

In developing a dog's instincts, the trainer must also introduce him to his working environment. Retrievers need a reasonable introduction to water. Some take to it more easily than others. A Chesapeake pup named Beaver introduced himself to water while I was closing his dogbox door. Looking up, I saw the little rascal some forty yards from shore, treading water and trying to uproot a dead tree. Brushing my hands deftly, I said, "Hey, can I introduce pups to water, or what?"

Many beginning retriever trainers forget to introduce their pups to cover, then expect them to retrieve from it—almost invariably with disastrous results. Bird-dog and spaniel trainers do a much better job here. Before starting birdwork, they familiarize their youngsters with all manner of cover through long walks in various fields.

CONDITIONING

We condition our dogs to behave in ways nature does not incline them to behave. Examples: basic obedience, steadying, force-breaking, switch-proofing, all blind retrieve training.

The conditioning process consists of repetitions of stimulus-response-result. In teaching a puppy to sit, the stimulus is the command sit; the response is the pup's reaction (he does or doesn't sit); and the result is a reward (if he sits) or a correction (if he doesn't). After a few repetitions, the pup learns which response gets the reward and avoids the correction. With enough repetitions, his response becomes automatic, or "conditioned".

You can often, but not always, precondition a dog to respond correctly through "training by association" or "leading-through." In training by association you give the command only when the dog is already doing what you want. For example, you say sit when your puppy sits on his own, then reward him with praise, petting, or even a treat. Do this consistently and he will soon associate your word with his action. Then he will sit "on command." You can precondition many commands by association: Say kennel when he enters his crate or kennel run on his own; say shake when he shakes water from his coat; and so on.

You can work association into more advanced training, too. For example, in training a spaniel or retriever to quarter with the "shaking" technique (see my column on "Quartering" in the October/ November 1993 issue of Gun Dog), *pip-pip* on the whistle every time the youngster turns from one assistant to run to the other. By association, that pip-pip becomes his turn whistle command. Another example: When releasing a young bird dog at the start of a run, use the word or whistle signal you will later use to send him out farther. And so on. Opportunities for training by association abound, and the technique is both positive and effortless.

You can sometimes precondition your dog by leading him through the proper response as you repeat the command and praise him. For example, in force-breaking, you start out holding the buck in his mouth as you say fetch— good dog over and over. The dog has no choice but to comply, so he makes the connection between fetch and holding the buck. Another example: In training a bird dog to whoa, you start out restraining him physically while you repeat whoa and praise him. And so on.

In many cases, preconditioning can be the same process. For example, in teaching a dog to heel, you can start out by using little jerk-and-release corrections with the chain training collar whenever he strays from the proper position. Of course, you should also praise him when he is where he belongs. The combination of praise for proper heeling and irritating little tugs for mistakes will convey the meaning of heel. Many TPR advocates suffer the vapors at the mention of this "negative" approach, but it works. Always did, even for obe-

> Proofing is negative training, pure & simple.

> This is delicate work, for if you overcorrect, he may refuse to leave your side in the rerun.

dience trial competition, where my dogs have won plenty of trophies. Anyone who has watched them in the ring will tell you they were bouncy, high-spirited animals, in fact, always on the edge.

Preconditioning, by whatever method, only prepares your dog for complete conditioning. Although he understands what reaction you expect to a particular command, you must still convince him that that is the only acceptable reaction, that any other reaction will bring unpleasant results. For this you introduce conditions that tempt your dog to ignore your command. Whenever he does so, you correct him appropriately (which does not necessarily mean severely). For example, after he understands fetch, whenever he refuses, you apply force ear-pinch, paw-squeeze, etc. After he understands that pip-pip means turn, whenever he ignores the whistle, you shake him up a bit. After he understands whoa, whenever he "goes deaf," you send him some e-mail from your transmitter. (I call my electronic collar "Erick's hearing aid," Erick being my German shorthair.) And so on.

PROOFING

Proofing is a specialized form of conditioning, used for teaching a dog to avoid places, things, or animals. Retriever trainers switch-proof their dogs and proof them against bank-running. Bird dog trainers deer-proof and rabbit-proof their dogs. Spaniel trainers may deer-proof, but may or may not rabbit-proof. All trainers in certain areas snake-proof their dogs. And so on. Proofing is negative training, pure and simple. Why? How else can you train a dog to avoid something? How many cookies would it take to condition a normally curious dog to avoid snakes?

Dogs are extremely "place conscious." They avoid places where they have been punished. To cure bank running, you should correct your dog while he is running the bank, then rerun the test. In the rerun, to avoid the place of chastisement, he will jump in and swim. This is delicate work, for if you overcorrect, he may refuse to leave your side in the rerun. Similarly, switch-proofing takes advantage of the dog's place consciousness, and requires almost as much delicacy.

Deer-proofing, rabbit-proofing, snake-proofing, and so on, are similar, but do not require a light touch. Far from it. You want your dog to associate "memorable" punishment with a particular animal. When he both sees and smells the critter, you reach out with a heavy hand (typically an electronic collar set at a high intensity level).

THEORY PROBLEMS

TPR has some good points. Who can disagree with positive training wherever it is effective? Certainly not I, as any regular reader of my work surely knows. However, TPR founders because it addresses primarily the trainer's ego rather than the trainee's nature. It ignores bred-in hunting instincts—probably because most TPR evangelists train only for the obedience ring. It ignores, or misreads, the packing instinct—probably because that instinct gives lie to totally positive anything in dog training. It ignores the effectiveness of corrections in the conditioning process. In short, it ignores too much.

Cat. II-F-4
Ind. Feature in Canine Newspaper or Newsletter

FREE TO A GOOD HOME: A DEATH SENTENCE

by Cara C. Christenson

(TEXAS DOGS)

(Inspired by a story in the Philadelphia Daily News by Stu Bykofsky)

Mary and Pat Callahan had raised seven children in a large Huntington Valley, Philadelphia home. Their youngest daughter, Katie, had just graduated from high school. Like many parents when their kids have grown and left home, Mary and Pat were moving. They had found a condo that would be just perfect for their situation, but there was one problem. No pets were allowed. They had to find a home for Duke, their beloved liver-and-white 6 1/2 year old Dalmatian. Duke had been a Christmas present to Mary from her children, and she adored him. Mary had a hard time with the idea of giving Duke up, but she consoled herself that they would find him a good home where he'd be happier than in a small condo.

The Callahan's youngest daughter, Katie, was having a graduation party. One of her friends brought Roy A. Elliot and Jason Tapper, age 21, and Jan Pyatt, Jr., 23, to the party. Pyatt and Tapper expressed great interest in Duke, telling Mary of their 10 acres of land where Duke would be able to run and exercise. They spoke of their other animals, and assured Mary that Duke would have a great home. Mary was immediately taken with the idea, as Pyatt and Tapper lived near the Callahan's new condo, and she would be able to visit Duke often. Without checking out Pyatt and Tapper's home and situation, she allowed them to take Duke home that night. This was a fatal error, a death sentence for the Dalmatian who Mary professed to love. If she had only asked more questions. If she had only checked out Pyatt and Tapper's story. If she had only requested references. If she had only made a home visit to see this farm and Pyatt's other animals. Mary would come to regret a lot of "what-ifs."

Duke never made it to the idyllic farm setting Mary had been promised for him. One of Katie's friends told the Callahans that Pyatt and Tapper had lost Duke, that he had jumped out of the car on the way to his new home. The Callahans immediately began searching, tacking up posters and knocking on doors all over the area where Duke had supposedly escaped. "Their search was in vain," writes Bykofsky, because they were searching for something that was not lost."

One week after Mary had turned Duke over to his "adoptive family," his mutilated remains were found in a field behind Pyatt's house. An eyewitness relates that the same night that Mary handed Duke over to what she thought was a good home, his mouth was taped shut, he was tied to a tree, and Pyatt's fighting pit bull was turned loose on the 6 1/2 year old family pet, who was rendered absolutely defenseless without the use of his teeth and unable to run. Duke's torment — and life — were not ended by the pit bull, but by a human being. The vet who examined Duke's remains reports that after the pit bull attack, his tail was cut off, his belly was cut open, his throat was slit, and his skull was crushed. Then "he was discarded like so much trash," relates Bykofsky.

The suspects are in custody. Their preliminary hearing is scheduled for October 21st. The three face felony charges for dog fighting ($15,000 fine, 3 1/2 - 7 years max), misdemeanor charges for killing, maiming and disfiguring a domestic animal ($5000 fine, 12 year max) and summary animal cruelty ($300 fine, 90 day max). Mary Callahan says, "I will never forgive myself for giving him to those bastards." She has made it her mission now to warn people never to surrender family pets "free to a good home" to someone they don't know.

This story has caused extreme reactions in Pennsylvania and on the many computer bulletin boards where it has been retold and reprinted. Throngs of people turned out with their pets at the courthouse where the accused men were brought to trial. Petitions were signed with thousands of names, demanding justice. A famous sculptor is erecting a statue of Duke. Duke T-shirts and pins are being sold to commemorate the event. Condolences rain down upon the Callahans, who have appeared frequently in interviews about their traumatic experience in losing their pet.

I offer a different viewpoint here. Although it is tragic that the Callahans made a fatal error in giving Duke to his executioners and that they will have to live with the knowledge of his painful death for the rest of their lives, we should remember that it is Duke who was the victim here. The family had decided they no longer wanted Duke, a family pet who had, by Mary Callahan's own admission, gone above and beyond the call of duty in his six-and-a-half years, and the family — certainly, unknowingly — placed him without a thought to the possibility that the new home should be checked out for suitability. Although I am sure that this family now realizes the importance of screening prospective adopters, I am afraid that the moral to this story is becoming lost in the media fanfare. The situation has almost become a carnival — proposed Thanksgiving Day floats with Dalmatians to honor Duke, Duke items and souvenirs, etc. What will be most tragic is if Duke died in vain.

Can nothing be learned here? Even if Pyatt and Tapper were hung from the highest tree, there are other Pyatts and Tappers. These men did a terrible thing, but theirs is not a singularly unusual story — they just got caught by some twist of fate. How many other pets are similarly slaughtered when given away "Free

> These men did a
> terrible thing,
> but theirs is not a
> singularly unusual
> story—they just
> got caught.

to a Good Home"? How many families even follow up to find out if a situation worked out, or are they just glad to "get rid of" the nuisance pet, who has become a burden? How many pets are euthanized by Animal Control, after new homes — even legitimate ones — do not work out — unless the family specifies to bring the dog back if there are any problems, hopefully even having a contract of adoption; many frustrated new owners of second-hand dogs automatically decide to drop the dog off at the pound. And what about the baby puppies toddling out into the world, many sold by backyard breeders whose "screening" of buyers is limited to possibly calling the bank to see if their check is good? (I won't mention the show fanciers or national breed club member/breeders who should know better).

The moral here is RESPONSIBILITY. It is not just a terrible tale of dreadful dog fighters accruing family pets to train their fighting dog. That is the stuff hot news stories are made of — but, a year from now or possibly even a month from now, no one will remember the story. The details will be fuzzy. Perhaps you'd remember that it was a Dalmatian, but maybe you will have even forgotten that his name was Duke. However, if you can learn from Mary Callahan's tragic experience, perhaps the next news story won't be about YOUR puppy, or that retired champion you had to place. This story is a sad reminder for the necessity of screening puppy buyers and prospective adoptive homes for older pets, a statement for the use of adoption contracts, a memo to check references. We work so hard to breed a better dog, then when a fantastic dog like Duke comes along we let him die a painful death because an easy solution presented itself.

How can you prevent this from happening to you?

1. NEVER advertise "Free to a Good Home" even if you don't want any money for the animal. People who answer "Free to a Good Home" ads are many times:

a) people who cannot afford a dog in the first place.

b) "weekend shoppers" who are bored, collect a "Free to a Good Home" dog or cat for the weekend, then take him to the pound or toss him out on the highway come Sunday night.

c) "B" dealers collecting animals for laboratory research — these people WILL pose as a family searching for the perfect pet.

d) children, teens, or spouses who have not given thought to the responsibilities of caring for the pet, what the rest of the family wants, etc. If Dad doesn't know about the new Cocker Spaniel, chances are that when he gets home and finds out about it that the new Cocker Spaniel will end up at the animal shelter, or tossed out in the country so that he can have room to run" and "find a home on a farm" where most likely he will be gunned down by the first farmer or rancher who spots him (loose dogs DO kill livestock, even dogs you think would never do such a thing.)

e) college students or military buying a dog for the summer or term of service in the area.

f) backyard breeders who want the dogs not for their pet appeal but for breeding machines.

g) dog fighters, Satan worshippers, and other people who enjoy seeing animals in pain.

h) people looking for guard dogs for junkyards, car lots, etc. and a myriad of other inappropriate homes.

SURE, you MIGHT luck out and find that perfect family, but why take the chance? You can eliminate MOST of the aforementioned bad homes/situations by NOT putting your dog in a "Free to a Good Home" ad. If you really don't want the money, send it to your rescue organization.

2. Be totally honest with the prospective adoptive family. I once had a rescue Sibe here at my house, and we were having a great deal of trouble placing him. A non-doggy friend was here during one of the unsuccessful encounters, and after the man left, she asked me, "Why do you tell them about the digging? If you hadn't told that man about that, he would have taken the dog." Well, aside from the fact that my backyard looked like Carlsbad Caverns (which is kind of a hard fact to hide), I have always made it my policy to be honest with potential adopters.

I have NEVER had a rescue dog returned to me out of around 30 rescues, and I DO have a contract that states they must be returned if the family chooses to give the dog up. The family will find out about the dog's behavior problems when they get home, anyway, so make sure that it's something they can live with. Otherwise, they will dispose of your dog when they find out he's not the perfect pet you made him out to be.

3. Use a contract for adoption. No, it might not hold up in court. However, it will PROBABLY make the person think twice about testing this theory. Be sure to include a clause that the dog must be returned to you if the family gives up the dog, and also state that if the dog is being mistreated or neglected in any way that you have the right to reclaim the dog.

4. Talk with the prospective adopter and make sure you agree on contracts & screening policies BEFORE he/she sees the dog. When the dog is brought into the room, the person will no longer be giving you his full attention.

5. Ask questions! Ask if this person has ever had a dog before, and what happened to it. Dying of old age is a good answer, but you will hear the gamut from "Hit by a car" to "I took her to the pound." Obviously, if the person's last dog was dumped at the animal shelter or if it died from running loose in the neighborhood, this is not a good home.

Ask where the person intends to keep the dog; "chained up in the backyard" should end the adoptive interview. Ask about other pets this person has.

Ask for three references — neighbors, veterinarian, groomer, kennel club members, anyone who could tell you that this would be a good owner.

Ask the person why they feel they might want a dog of this breed, and see how much they actually know about Chinese Cresteds — "I saw a picture in a book," or "Aren't they good guard dogs?" should lead you to believe this person needs more education before getting a dog of your breed. A fenced yard should be a must.

6. Check out all information for yourself — do NOT take these people at their word. Your dog's quality of life — or even his life itself — may depend on your actions at this time. Drive by the house, attempt to arrange a home visit before adoption, call the references.

7. Follow up! Call the new adoptive family to check on the progress, assist with problems, and be sure that this is the absolute best home possible for your former pet.

Category II-F-5
Ind. Feature in Special Interest Animal Mag.

MY PRECIOUS GIFT
by Elizabeth Barlow

(OUR ANIMALS)

When George Reid was 18, doctors listened to his irregular heartbeat and pronounced imminent doom for the young man. George found the spiritual strength he needed shortly thereafter, through his newly chosen profession — the ministry.

At age 32, George was told by doctors that he had terminal cancer. After seven operations in three weeks, the doctors changed the prognosis, but not by much. George was informed that, if he survived, he would spend the rest of his life in seriously constrained circumstances. He would never be able to drive again, or travel for that matter. The ordeal required all the physical and emotional resources he could muster.

Today, at 69, George Reid still takes pleasure in having

Reverend Reid & Bingo

proved his doctors wrong. Not only has he survived, he has thrived. His vocation as an evangelical minister (he is a bishop in the United Metropolitan Spiritual Church of Christ) takes him on frequent ecclesiastical travels across much of the United States.

George lost most of his hearing while a youngster. He wears hearing aids and uses a special amplifier on his telephone. But clearly, this disability has not impeded his life or career. Just a couple of years ago, though, George had another brush with death.

He was in a hurry and stepped off the curb sooner than he should have. If the driver honked at him, he didn't hear it. The car ran over his foot and he fell into traffic. While not seriously injured, George was shaken into realizing that his own spiritual, physical and emotional strength wasn't enough. He needed help.

"Not too long after that," recalls George, who speaks in the same deep, resonant tones as actor James Earl Jones, "I saw an advertisement for Guide Dogs for the Blind, and I thought that they might know something. I said to the lady who answered the phone,

'What I'm about to ask you may sound silly. I'm not blind, I'm deaf. Is there such a thing as guide dogs for the deaf?' She said yes and gave me a number to call."

After several more calls, George reached The San Francisco SPCA Hearing Dog Program and was promptly sent an application. So thorough was he in completing it (even anticipating the need for proof of his landlord's pet policy) that he was accepted as a candidate for a Hearing Dog in record time.

Meanwhile, the dog he would eventually be paired with also had a close call, and very nearly missed out on becoming George's friend and helpmate. Although Bingo is highly intelligent and eager to please, he was almost dropped from the Hearing Dog Program.

Ralph Dennard, the program's director, remembers discovering this discarded dog at the Yolo County Shelter in Woodland, northwest of Sacramento. "He was very friendly, and barked and pawed at the gate for attention, which is just what I was looking for. Bingo did everything well; he had good sound curiosity, he walked on the leash calmly, he was mature and energetic, but not silly. So we adopted him and took him into the program."

Bingo's first hurdle was a bevy of medical matters. The four-year-old dog had giardia (an intestinal parasite) plus a few other problems. Over a two-week period, SF/SPCA veterinary staff gave him antibiotics, performed dentistry, vaccinated him, wormed him, neutered him, took X-rays, treated the conjunctivitis in his right eye, and removed a large tick from his left ear. One more stop, at the Society's Grooming College, and Bingo was ready to start four months of training.

Hearing Dogs are taught to alert their hearing-impaired guardians by making physical contact, jumping up against the person to get their attention, then running to the source of the sound, and back again until the person answers. To entice the dogs into responding to common household sounds (such as the doorbell, telephone, and alarm clock), the trainers begin by using food treats. Bingo, however, wasn't very interested in these morsels.

"We had some discussions about Bingo and whether or not he was trainable," recalls Dennard. "But my intuition told me that 'the lights were on' with Bingo, and that we were just going to have to do things differently for him." It turned out that Bingo adores tennis balls. So much so that by using tennis balls instead of treats, trainers had no trouble teaching Bingo everything he had to know to be a Hearing Dog. Bingo graduated canine cum laude.

Dennard and the other trainers also put much time and thought into selecting an appropriate human partner for Bingo. Bingo was mature, smart, alert, and very well-mannered — characteristics that went well with George Reid's dignified yet active lifestyle. Sure enough, when George and Bingo finally met, they bonded instantly.

SF/SPCA Hearing Dog Program staff told George that Bingo is a sociable dog who loves to show off his obedience training. Because Bingo is a border collie, he has a natural herding instinct, he uses his eyes to communicate a lot.

George laughs a deep, musical laugh. "He really does use his eyes. He tells me with his eyes when he wants to go out, or when he wants to play. Sometimes when it is time to go to bed, I will hide his ball. When we wake up in the morning, Bingo looks back and forth quickly from the hiding place to me, to let me know that he remembers exactly where it is."

Last March, George and Bingo celebrated their first year together. In that time, George has noticed two important changes in his life.

The biggest difference is that he simply feels more secure, more in touch with his surroundings. "Bingo knows a lot more than just the things he has been taught," George says. "There are certain streets that Bingo doesn't want to walk down, and I trust him. He senses things that I'm not able to. I've learned that when Bingo puts his ears up, there is a reason. Bingo is normally a very friendly dog, but he is also very protective of me," George adds. "When we meet someone for the first time, he looks up at me as if to say, 'Is it all right for me to speak to him?'"

George's friend, the Reverend Marie Bolden, minister at San Francisco's True Light Spiritual Temple of Christ, sees a newfound sense of confidence and security in her colleague. "He steps out so proudly with Bingo," she says. "George used to be a little worried about traveling alone, but now with Bingo, he goes everywhere so proudly."

The other big change centers on a very practical part of George's life: the telephone. "When Bingo hears it," George reports, "he is Johnny-on-the-spot. He pushes me with his nose, or if I don't respond quickly enough, he will jump on me." George isn't as tense any more, and gets fewer headaches because he no longer has to worry that someone might have rung the doorbell or called on the phone.

Bingo's presence even has a positive financial effect. "Until I got Bingo," says George, "I had no idea how many telephone calls I missed and how much that cost me. Because I don't have to call everyone back now, I have saved four or five hundred dollars in telephone charges."

Like any proud "parent," George takes exquisite care of his prized companion. He keeps meticulous records about Bingo, stored carefully in "Bingo's briefcase." Without fail, George walks Bingo four times a day. He takes Bingo to the groomer for a bath and flea dip every month. And when they travel, Bingo drinks and eats from a set of stainless steel bowls that George keeps spotless.

Rev. Marie Bolden can testify to the loving treatment this dog receives from George. "He always takes care of Bingo first," she says. "When we are at a meeting or convention, he gets Bingo something to eat before he has his own lunch."

George is so conscientious that when they visit a city in a different time zone, he keeps Bingo on a California schedule. Bingo's regular breakfast time, for example, is 7 a.m.; when they're in the Midwest, George rises to feed him at 5 a.m.

> George used to be a little worried about traveling alone, but now with Bingo, he goes everywhere.

Next year, George will celebrate 50 years in the ministry. He was recently named to a national post and his expanded duties will take him on at least ten trips, including a few to the San Francisco area and one to the church's national convention in Baton Rouge, Louisiana. Bingo will go with him everywhere, of course.

When they travel by plane or Greyhound bus, Bingo lies on the floor at the foot of an empty seat next to George. "He is quiet as a gentleman," says George. "Once, we traveled by Amtrak, and we were on the train for a very long time with no stops. Bingo didn't whimper a bit, and the staff all marvelled at how gentlemanly he was."

Bingo has a specially appointed place in George's church. "I put his crate behind the altar, and he stays there quietly throughout the entire service." George adds jokingly, "He's better behaved than some of the parishioners!"

People are used to seeing the two of them together, but during last winter's rainstorms, George occasionally left Bingo at home to protect him from the weather. When George went to his doctor's or dentist's office, "the first thing the receptionists always asked me was, 'Where's Bingo?'" he laughs.

George also accompanies Bingo on his regular visits to the veterinarian. "I do for Bingo just like I do for myself — we go in for regular checkups." Bingo's doctor is a 2 1/2 hour bus ride away (that's one way) from George's downtown Los Angeles apartment, but the long trek is worth it to George. "Bingo's vet is deaf, too, which is a great support to me. I think that he can under stand things about Bingo and myself that a 'normal' doctor wouldn't."

All Hearing Dog/human partnerships are close ones, with deep and emotional ties strengthened by mutual need and support. George calls Bingo "a joy and a pleasure," and refers to him as "my precious gift."

"People say that we match each other," George says, referring to his own black and white clerical outfit and to Bingo's black and white coloring. "We are both shepherds," he comments. "Bingo is a shepherd dog. And I am a minister — a shepherd of people."

With these two steadfastly looking out for each other, one can't help wonder if this isn't a match made — well, in heaven.

Any California resident with a hearing impairment can apply for an SF/SPCA Hearing Dog. Call (415) 554-3020, TDD (415) 554-3022.

> **People say that we match each other," George says, "We are both shepherds,"**

> **"Bingo is a shepherd dog. And I am a minister, a shepherd of people."**

Category II-F-6
Individual Feature in General Interest Magazine

A TERRIBLE BEAUTY
by Michael D. Lemonick

(TIME MAGAZINE - DEC. 12, 1994)

FOUR YEARS AGO, AMANDA AND BOB Metzger of Exton, Pennsylvania, saw an ad for golden retriever puppies in the local newspaper and went to have a look. "Once we saw them," says Amanda, "we fell in love. We couldn't have left the place without one." They decided on a dog they named Jake— but being careful consumers, the Metzgers made sure the breeders had a solid reputation, insisted on an American Kennel Club certification of Jake's pedigree and got assurances that his parents were free of health problems before they handed over $325 for their dog.

Their troubles started three months later. Jake began to limp on his left front leg; the vet diagnosed osteochondritis, an inherited bone condition, and had to operate. The bill came to $650. Six months later, Jake went lame again, and X-rays showed severe dysplasia, a hereditary weakness of the joints, in both hips. A $750 operation relieved his pain, but even with a dose of aspirin almost daily, Jake still walks stiffly. On top of that, he has severe allergies, dry skin and a poor coat. He has recently started having seizures as well. "He's a medical mess," says Amanda Metzger. "It just breaks my heart because he wants to play like a puppy, but he can't."

It would be tempting to put Jake's problems down to plain bad luck—but in fact the odds were against him from the start. While most golden retrievers are healthier than Jake, a shocking 60% of them end up with the dysplasia that may yet cripple him,

according to the University of Pennsylvania's School of Veterinary Medicine. Many are born with an undescended testicle, another hereditary condition vets say can cause the gland to become cancerous.

Yet even if they had chosen another breed, the Metzgers would have been taking a chance. The appalling truth is that as many as 25% of the 20 million purebred dogs in America— 1 in 4 animals — are afflicted with a serious genetic problem. German shepherds, for example, run an even higher risk of hip dysplasia than do golden retrievers. Labrador retrievers are prone to dwarfing. At least 70% of collies suffer from genetic eye trouble, and 10% eventually go blind. Dalmatians are often deaf. Cocker spaniels tend to have bad tempers. Great Danes have weak hearts. English bulldogs have such enormous heads that pups often have to be delivered by cesarean section. Newfoundlands can drop dead from cardiac arrests. Chinese Shar-Peis, the wrinkly dogs that don't seem to fit into their skin, have congenital skin disorders. And Irish setters, laments veterinarian Michael Fox, a vice president of the Humane Society of the U.S., "are so dumb they can't find their way to the end of the leash."

The list goes on and on, running to more than 300 separate genetic disorders that subject dogs to enormous pain, roil the emotional life of their owners and, estimates Dr. William Schall, a genetic specialist at Michigan State University, cost almost $1 billion in vet bills and lost revenues from stillborn pups, which cannot be sold.

Bad genes are a universal hazard of life, of course; practically every species suffers from inherited diseases. But golden retrievers and other purebreds are not like most other animals. They are in a very real sense artificial, molded over thousands of years through selective breeding to satisfy human needs. For most of that time, those needs have largely been companionship and labor, and dogs have prospered.

Within the past century, though, and especially over the past 50 years, the most popular types have been bred almost exclusively to look good—with "good" defined by breed-specific dog clubs and the American Kennel Club (AKC). "Form has been separated from function" says Brian Kilcommons, a dog trainer in Middletown, New York. "Styles come in vogue. The competition at dog shows is geared almost exclusively to looks." This focus on beauty above all means that attractive but unhealthy animals have been encouraged to reproduce— a sort of survival of the unfittest. The result is a national canine health crisis, from which few breeds have escaped.

The astonishing thing is that despite the scope of these diseases, veterinary researchers know next to nothing about what causes them or how to cure them. Only 23 of the hundreds of known disorders can currently be picked up by genetic lab tests. Biologists know far more about the heredity of the fruit fly, in fact, than they do about canine genetics. That is because there are fewer than 100 canine geneticists in the world, working at just a handful of major universities—and they are constantly scraping for funding.

The lack of research money is especially disconcerting when one considers that dogs are the nation's most popular pets. Almost 36 million households have them, compared with the 29.2 million that keep cats, according to the Humane Society of the U.S. Americans spend more than $8 billion a year on their dogs, not counting the initial purchase. The AKC alone raked in $29 million last year, about three-fourths of it from the $25 or more it charges to register each pedigreed pup and provide a copy of its family tree. But the AKC annual report shows that the club cut its grants for education and research into the health of dogs from $1.675 million in 1992 to $575,000 in 1993.

Who is to blame for the shabby treatment of humanity's best friend? The AKC, with its focus on pedigrees and beauty pageants rather than canine well-being? Legitimate breeders, who supply customers with beautiful but sometimes damaged puppies? Puppy mills, which do the same but at much higher volume and in search of greater profits? Or the public, more insistent with each passing year that a mutt—a "randomly bred dog" to be politically correct— simply won't do?

They are all partly at fault. But it is hard to avoid putting the AKC high on the list. While the club is not the only dog registry in the country, it is certainly the biggest, best known and most powerful. It is because of this power that the AKC has been largely unchallenged over the years. "Criticize the AKC, and there will be retribution," says one New York dog trainer. "Judges may find they are no longer getting assignments. Breeders might discover their dogs are no longer winning prizes." The AKC acknowledges that it is perceived as overbearing. "I think it's a fact of life that people have that fear, and it's unfortunate," responds John Mandeville, the club's vice president for planning.

The AKC does not need to resort to intimidation, however, to have an overwhelming influence. It sponsors most of the nation's dog shows, events that reinforce the insidious notion that beauty is a dog's paramount virtue. It also keeps track of purebred pedigrees, yet it requires no proof of good health to certify an animal. All it takes to get AKC certification is proof of pedigreed parentage. Says Fox: "The best use of pedigree papers is for housebreaking your dog. They don't mean a damn thing. You can have an immune-deficient puppy that is about to go blind and has epilepsy, hip dysplasia, hemophilia and one testicle, and the AKC will register it."

No one at the kennel club denies this. AKC certification "is absolutely not a Good Housekeeping seal of approval, unfortunately," says Mandeville. "It's acquired a lot of these trappings because the idea of 'AKC-registered' is so widely known."

Or, to be blunt, because it has such snob appeal. The American Kennel Club was founded 110 years ago by a group of American bluebloods who pledged "to do everything to advance the study, breeding, exhibiting, running and maintenance of purity of thoroughbred dogs." At the time purebreds were status symbols, owned exclusively by the wealthy and prized for their strength, skill and intelligence as much as for their looks.

But during the 1940s, as the middle class sucked in vast numbers of new members with aspirations of gentility, these Americans began to insist on purebreds too, and their popularity took off. In 1944 the AKC registered 77,400 dogs; that jumped to 235,978 in 1949, and by 1970, the club was issuing papers on a million dogs a year. (The total last year: 1.4 million.)

The number of AKC-sponsored dog shows has increased just as dramatically. In 1894 there were a mere 11 all-breed shows. By 1954 there were 384, and last year a total of 1.3 million dogs competed in 1,177 different exhibitions. Then as now, the idea was to show off the owners' prize breeding stock.

But the concept of what makes a dog valuable for breeding has changed. While obedience and field trials were once considered at least as important as beauty contests, the canine equivalent of the swimsuit competition has all but taken over. Historians have yet to explain this ideological shift, but the AKC has one idea: "You could almost say this venerable institution with its great credibility and history has been infiltrated slowly by the type of people it was not intended to deal with" says Wayne Cavenaugh, the group's spokesman. Whatever the reason, animals with names such as Rainbow's Maggie Rose O'Koehl and Jrees Buddy Holly are brushed, hairsprayed, beribboned and otherwise tarted up before going in front of the judges. Says Buddy Holly's owner, Jan Smith of Wichita, Kansas, a longtime exhibitor of Great Danes (and herself the runner-up for Miss Congeniality in the 1965 Miss Arkansas pageant): "When the ears are too flat, we use cement to make them perky. We use chalk to color the legs, which is fine as long as you don't use copious amounts."

That's just the final polish, though: no dog can hope to be a champion without conforming to a very narrow standard of physical perfection set by individual dog clubs and ratified by the AKC. And customer-conscious breeders have obliged by creating prizewinning dogs with specific traits, such as long ears in cocker spaniels or sloping hips in German shepherds.

Biologically, this is just asking for trouble. For one thing, the characteristics judges and clubs have decreed to be gorgeous can themselves be bad for the animals' health—huge heads on bulldogs that make it difficult for them to be born naturally, for example, or the wrinkled skin on Shar-Peis that sets them up for rashes. For another, the best way to produce a puppy with a specific look is to mate two dogs who have that same look. As with any species, though, the closest resemblances are found among the closest relatives. So breeders often resort to inbreeding, the mating of brothers and sisters or fathers and daughters. Or they "linebreed", having grandparents mate with grandchildren or cousins with each other. "If we did that in humans," says Mark Derr, who wrote a scathing indictment of America's dog culture for the March 1990 Atlantic Monthly, "we'd call it incest."

Both practices increase the likelihood of genetic disease. It is not that purebreds have more defective genes than other dogs, or that inbreeding somehow causes healthy genes to go bad. Most hereditary disorders in dogs are caused by recessive genes, as long as an animal has a good copy of the gene from one parent, it will override a bad copy from the other parent. But if both parents pass on the same bad gene—which is more likely if mother and father come from the same family—the puppy has a problem.

The problem intensifies with what experts call "the popular sire effect," the result of a single desirable male's being used to sire a large number of litters. Says Michigan State's Schall: "If it is later determined that the male that looked perfect has a genetic disease, he will have dispersed it widely before it gets discovered."

Hereditary weakness can be introduced even when there is no underlying genetic defect at all. The biological interplay between individual genes can be extremely complicated, and breeding to enhance one characteristic can have unintended consequences. Vets believe the retinal disease that afflicts most collies may fall into this category. The gene responsible may lie very close to the one that gives collies their long noses and closely set eyes—traits that have been deliberately emphasized by breeders. Says Dr. Donald Patterson, chief of the medical genetics section at the University of Pennsylvania's School of Veterinary Medicine: "Many people have bred dogs for desired traits, but in the process of doing this

they have also got undesirable ones. The objective should be to combine breeding for good traits with more careful planning to get rid of genetic defects. Unfortunately, not much attention has been paid to that."

The AKC insists that it is not at fault: the breeders are. Asked why club-sponsored shows put much more emphasis on appearance than health, Mandeville responds that "this is America. If this size is good, this size is better. We reflect, unfortunately, the breeding of dogs [that] people register with us. Are there genetic problems? Absolutely. Are there temperament problems? Absolutely. Are there people making poorly informed breeding decisions? Far too many."

The club is just a registry, he says, so "don't rely on a registry to make an informed decision for you." Why don't AKC registrations carry health and temperament requirements—as comparable certification does in Germany and Sweden? Says Mandeville: "It's the Big Brother argument. At what point does regulation of the individual for the greater good step on the individual's toes?"

Mandeville also claims that any attempt by the AKC to limit registration would trigger government sanctions. "We would like to be able to say, 'I'm sorry, we're not registering your dog' but we would be in court faster than your head would spin. The Federal Trade Commission has rules and regulations in this country about restriction of trade."

Plenty of dog owners reject this sort of reasoning—and shun the blessings of American Kennel Club membership as well. The U.S. Border Collie Club is vigorously resisting AKC efforts to add border collies to the 137 breeds it formally recognizes (there are more than 300 breeds worldwide). The border collie owners and breeders are convinced that AKC recognition would create pressure to breed the dogs for their looks at the inevitable expense of their intelligence and herding instincts. "We are concerned that the working ability of our dogs would be completely lost" says Donald McCaig, a breeder in Williamsville, Virginia, and a spokesman for the club.

The Cavalier King Charles Spaniel Club voted overwhelmingly last May to reject AKC recognition for another reason: their conviction that the AKC values its own revenues over a dog's welfare. Cavalier breeders do not allow the dogs to be sold in pet stores, which are infamous for buying animals from shady sources, including puppy mills. In fact, most dog experts routinely warn buyers not to deal with pet stores at all. The AKC insists, though, that the Cavalier club drop its prohibition as a condition of affiliation. Why would it take such a position? Perhaps because some 7% of the group's $21 million in dog-registration earnings comes from pet-store sales. "They simply want to gain as many registrations as possible because money is power,' says the Humane Society's Fox.

Greed cuts both ways, of course. Six Labrador retriever breeders say they have filed a class action against the AKC and the Labrador Retriever Club Inc. for changing the breed standard to favor slimmer, longer-legged animals over the traditional stockier, shorter ones — thereby devaluing the out-of-date model. And some owners of a relatively rare dog called the Havanese, which arrived in this country from Cuba in the mid-1970s, are actively seeking AKC recognition, despite worries by other owners that they are inviting overbreeding and genetic problems.

"It's a competitive world, and money talks," says one Havanese breeder. "For many people, winning dog shows is a thrill and makes them proud, and the AKC has a lot of shows" Perhaps more to the point, once the Havanese join the high-profile AKC fold, the going rate for puppies, according to some breeders, could go as high as $2,000, up from about $750 now. On average, registered puppies go for 10 to 20 times the price of

paperless dogs, and champion purebreds can sell for as much as $50,000.

Most of these genetic problems would disappear if Americans could somehow be persuaded to abandon purebreds in favor of mutts. While individual mixed-breed dogs have problems, the animals on average are a lot healthier than their high-class cousins. "Mutts are the Hondas of the dog world" says syndicated animal columnist Mike Capuzzo of the Philadelphia Inquirer. "They're cheap, reliable and what nature intended in the first place. They are what you would get at a canine Club Med if you left them alone for six Years." There are "breeds" in the mutt world, just as there are among purebreds. The most popular: a cross between a Labrador retriever and a German shepherd.

But even if the U.S. cannot be cured of its addiction to purebreds — probably a safe assumption—there is plenty that can be done to improve overall canine health. One factor that is forcing breeders to pay closer attention to genetic problems is the emergence of puppy lemon laws in a dozen states, including New York, Massachusetts, California and Florida. If a dog is found to have a debilitating defect, owners can get a refund or a healthy dog in exchange, or they can force the breeder to pay the vet bills to repair a problem.

The laws are not entirely fair to breeders, though, says George Padgett, a veterinary pathologist at Michigan State University. "Some may be penalized unfairly because no one has taught them about genetic defects:' Agrees Penn's Dr. Donald Patterson, founder of the genetic section of the University of Pennsylvania's School of Veterinary Medicine and widely acknowledged as the dean of canine genetic research, "The common misconception is that breeders are cavalier" The real problem, he says, is that they have not had the scientific information to detect hidden defects and thus avoid bad breeding decisions.

That is starting to change. One new tool that should prove helpful is a computerized genetic-disease data base developed at Patterson's lab that lists more than 300 genetic problems plaguing dogs. Another is the university's PennHIP program, a hip-disease detection system that took 11 years and $1 million to develop. It involves taking detailed measurements of hip X rays to grade the severity of dysplasia. The program is being marketed by International Canine Genetics Inc., a research company based in Malverne, Pa., which is already training vets to use it. "A tighter fitting hip joint is better, and we now have the technology to determine which hips are tighter" says Dr. Gail Smith, an engineer and veterinarian who developed the test. "This will help people select the best breeding dogs."

Lists and detection systems are not the same as cures, but Patterson points out that veterinary researchers are finally beginning to have some insight into the causes of these disorders. "Canine genetic diseases" he says, "are now being defined at the molecular level, and the mapping of the canine genome is at last under way." Scientists have located the genes that cause muscular dystrophy in golden retrievers, and "shaking pup" syndrome in Welsh springer spaniels. They're working on identifying the genes responsible for failure-to-thrive metabolic problems in giant Schnauzers, bleeding disorders in Scottish terriers and Doberman pinschers, and the hereditary deafness that affects about 30% of Dalmatians. And they believe hip dysplasia, the crippling condition that afflicts Jake the golden retriever and his kin, may be the result of several defective genes working in concert—not an unusual situation with hereditary disorders.

On the supply side, critics of the AKC argue that the kennel club should follow the lead of its European counterparts by imposing health standards as part of its registra-

tion process. Rather than wait for that step, individual-breed clubs are taking their own action. At least three Rottweiler clubs have ruled that dogs missing more than one tooth, which can be a sign of a genetic defect, may not be bred. English springer spaniel owners are encouraging one another not to breed dogs with temperament problems; they want to eliminate what they call the "rage syndrome" a type of brain seizure that makes some dogs lose control. And the Portuguese Water Dog Club requires breeders who advertise in its magazine to submit copies of hip, eye and heart clearances to prove that their dogs are not suffering from genetic defects.

The Portuguese Water Dog Club is perhaps the most active organization in policing genetic defects. Water dogs tend to suffer from progressive retinal atrophy, which causes blindness, and from an enzyme deficiency that can kill dogs by storing toxins in the nervous system. The club offered in 1987 to finance several researchers at major veterinary schools to develop screening tests for the diseases. The result is a blood test that found 16% of the dogs to be carriers in 1990. Club members stopped breeding the afflicted animals, and by 1993 the incidence had dropped to 7%.

With such grass-roots pressure, and perhaps a bit battered by bad publicity and lawsuits the AKC has lately shown some interest in promoting this kind of research itself. In October it sponsored its first-ever canine-genetics conference, where as leading researchers gave talks to an audience of some 150 veterinary scientists from around the world. And during the past month there have been discussions within the club about setting up a scientific advisory panel that would recommend research projects the club might support. If the ancient American Kennel Club is finally thinking of altering its culture, there may yet be hope for the family dog.

Category II-G — Editorial/ Opinion Piece /Essay

IS THAT A PIT BULL?

HOW ONE FRIENDLY DOG HELPS EDUCATE THE PUBLIC

by Marion Lane

(THE AKC GAZETTE)

I'd had my new puppy for only a week when I heard the question for the first time.

"Is that a pit bull?"

I knew people would wonder, and I was ready. "No," I said brightly, so pleased to be asked. "She's a Staffordshire Bull Terrier. Staf-ford-shire Bull Terr-i-er."

The boy looked disappointed. "Staffer—what?" He studied the black puppy as she tugged the drooping laces of his Reeboks. I could see him calculating. "You sure?" he finally asked.

After my Poodle died, I spent a long time thinking about what breed of

Lane & Nell
- photo W. Harpotian

dog to get next. Not many of my friends could understand why I'd settled on a Stafford. Most had never heard of the breed, so I carried around a picture from "The Complete Dog Book," pulled it out and watched their eyebrows soar.

Suddenly they knew. "It looks like a pit bull," they said without exception. "Why do you want a dog like that?"

I explained that I liked terriers but wanted one with no caffeine. I also wanted a midsize dog with a low-care coat, a dog I could pick up and carry, but enough dog to discourage muggers. Because I live in an apartment building with neighbors on the other side of the walls, I needed a dog that wouldn't bark.

All in all, I had quite the speech. I don't recall convincing anyone.

In fact, there was one more reason I wanted a Staffordshire Bull Terrier, but this one I kept to myself. Staffords, of course, are one of the "bull and terrier" breeds that are often all tossed into one criminal class and tarred with the pit bull brush. Yet I knew Staffords are just like other dogs, no worse and no better than they are bred, raised and trained to be, and I wanted to help convince the public of that.

My plan was simple: Take one friendly dog that looked just the opposite, let it meet and greet the person in the street and before long, you've converted the world. Or at least the neighborhood.

Little Nell did her part. In the elevator, at the vet's, in the Laundromat, she made friends with everyone. At the Tip Toe Inn on my block, she soon became a fixture, sitting up smartly on a bar stool to beg a bowl of ice cubes or prowling the floor beneath the peanut dispenser. I'd taught her a few party tricks and she'd roll over, pirouette or give the high five to anyone who asked. Over time, a few people at the Tip Toe confided that until they got to know Nell, they'd been afraid of "dogs like that."

Still, with every new person the question was the same: "Is that a pit bull?" Or, more politely, "What kind of dog is that?" Usually, after I'd intoned Staf-ford-shire Bull Terr-i-er, the follow-up question was, "But isn't that a pit bull?"

I did my best to educate the public, explaining that a pit bull was what a dog did, not what it was, just like a guard dog, or a gun dog, or a guide dog for that matter. I had quite the speech. One man up the street was petting Nell and marveling at how strong she was when his friend whispered that she was a pit bull. The man jumped back as if bitten and now flees

when he sees us coming. And a woman in my own building who used to give me bits of liverwurst for Nell when she was a puppy now seems to suspect that Nell may have grown up into something dreadful. When she sees us in the elevator she retreats into the corner and asks if the dog is a pit bull; when I shake my head, she slumps against the wall in relief.

Nell is 4 years old now, and I've gradually come to care less and less what people call my dog. Overwhelmingly, people who like dogs like her and people who don't like dogs, don't. I still try my best to educate the public about what Staffords are, and what pit bulls are, and aren't.

One recent afternoon, though, I wasn't up to the job and I took a different tack, one I'd often been tempted to take. It was a sweltering hot summer day. I was unwinding at the Tip Toe and Nell was up on the stool beside me, crunching ice cubes and accepting pats from all her pals as they came in. A newcomer watched us sternly from across the noisy room and finally had to have his say. "Lady, is that one of those pit bulls you've got in here?"

In that instant, I realized this was not a question at all, and maybe never was; it was an answer, sometimes an accusation. "Yes, it is," I answered, so pleased to be asked. "Awfully nice dog around people, don't you think?"

> Overwhelmingly, people who like dogs like her and people who don't like dogs, don't.

Category II-H — Subject Related Series

ON GOOD BEHAVIOR
by Gary Wilkes
CLICK INTO MODERN TRAINING METHODS
(DOG FANCY)

"The more things change, the more they remain the same."
— Old proverb

While this common cliche may be true for things such as love, war and politics, one thing that is really in the process of changing is dog training.

For thousands of years, the primary means of controlling dog behavior has been with a collar, a leash and the strength of the trainer's hands. For pet owners who do not have the strength or skill to succeed with traditional training methods, there have been few alternatives. Some owners abandon the concept of training altogether and live with an unruly dog. In an effort to provide alternatives to old-style training, many trainers are abandoning more physical methods for something entirely different—toy clickers and hot dogs.

Over the last 10 years, a new form of dog training has developed as a result of the demand for gentler methods. This new method, called "click and treat" training, is the result of blending the rules of behavioral psychology with the practical teaching techniques of marine mammal trainers. The first dolphin and whale trainers laid the foundation for this method out of simple necessity. Karen Pryor, pioneer marine mammal trainer, summed up the problem in her book Don't Shoot the Dog.

"You cannot use a leash or bridle, or even your fist, on an animal that just swims away. Positive reinforcement—primarily a bucket of fish—was the only tool we had."

This dependence on fish, rather than force, led to the creation of a new technology of teaching. Pryor's experiences and her book planted seeds in the minds of many dog trainers. "If marine mammal trainers could control 600-pound sea lions without force," dog trainers asked, "why not try to adapt the same techniques to dog training?"

The result of this simple question is the growth of the click and treat movement. It has its own trade paper, the Clicker Journal, and thousands of devoted followers. More importantly, it provides a training method that is ideal for people who want a relationship with their dogs based on trust and affection rather than force and compulsion.

To see the benefits of click and treat training requires three things: a dog, some treats and a few minutes of your time.

First, pretend that you are training a dolphin to jump out of the water. You have a psychology text that tells you to wait until the animal does the behavior (jump) and then give it a fish (reinforcement). If you do this many times, according to the book, you increase the chance that the dolphin will jump. Three days later, having reinforced every jump, your dolphin is fast becoming a jumping fool. Every time you show up at the practice tank with a bucket of fish, Flipper starts jumping. There is only one problem with this little routine: the jumps are so low that no one will be willing to pay to see such a performance. The challenge now becomes getting Flipper to jump higher.

The solution to this problem starts with refining an ancient training tool — verbal praise. While dog trainers often use verbal praise to tell an animal "I liked that," dolphin trainers are forced to do something different. In the time it takes to say "good boy," Flipper can travel 20 feet through the air. He can't possibly understand exactly which part of the behavior "caused" the praise unless the "good boy" signal is fast enough to single out the split second in which the behavior occurred. Marine mammal trainers use whistles and clickers for this purpose.

Now when Flipper jumps, you can hit the clicker at the instant he reaches the highest part of the jump. Over a series of repetitions, he will know that unless he hears the click, he gets no fish. Trial and error will tell him that low jumps never cause the click, but high jumps do. As the clicker becomes a part of his training routine, it starts to guide his responses. The click tells him what works, while the absence of the click tells him he is off track.

To start clicker training your dog, it is not really necessary to have a clicker. Merely shortening your praise to "good," rather than, "Oh, what a sweet baby, my good little boy," is acceptable. For those of you who are adventurous and have a clicker, begin by presenting the click and then giving your dog a small treat. Make sure that you click first, then give the treat. Repeat this sequence 10 to 20 times, until you notice that the sound of the click causes Fido to visibly startle. Once the dog has made the association that the click means "a treat is on the way," your tool is ready to do some work. For those of you without clickers, substitute the word "good" in place of the click.

Shaping your first behavior: When offered a favorite treat, most dogs will sit expectantly and wait for the treat. After a few seconds of waiting, Fido is likely to get impatient and fidget in some way. He may turn his head, back up, speak or lift a paw.

For this first session, the behavior you choose is not important. Wait for the first thing he offers, click and treat. If Fido turned his head a little bit for the first click, wait a few seconds; he'll do it again. Click and treat. Continue this process and watch how his behavior changes. If you continue to click and treat each time he moves his head, the behavior will become stronger. Now try waiting a second before you click. Try to get two "head turns" for the price of one treat.

Once you have a clearly definable behavior going (head turning), start saying "Turn your head" just before you think Fido is going to do it. If the behavior you shaped was lifting a paw, say "High five" just before you think he is about to perform the behavior.

Learning to use positive reinforcement to shape behaviors is a fun process. For your first project, relax and see what behaviors your dog wants to offer. Your initial goal should be to watch how your dog's behavior changes, and see how the clicker helps you identify correct responses.

Next month, I will provide some details on adding commands to your new behavior and getting better control over some classic obedience behaviors. After that, I'll cover how to get great response, even when you don't have treats, improving performance and some tips on "stupid dog tricks."

WHAT IS A TREAT?

A proper treat is anything your dog will actively work to get. Treats should be small bite-sized and easy for the dog to swallow. Whole soft treats can be swallowed quickly and are preferable to harder treats which require time to chew and swallow Be careful not to feed your dog too many treats; try dividing a treat into several pieces.

WHERE TO BUY A CLICKER

Toy metal clickers are available in some novelty shops. Karen Pryor's book, *Don't Shoot the Dog,* and reliable, hard plastic clickers are available from Direct Book Service, (800) 776-2665, and Sunshine Books, (800) 472-5425.

The Clicker Journal is a national monthly publication for click and treat trainers. For more information, contact the editor: Corally Burmaster Coldstream, Rt. 1, Box 349E, Leesburg, VA 22075.

Part Two

LAST MONTH WE BEGAN A SERIES ABOUT "click and treat" training. This month we'll look at how to connect commands and signals to our dogs' new behaviors.

A common training practice is to chant commands while attempting to push, pull or tug the dog into the desired position. For instance, the trainer says sitsitsit while pushing the dog's rear end to the ground. With this method, the animal is forced to choose between paying attention to the trainer's words and learning the behavior

This practice often leads to one of two problems. Either the animal understands the behavior but must be told several times to do it, or the command is obeyed instantly but in a sloppy fashion.

These methods can be the foundation of fun for you and your dog.

If teaching the command and the behavior simultaneously causes poor performance, the obvious solution is to teach them separately. Since a command without a behavior is useless, a reasonable sequence is to teach the behavior first, and then add the command.

While this may sound logical, the implications of this concept may seem alien. If one does not talk to the animal first, how can the behavior be taught? If one trains silently, how does the command become connected to the behavior? Before the strangeness of this concept causes you to reject it, consider how you taught your first "click and treat" behavior last month. Your first goal was to select a behavior such as "shake" or "head turning" and reinforce each occurrence. Within a few repetitions, your dog offered the behavior consistently.

After the animal began to offer the behavior, I suggested you add the cue—just before you thought the behavior was about to occur. As you tried this method, you probably found that teaching the behavior without chanting the command was incredibly easy.

Step 1. Now that Fluffy turns her head when you touch a treat to her nose (or offers her paw, or whatever behavior you selected) try to get her into a cycle. First, let her know that you have a treat. Now wait for the behavior. When she does the behavior, click and treat (or say "good" and give a treat). After a few repetitions, the sequence becomes automatic: When the behavior occurs about every 10 seconds, you are ready to attach the command.

Example: Touch a treat to Fluffy's nose; she waits a few seconds, then turns her head; and you click and treat.

Step 2. For this step, change the routine slightly. This time, give a "command" just before the behavior starts. (The command can be any word that you choose.) Since the behavior is happening on a 10-second cycle, it is easy to predict when the behavior will occur.

Example: Touch a treat to Fluffy's nose; say "turn your head"; she waits a few seconds, then turns her head; you click and treat.

At this stage of the process your goal is simply to attach the command to the behavior. The command is not yet "causing" the behavior to happen. Fluffy turns her head because it "causes" clicks and treats. It will take a minimum of 20 to 50 repetitions before the word begins to cause the behavior. Be patient and watch for the "light bulb" glimmering over your dog's head.

These methods can be the foundation of fun for you and your dog. While pushes and shoves can develop control over behaviors, hands-on training is limited. By using the click to signify "Yes, do that again" while reinforcing the behavior, you are limited only by your imagination and your dog's physical and mental abilities.

To expand your dog's repertoire, try this new behavior: have your dog identify an object by name. Hold an object (car keys, wallet, newspaper, etc.) in front of Fluffy's nose, and click and treat if he investigates it. Repeat this process several times. When Fluffy is repeatedly touching the object for treats, start naming it just before he touches it. Teach at least two more object names, then put all three objects on the ground in front of Fluffy. Ask for one of the objects by name and reinforce (treat) only correct identifications.

Next month we will examine how to vary the reinforcement so Fluffy will give better performance and not be dependent on treats.

Part Three
GET REAL! REINFORCING BEHAVIOR IN THE REAL WORLD

The focus of our third article on "click and treat" training is learning how to vary the reinforcement to get more and better behavior. It may help you to have the last two issues handy to use as a reference as you try this month's exercises.

Click and Treat trainers are often chided by traditional trainers who tell us to "get real." Traditionalists argue that using food causes weak performance and a fixation on the food rather than on performing a behavior. Ultimately, they say, food loses its reinforcing effect as the animal becomes satiated. Fair enough.

However, if the reinforcement is varied, this loss of the effectiveness of food rewards will not occur. In fact, the reinforced behavior will become more enthusiastic. Let's look at nature. Nature requires animals to work for food as an essential requirement of survival. For example, a pack of wolves attack 20 moose, on average, for every one they actually kill. How is it that nature does not have the same limitations that we trainers do concerning behavior reinforced by a food reward? The answer lies in finding the difference between the artificial world of training and the "real" rules of nature.

In the real world, animals must respond correctly to situations that offer reinforcements such as food, water and shelter. They must learn which behaviors are most likely to pay off, and which ones offer a "low yield." A wolf that ignores a moose in order to hunt a mouse will soon perish. Even though moose hunting is far more hazardous than mouse hunting, wolves prefer to hunt larger game whenever they can. Big game offers the opportunity for big payoffs.

MOUSE OR MOOSE

To better illustrate this process, let's look at two types of machines that create "mouse and moose" situations for humans — Coke machines and slot machines. The "mouse" is represented by the Coke machine, while the "moose" is the slot machine.

Here are the rules of Coke machine reinforcement: Coke machines pay off each time you deposit your coins. A fixed number of coins buys one Coke. If the machine does not give a Coke in exchange for your money, you are unlikely to deposit more money. Also, you will deposit money based on how many Cokes you can drink at any one time. Once you are no longer thirsty, you will stop buying drinks. These reactions sound remarkably like the traditional objections to using food in training: weak performance, a fixation on food and reduced effect due to satiation.

In contrast, a slot machine offers a more varied result if you put coins in its slot. You may receive a huge number of coins in return or nothing at all. The slot machine controls your behavior by offering a chance to gain a dramatically large reinforcement in exchange for a nominal bet. A natural reaction for humans is to prefer the variable reinforcement of the slot machine to the fixed reinforcement of the Coke machine — just as the wolf prefers moose over mice.

Whether you are using food, praise or physical affection as a reward, it is the predictability of consistent reinforcement that creates lackluster performance and a dependence on "treats," not the type of rewards used. To get enthusiastic behav-

ior from your dog even when you don't have treats requires that you imitate the more varied reinforcements of nature — you must indeed "get real."

RULES FOR REALITY

The rules for varying your dog's reinforcement can be spelled out using the word REAL.

R - Raise your standards. Make it harder to earn a click and treat. Ask for two or more repetitions of the behavior, faster performance or greater enthusiasm before you reinforce the behavior. Be opportunistic and hit any of these improvements with bonuses.

E - Extras for excellence. Start giving relatively large jackpots for exceptional performance. It helps to start your shift to variable reinforcement with a pretty big "positive kick in the pants," so throw a jackpot in as soon as you can. The most important purpose for these jackpots is to teach Fido that his efforts could pay off big, man, really huge.

A - Anticipate errors. As you vary the reinforcement, the dog will start to vary his behavior. Fido's first job is to figure out why the old level of performance is no longer working, or why some repetitions cause fantastic payoffs. He does not immediately know that you wanted a faster "down" or a quicker "sit." You are likely to see your animal offer a broader spectrum of behavior — responses start to vary — from garbage to greatness. Remember to give extras for excellence and garbage will turn to greatness.

L - Lots of repetitions. Allow the animal a chance to practice the behavior long enough to get comfortable with the new standards. Your immediate goal in varying the reinforcement is to get lots of repetition, not necessarily to get great performance. You are really trying to communicate "if at first you don't succeed, try, try again."

EXAMPLE BEHAVIORS

While these rules seem pretty straightforward, it may still help to see them in action. The first rule of variable reinforcement is to raise your standards. The easiest way to do this is to merely ask for the same behavior—twice.

For example: Say "turn your head" (or whatever behavior you are working on). Fido turns his head. (And then looks back at you, expecting a treat.) Say "Turn your head" again, and Fido will turn his head, somewhat hesitantly. Click and treat.

Congratulations! You just gotten two behaviors for the price of one. This shift from "one sit, one treat" to "two-fers" is a very important transition for your dog. In order to get away from continuous treats, you must teach your dog that he isn't going to get a treat every time or "if at first you don't succeed, try, try again." You can continue to raise your standards by reinforcing only the fastest behaviors, the quickest responses to the command or more responses in between reinforcements.

Our next rule for variable reinforcement is to give "Extras for Excellence." Getting an animal to modify the number of times it will work in the absence of reinforcement, or to expend additional effort to gain the same reinforcement depends on obeying this rule. In effect, raising your standards asks Fido to work harder than before. A corresponding increase in reinforcement is necessary to prevent him from deciding that the game is rigged.

The simplest way to start is to begin judging Fido's performance. Ask yourself if the most recent behavior was better or worse than usual. If the behavior was better, give extra rewards along with lots of praise. If the behavior was worse, ignore it. Let Fido know that additional effort will be rewarded, while minimal performance earns nothing.

For example: Ask Fido to sit, then click and treat. Ask Fido to sit again. If the behavior was better than the last sit, click and give Fido 10 times the normal amount of treats. Include wild and crazy praise and petting for about 15 seconds. But, if the behavior was about the same as the last repetition, click with no treat or say "good dog." That's all Fido gets for marginal performance.

If Fido does worse than his usual performance, say "Sorry Charlie," "uh-uh," "tsk" or "wrong" in a bland tone of voice. This cue is meant to say "That behavior wasn't good enough; try it again." Move a few steps away from him and try it again.

During the shift from consistent reinforcement to more variable reinforcement, Fido may get confused and a little frustrated. If he stops offering the behavior, drop your standards and go back to more consistent reinforcement. As he regains his confidence, gradually try to go back to "two-fers" and "threepeats." Behavioral psychologists who study variable reinforcement suggest that the more gradually you raise your standards, the more dependable Fido's performance will be.

The most difficult aspect of click and treat training is the move from consistent reinforcement to variable reinforcement. Don't be surprised if your dog has a little trouble with this—he's supposed to. Just be patient and work at the level that your dog is comfortable with.

Next month I'll cover the various pieces of this method, shaping the behavior, attaching a cue and varying the reinforcement, into a logical whole.

Part Four

BEHAVIORAL FLUENCY:
SHAPING CONSISTENT BEHAVIORS

The last section of this four-part series explains how to get reliable responses to any learned command, in any environment.

At this point in your Click and Treat program you have shaped a simple behavior, added a command to the behavior and varied the reinforcements for correct responses. By now, your dog should be willing to offer several repetitions of the desired behavior between reinforcements.

To start adding some structure to your dog's performance and make your dog's new behaviors readily available on command, look at another aspect of click-and-treat training—behavioral fluency. Just as a person can speak a foreign language fluently, animals can become fluent in their ability to respond to our requests.

Behavioral fluency is achieved when a dog is capable of responding correctly to a command for any of its learned behaviors, at any time. Each time a new behavior is taught, it temporarily becomes stronger than previously learned behaviors. The trainer must attempt to achieve a balance between old behaviors and new ones to allow the animal to become behaviorally fluent.

The easiest way to develop behavioral fluency is to start asking for the new behavior in a random fashion. If the new click-and-treat behavior you taught was "turn your head," start injecting this command into regular performances. Try this scenario: If your dog knows sit, down and come reasonably well, ask for the new behavior in a sequence such as this one: sit, down, turn your head, come, sit, turn your head.

Mixing new behaviors into your dog's repertoire may cause some initial confusion, and the dog may show a preference for performing established behaviors rather than trying new ones. Consistency and perseverance are the tools that will straighten out this problem. Once your dog realizes that only correct responses are reinforced, mistakes tend to fade away.

THE CLICK AND TREAT STYLE

Here's how to teach a behavior—click-and-treat style—from start to finish. To shape a down/stay, for instance, start with the dog in a seated position. Then touch a treat to the dog's nose and slowly move it straight to the ground, to a point between its paws, under its chest. As the dog's nose catches up to the treat, it should be seated and slightly humped over. Click and treat. Repeat this routine several times until the dog easily follows your hand to the ground. If it attempts to stand, say "uh-uh" or "wrong" and return her to a seated position. Try it again.

Once the dog consistently follows your hand to the ground, add a second stage to the behavior. Move your hand straight to the ground, and wait for the dog to touch your hand with its nose. Once its nose touches your hand, begin to move the treat along the ground, toward you. The dog's nose will follow the treat. If the dog moves either of its front legs forward as it follows your hand, click and treat. Try to get the dog to stretch a little farther on each repetition. It is unnecessary to get the whole behavior at one time. Be satisfied with steady, small progress. If the dog raises its rear end, say "wrong" and try it again.

As your dog stretches farther and farther, it will eventually walk itself into a "down" position. Click and treat. As the dog begins to gain some confidence and speed, wait a few seconds before you click and treat so that it must hold the "down" position for several seconds. If the dog jumps up, say "wrong," and repeat the behavior. Try to get 10 to 20 repetitions of this simple behavior.

Now that your dog easily follows the treat to the ground, make things a little tougher. Touch the treat to its nose and then quickly hide it behind your back. If the dog moves to get the treat, say "wrong," and try it again. Tease it in this way several times. If you see the dog make any attempt to lie down, click and treat. If it continues to try to circle behind you for the treat, lead the dog to the ground a few more times.

Once the behavior again happens consistently, go back to several teases. Give the dog about 20 seconds on each "tease" to think about the target behavior. If you follow this pattern, you will be pleasantly surprised. After one of the teases, the dog will lie down on its own. Don't be surprised if this process takes a whole training session.

Once the dog lies down each time you tease it, start saying the word "down," just before the dog completes the command. Click and treat.

Now stand up, and try the sequence again. Touch a treat to the dog's nose, and say "down." If it lies down, click and treat. If it loses the behavior, lead it to the ground a few times, and try your "teasing" routine again. Your goal at this stage is to get your dog to lie down on command, even if you are standing.

Start to vary the reinforcement. Look at last month's column if you need to refresh your memory. A simple way to vary the reinforcement is to ask the dog for longer or shorter "downs." Another approach is to give additional re-inforcements for better performance. The clicker acts as an "end of behavior" signal, so by withholding the click you can easily turn "down" into a "stay."

Next, introduce the new command in a session that includes other requests. If you taught your dog to "high five" or "turn your head," ask the dog to "down" after a "high-five," and then ask for "sit," "come" or any other behavior the dog knows.

BASIC RULES FOR CLICK AND TREAT

• If a behavior fails, drop your standards and review the behavior from the beginning. In the early stages of shaping a behavior, the dog can become easily frustrated by repeated failure. Dropping your standards allows the animal to get back on the right path. Once the behavior is reestablished, gradually raise your standards again.

• It is important to get "two-fers" (two behaviors in exchange for one rein-forcement) early in the shaping process. You must teach the animal "if at first you don't succeed, try, try again." Animals that have experience with this method of train-ing are often willing to perform long routines without actual reinforcements.

• Don't be afraid to shape behaviors just for the fun of it. Your skill and timing will only improve with practice. And learning tricks can be a rewarding, stimulating experience for you and your dog.

Information about click-and-treat training and catalogs that feature books, videotapes and reliable, hard-plastic clickers are available through Direct Book Service (800) 776-2665.

Category II-I Regular Column

*This year two columns tied for first place in this category:
Partners In Independence - Ed and Toni Eames - *Dog World*
Gun Dogs - Bill Tarrant - *Field & Stream*

PARTNERS IN INDEPENDENCE
by Ed and Toni Eames
(DOG WORLD)

(*March 1995*)

Last month's column found us in Annapolis, Md., visiting with our friend Ilene Caroom and her family. Our Golden Retriever guides, Ivy and Jake, were able to unwind after a hectic few days in Washington, D.C., with Ilene's Border Collies and Australian Shepherd. We had been attending the meetings of Assistance Dogs International (ADI) and the International Association of Assistance Dog Partners (IAADP) [DOG WORLD, February 1995].

On our way to Frederick, Md., our next port of call, we stopped off at the Hebrew Home in Rockville to visit Cecil Gelburd. Cecil was the mother of Toni's childhood friend Eileen Schonfeld, now living in Akron, Ohio. Toni fondly remembers Cecil for her warmth, cheerfulness and obvious comfort with Toni's blindness. Cecil had been admitted to this nursing home several weeks earlier after suffering a massive debilitating stroke.

In Ivy's long career as a guide, she visited many nursing homes and other health-related facilities. Ivy was an im-

> From Ivy and Jake's point of view, the highlight of the trip was access to the swimming pool.

portant adjunct to Toni's practice as rehabilitation counselor at a New York State psychiatric center. Jake, new on the job as guide, had never been exposed to therapy work. In true Golden Retriever fashion, both dogs reveled in the attention they drew. Cecil, no longer able to speak, enjoyed patting the dogs. Several residents stopped us in the corridors to receive a canine fix. Our pleasure in spending time with Cecil and bringing her some joy was strengthened when, several weeks after our return to Fresno, she died.

Our two days in Frederick were delightful. We stayed with Ann and Jeff Strathern, their children and six Golden Retrievers.

From Ivy and Jake's point of view, the highlight of the trip was access to the swimming pool. The dogs barely dried off before they were up and swimming again, but there was a serious downside of these water antics.

Several months before our trip to the East Coast, Ivy had been seen by Dr. Alan MacMillan, a leading San Diego ophthalmologist, who comes to

Fresno once a year to run eye clinics. Dr. Mac told us Ivy had completely lost vision in her right eye but still had good vision in her left. Toni had noticed some hesitation and slowing down in Ivy's guiding, but she attributed it to the arthritis Ivy had been diagnosed with. This Delta Society Guide Dog of the Year award winner had continued to perform her duties expertly and with such brilliance that Toni was unaware she was functioning with just one eye.

During the first few days of the D.C. meetings, Ivy was her usual outstanding self. On the last day of the conference, however, Toni noticed a marked deterioration in Ivy's ability to guide. She was fine in the narrow corridors of the hotel, but when entering the open lobby area she appeared confused and disoriented. At dusk she seemed particularly unsure of herself. Not wanting to put pressure on Ivy or endanger herself, Toni relied on sighted human guides and heeled Ivy for the rest of the trip.

Since Ivy was familiar with Ann's house and property, she used her residual vision to run around the yard and dive into the pool. When a bumper was thrown for her, she would dive after it but often swim right by it. She would eventually scent it, retrieve it and bring it to us on the patio. Ann noted in distress that at dusk Ivy was unable to locate the patio steps and tried to reach us by crashing through the bushes.

Before returning to Fresno, we took Ivy to Dr. Jane Sailor, the veterinarian in Frederick for whom Ann works as a technician. Sailor, a general practitioner, found no sign of glaucoma, an eye disease requiring immediate treatment.

Our trip back home was bittersweet. Toni knew the prognosis was not good, and plans would have to be made to train with Ivy's successor. Ivy was Toni's loyal guide for 11 years and had accumulated thousands of flying miles. Toni was teary-eyed throughout the flight knowing Ivy's retirement would soon be official.

In September we were scheduled to fly to San Diego to speak at the tristate (California, Nevada and Arizona) Veterinary Medical Association meetings and to receive a posthumous award for Ed's former guide dog Kirby. Kirby, a courageous Golden Retriever, battled bone cancer, underwent amputation of his left front leg and triumphantly continued his work as Ed's guide for more than a year. The California VMA inducted Kirby into its Animal Hall of Fame, presented Ed with a beautiful plaque and a check for $500. Waltham, a division of Kal Kan, sponsored the award and provided a year's supply of dog food.

Whenever we attend conferences or go on a lecture tour, we try to link up with friends or relatives in the area. San Diego was no exception. Our friend Mike Glass, the California representative of Paws with a Cause, the Michigan-based service and hearing dog training program [DOG WORLD, February 1993], picked us up at the airport and wandered through the exhibit area with us. As board members of IAADP, we approached more than a dozen animal drug and vaccine manufacturers with our proposal to reduce the financial burden of assistance dog partnership by reducing the cost for medical care. Most company representatives listened attentively and provided us with names of contact people at headquarters.

Mike, who had attended the ADI conference, was aware of Ivy's eye problem and offered to drive us to her appointment with Dr. MacMillan. We had fantasized about corrective cataract surgery or other miraculous medical interventions, but Dr. Mac had to break the bad news that Ivy would soon be totally blind. In addition to cataracts and uveitis, she had inoperable retinal deterioration. As he described the condition, Ed experienced deja vu. While consulting an ophthalmologist 20 years earlier, Ed had a heard a similar description of his failing eyesight!

The harsh and painful reality of Ivy's forced retirement was eased by our reunion with Robert Martinus, a British teenage friend who would be spending the next few months with us. Robert joined us in San Diego to do some sight-seeing but would make Fresno his home base. Robert took on the role of Toni's makeshift walking, talking, driving guide.

Several weeks after returning home, Ivy lost her remaining vision. She is now totally blind. Our hopes that she would be Jake's mentor have now been reversed; we hope Jake will settle in and become the mentor for Ivy's successor.

Ivy has adjusted well to her disability. We are the ones struggling with deep emotions. Although Ivy will remain with us in her retirement, the pain of shifting the bond from working partner to beloved pet is wrenching.

> Dr. Mac had to break the bad news that Ivy would soon be totally blind.

(*DOG WORLD* - JULY 1995)

As my wife, Toni, and I walked through the Chicago airport to catch our next plane, my thoughts were swirling. Several weeks before this trip, I had made the decision to retire my Golden Retriever, Jake, from guide service. As he competently guided me through the congested, noisy airport, I began to have second thoughts about this decision. However, by the time we returned to Chicago two days later on our way home, my doubts were gone.

From the time I began my partnership with Jake in July 1994, he became somewhat distracted in the presence of dogs and cats while guiding me. He pulled so hard in harness, I frequently felt off balance and uncomfortable. Unlike most Golden Retrievers, he did not enjoy being groomed, and daily obedience training sessions were a chore. Unlike most guide dogs, he resisted having his harness put on.

Despite these problems, Jake knew his basic guide work. His street crossings and traffic work were excellent. He was extremely bright and quickly learned new routes. In addition, he was a real gentleman in the house. He had been trained to relieve on leash and never forgot his early house breaking. He did not chew our possessions, did not steal food from tables or counters and was quiet and settled at home.

Not willing to give up easily, I sought help from several sources. Brad Scott, the director of training at Leader Dogs for the Blind in Rochester, Mich., was in phone contact with me from the start. Brad, who had trained me with Jake, flew out to California in December in an effort to salvage us as a team. He was able to combine this after-care visit with the introduction and training of Toni's new guide, Escort.

An extremely flexible and experienced guide dog trainer, Brad was willing to incorporate many of the suggestions made to me by leading animal behaviorists. At first Brad and I tried breaking the distraction and pulling problems through the use of the Halti (a halterlike device similar to that used to control a headstrong horse. Unfortunately, Jake's reaction to the Halti was so negative, his guide work deteriorated even further. One of several techniques we employed was to drop the harness handle and put Jake at a sit when he began pulling.

Another method was to drop the harness handle and heel Jake for several yards before picking up the handle and resuming formal guide work. A third suggestion, patterned after the way puppies are trained to heel, was to give Jake an about-turn and reverse our direction. After walking several yards, we would do another about-turn and resume our original direction. The premise for all these recommendations was the need to break Jake's concentration on whatever was distracting him and refocus his attention on me.

For eight months I experimented with these techniques, but it became increasingly apparent that Jake was breaking down and I was losing confidence in him. At home he ignored our cats, Cameo, Kimmel and Kismet, but outside our home cats became objects of fixation. Guide dogs are supposed to

stop for curbs and steps, but not for cats streaking across their path. Noises began to stress Jake, and he responded by becoming even more pully when he heard a screeching siren, a slamming car door or barking dogs. If his work had been consistently bad, my decision to retire him would have been easier and been made earlier. However, he did have good days and each such day gave me hope we were on the verge of a breakthrough.

In late January, Toni and I went on a nine day trip to Michigan, Florida and Texas. Like most of our trips, this one combined visits with friends and relatives with professional speaking engagements. In Lansing we spoke at the Michigan Veterinary Conference. Brad took this opportunity to join us for additional work with Jake and Escort. Although pleased with the progress Escort was making since joining our family six weeks earlier, Brad was distressed with the lack of progress Jake and I were making. For the first time in our many discussions about Jake, the subject of retiring him from guide work was introduced. I felt guilty that my poor dog-handling skills had exacerbated Jake's problems. Brad reassured me the problems were not created by me, and my attempts to solve them showed a tremendous commitment to the relationship.

I still wasn't ready to consider breaking the bond until we flew from Michigan to Florida. Jake became uncontrollably anxious when our small commuter plane landed in Sarasota. When the plane door opened Jake became so frantic to get out, he neglected his role as guide. This incident confirmed my growing belief that Jake was no longer a safe and reliable guide.

Once I faced the possibility of Jake's retirement, I could talk about it openly. At our lecture to the veterinary students at Texas A&M, I reflected upon the probability of the early retirement of Jake for work rather than health reasons. I received a great deal of support and understanding from the more than 100 students in attendance.

Brad did not seem surprised when I called with the news I had decided to retire Jake. He respected my decision and said he would start looking for another dog. Realizing it would take some time before a new match could be made, I decided to continue working with Jake on a limited basis.

A month later Brad called with the news that Golden Retriever Echo, my soon-to-be partner, would arrive in Fresno on March 18. Brad had plans to attend a meeting in Los Angeles, providing the opportunity for him to train me in my home setting. Jake was scheduled to go to his new home on March 17.

So here we were on March 14 in the Chicago airport changing planes. We were on our way to Champaign-Urbana where we were scheduled to present a workshop at the University of Illinois. Even though our retirement plans were already set, Jake's excellent job of guiding through the airport rekindled my feelings of ambivalence. Even at this late date, I fantasized about a magic solution to our problem.

During our two-day stay in Champaign, Jake showed all the old

> By the end of this trip, I acknowledged my fantasies of Jake's resuming his role as guide were just that, fantasies.

signs of stress and anxiety. His guiding duties were kept to a minimum since Joseph Hahn, a first-year veterinary student, offered to be our host and chauffeur during our stay. We had been invited to speak at the SAVMA (Student American Veterinary Medical Association) annual conference, which is held on a different campus each year.

Our return trip to Fresno on March 16 was a mixture of sorrow and relief. By the end of this trip, I acknowledged my fantasies of Jake's resuming his role as guide were just that, fantasies. Because our working relationship was rocky from the start, I never fell in love with him, but still grieved at the thought of breaking the bond.

Our friend Sheila Cary joined us for breakfast on the morning of March 17. Learning of our need to retire Jake, Sheila had offered to adopt him. Sheila planned to take Jake with her to work on a regular basis. Her house has a large yard in which Jake could romp with P.J., a Lhasa Apso. We knew Jake would be in good hands. but all three of us cried as Sheila prepared to leave with her new charge.

With the arrival of Echo the next day, my emotions shifted from sadness to anticipation. At the time of this writing, Jake has made a wonderful adjustment to his new lifestyle and Echo promises to be an outstanding guide.

Category II-I — Regular Column

GUN DOGS
by Bill Tarrant
(FIELD & STREAM)

(MAY 1995)

THE RABBIT HUNTER

To my ear, anymore, many city folk's words come shrill, sharp, fast, and adamant. But my friend John L. Lewis is not of the city; but of the earth and country and deep family roots and his words come slow like the rivers flow in Dixie, rich and laden and full of deep wonder. Words often punctuated with a laugh on himself or life in general, and John's smile is always there.

This evening I'm sitting in this 57-year-old Grand Junction, Tenn., handyman's kitchen where we're visiting. Through the window behind John's thick left shoulder I watch a pale setting sun, smell the night's dinner steeping on the stove, and hear grandchildren playing in a closed-door bedroom.

> His words come slow like the rivers flow in Dixie, rich and laden and full of deep wonder.

I hear the dogs bark in the backyard and ask John, "When you going to get an old dog to train those beagle pups?"

He laughs and tells me, "Soon as I see one to buy. They scarce you know."

"Why do you need one anyhow, why don't you train them pups yourself?"

"Cause that's the slow way to do it. You get a good ol' trained dog and he can do the job in half the time. For the pups follow him and do everything he does. But I have trained em myself... just get out early in the morning and see where a bunny's been playing all night and put the dogs on the scent."

"Well by using an old dog for a teacher, what contribution are you making to those puppy's training?"

"Once the ol' dog get em started most of the time, the puppy, especially on deer — they goina have a fit. Take off on the deer. And my job is to try to head em off and stop em. Sometimes I have to get a little switch to do it. Got' ta get em where they hear me and understand what I'm talking about."

"What gun you carry to do this training?"

"I start off shootin' a .22. Because the reason I start off with a .22 is it don't make a loud fuss as a 16 gauge. And I get em used to that noise and when they start running good I'm shootin' the big gun like a 16 gauge, or 20."

"You always told me rabbits circle back."

"They will... now if an old rabbit don't have no where to go he'll make a circle. But if he got somewhere to go like wherever his hide is, he'll take off... and he liable to run a quarter a mile or so before he run back. But if you'll just stand there and you got a good dog that rabbit will be coming right back to that same spot. All you got to do is wait for him."

"I never thought to ask you this John, but do you call these rabbits here cottontails?"

"No, I call the little ones hillbilly rabbits and when I go to the bottoms and I get a big rabbit, I call him a swamp rabbit."

"And you like your wife to boil them?"

"Parboil em, that's what she do. Then take em out and fry them and put a little gravy and onions and pepper around them. That parboiling make em tender."

"You got swamp rabbits around Grand Junction?"

"I go to the bottoms about 7 or 8 miles from here. When you take a dog to the bottoms he's going to run better for there's scent in those damp bottoms and that dog goina work better. And when they're hot, kind of warm from running, he's got water there to drink."

"Being out like that, you ever have trouble getting on people's land?"

"That's a real problem. You know I put them in the honey suckle and grass patches and that's a big problem cause a lot of times I'll be hunting here and the next thing the rabbit's over there and I can't hunt over there. And your dog get off on that prohibited property and people getting mad saying the dog's running the deers off. Or they say we're disturbing the birds if they got some there."

"Can't you whistle them back?"

"You got a good dog you can blow yourself silly for they ain't going to come back right then... they're chasing that rabbit. They'll follow him for a piece until he makes a turn. Most of the time when they're cut off by his tricks that's when you can call em back in."

"Tell me about cold tracking."

"You take a dog out in the morning and the rabbit will be playing all night...

he'll prowl all that night... and that ol' dog will get a scent of it. He'll go trailing it and bawling, whoo, whoo, whoo. He'll bawl real course and hollow."

"Then when the dog finally get on the hot scent and starts running the rabbit... he can see him... that's hot tracking and his voice changes to a high yip, yip, yip, and you can really hear him go."

"How much training do you do before season?"

"Lots. I walk em in the evening every night. On the frost it's easy to train. The reason I go out hunting in the frost, you know, and after the rain, because in the spring and fall of the year the grass is real dry and when the dog is running and he try to smell he get all those loose debris up his nose and start him wheezing and coughing and stuff like that."

"How far you seen a beagle smell a rabbit?"

"If a dog's not got a cold and they got good smelling he can track on the thinnest scent. If that rabbit played any time at all that night. Now that is if you got a good jump dog. And they'll mess around there and go in circles and know the way the rabbit went.

"But you got to remember a beagle is a ground-scent dog. He ain't smellin' far off like a pointer. All the time he got his nose to the ground. He keep his head down."

"How many dogs do you hunt with?"

"Now once I get em trained I hunt about four dogs in a pack. But when I'm training I just hunt two together, the old dog and the pup. They get on a deer and there's always going to be a hard head in the bunch and they're hard to stop. I don't want too many dogs out there."

"Didn't you once tell me a beagle could catch a rabbit?"

"Oh yea. A beagle a lot faster than

he look to be. If he jump that rabbit up hot and he don't go through some thickets or something they can keep on him real fast. A rabbit can't run very far on a straight away. Now if he can get way ahead he can hop along and get his wind back. But straight out running he can't run very far. And they can catch him."

"You eat all your rabbits?"

"I want to, I tries to. But sometimes they all got the wolves. November the wolves still in the rabbit. And always you need three or four hard frosts come and stay cold like a week or two weeks and then I start hunting because before that you find wolves in them then."

"Wolves? What on earth you talking about?"

"Wolves, you know. A bug under the skin. It infects the rabbit and you don't want to eat him."

"S'cuse me," I say, and go to the phone to call Thomas Newton (remember, we wrote about him in April, 1994) and tell him, "I'm with John L. Lewis and he's telling me about the wolves. What on earth's he talking about?"

Thomas laughs and says, "John's talking about the warbles. The maggot of a bot fly that's burrowed under the rabbit's skin. Those maggots have breathing holes in the skin and bore out when ready to emerge. By Christmas the rabbits have recovered and are good for food. Wolves is an old-time Southern name for them. They're ugly stuff."

I hang up and turn to John saying, "I don't blame you for not wanting to eat them. You find that often?"

"Too often. But come a frost and the wolves come out."

"John," I ask, "any problems hunting rabbits?"

"That's the coyotes nowadays.

They got real common. And I've had em kill a dog. They just slash em to pieces. The pack do. The dog don't know he's runnin' into a pack and then there he is and they just tear him up."

"Other than deer what else does a beagle take off on?"

"Well you know when I ain't rabbit huntin' I'm coon hunting. And the beagle will take off on a coon if they find him in daylight. But then they think the better of it. For you know a beagle afraid of a coon. Yes he is. Plumb afraid."

"And what about hunting a dog or a bitch?"

"There's a whole lot of difference. A bitch will learn a whole lot quicker than a dog will. And she'll make a better track dog. And a dog will run slower than a bitch. I'd rather have a bitch."

I prefer bitches too, so I say nothing more, and cozy in the knowledge I'm in the presence of a master hunter. Then I make a note to go rabbit hunting come Christmas with John L. Lewis. From what he's told us it's a sure thing we'll be eating parboiled rabbit.

(JULY 1995)
THE LEGACY

Clyde Morton came to dogdom through hardship and sorrow, but fate quickly changed that to luck, competency, and a knack for gaining the confidence (if not the love) of most everyone he met.

For Clyde Morton was destined to become the winningest handler in history when he garnered his eleventh National Bird Dog Championship with 7 dogs.

All of which is made more miraculous when you factor in the era he competed (the second quarter of this century): when the vogue for New York millionaires was owning Southern Plantations filled with "pottges." When certain field trial handlers could demand chauffeured cars, house maids, and free housing on the estate. And when bob white were so plentiful you could call them a burden on the land. And yes, there were limitless venues where each weekend you could have a go at it. And the big boys with the big dogs did.

So here comes this 18 year old boy who's father died when he was 12, a high school drop out who has worked the bottoms the past six years raising cotton near Myrtle, Miss, to help care for his widowed mother and six sisters. Here he comes walking from Myrtle to Cotton Plant, Miss., to ask Er Shelley, the renowned dog trainer for the wealthy sportsman, Paul Rainey, if he could help work the dogs.

Dogs had always been Clyde's first love, and as his sister Eloise Meagher and her daughter Paula Sensing, both of Memphis, tell me, "Uncle Clyde was given a bike by his mother and he immediately traded it for his first pointer. He named that dog Frank after his deceased dad."

But Er Shelley (see F&S, Jan, Feb '90) told Clyde there was no work to be had.

So young Clyde pleaded, "I'll do anything you want with the dogs... I especially like fox hounds."

And Er told him, "Good for you...I do too."

But the boy was turned away. Yet Paul Rainey, owner of the vast plantation with it's 100 dogs, had taken a liking to the boy's appearance and came over to ask Er what he wanted. Er told him the boy wanted a Job, and Paul requested, "Well saddle a horse and go bring him back."

Er Shelley came to a fork in the road and had no idea which way Clyde had turned. So he flipped a coin in his head and turned left...which was right, for he soon caught Clyde. Er always said, if he'd turned right the world of dogs would never have had it's master champion.

So here this teen-ager was working for the greatest bird dog handler of all time. And when Er left Paul (because Er's wife objected to him being gone on safaris with Paul so much), Er took Clyde with him. They custom trained for a while in Columbus, Miss., to later enter the employ of another millionaire sportsman.

Then it came to pass A.G.C. Sage of Sedgefields Plantation, near Alberta, Alabama—and also of New York City—heard of young Clyde and offered him a job. But Clyde didn't know. Yet both Er and Ed Mack Farrier (see F&S, Sept, 94) encouraged him to take it. So Clyde moved to Sedgefields—which stands today as one of America's premier field trial venues.

Sage had J. Louis Holloway as plantation manager (see F& S Oct '89) who also trained the field trial dogs, so Sage put Clyde with the shooting dog string. Yet, Sage immediately took a lik-

> **Uncle Clyde was given a bike by his mother and he immediately traded it for his first pointer.**

ing to the boy so in Clyde's second season, when a litter of field trial prospects was born, Sage gave Clyde two pups to train. And what two pups! They were Lullaby and Rapid Transit (the latter becoming national champion, 1933).

How would you like your first pup to be the champ?

Well history fascinates me and maybe you, but dog training is our quest. So with the recall of Eloise and Paula we're shown just how Clyde Morton trained.

These two women have brotherly love, that's for sure, but it's more than that. They idolize the late Clyde Morton. Paula, as a girl in the 40's and 50's visiting each summer at Clyde's place, was so enamored she can tell me which gates were double, what pastures were used to train with pigeons, the ingredients of the dog food made on the premisis, and on and on.

> He later told me, 'If I'd touched that dog, I'd of ruined him. It's more important I control myself than control that dog.'

Listen. Their account will reaffirm how correct you are in your training methods. It did for me.

Paula, who recalls herself as a tom boy, says, "Uncle Clyde was a detailed man. He oversaw the cooking of the dog food, he took each dog into the hospital after each run and checked him over head and foot... he just never left anything to chance. It had to be right. And it had to be checked.

"When he worked the dogs he was stoic, quiet, steady, and consistent. I was training with him once," says Paula, who has since become a racking horse expert and her daughter owns a world champion, "when a dog just infuriated him. So what did he do? He got off his horse, walked to a nearby shade tree, scootched down its trunk and breathing hard, just sat and stared. He later told me, 'If I'd touched that dog, I'd of ruined him. It's more important I control myself than control that dog.'"

That paragraph alone is worth the telling of Clyde's history. That paragraph alone is probably the best dog training advice you'll ever read. For remember, if a dog makes you mad he's defeated you. If you strike back, it's possible you've ruined the dog for life.

"Man Rand (Clyde's field trial scout) broke all the puppies to retrieve in that big old hollow barn." says Paula. We've gone there before and learned how Man hitched the dog's collars to the wall and introduced the buck — all the while gently telling them to fetch. It's interesting that Clyde demanded each pointer to fetch in an era when no field trial contender was ever asked to do so.

The reason was to handle the dogs, get close to them, get down in their face, and to bold them up through discipline: yes, discipline does bold a dog up. And Clyde knew it.

Paula continues, "Sometimes at night we'd all get into the pickup and follow the fox hounds. You'd better not cough, better not talk, and you'd better not move, 'cause he was listening to those dogs. And when you followed them on horse, those horses couldn't eat grass, couldn't swish their tails. That horse had to keep silent so Uncle Clyde could listen to those dogs."

It's evident then, Uncle Clyde was a very intense man. His joy was in concentration and observation. He brooked no nonsense. And I can imagine when he was training pointers, he demanded the best of himself and we know he got the best of his dogs.

Paula points out, "Uncle Clyde would let us kids go down to the kennels and pick out our own puppy for the summer. And we took that puppy to the house and played with it, and we'd tie a string on it and lead it all over the place and make a pet out of it. Then lo and behold, it happened time and again, he'd end up selling that puppy.

"What I didn't know 'til later was we were humanizing those pups. And when the people came to buy, that was the pup they wanted." Uncle Clyde was a rascal. "And I'd come back next summer," continues Paula, "and want my pup and he'd tell me just go down there and pick yourself out another one. I didn't want another one, I wanted the one I had made a pet."

Uncle Clyde was shrewd. There is no one who can bring along a pup like a child, next would be a woman, last would be a man. Pups love a female's energy and giddiness and high-pitched voice; plus their tenderness. Uncle Clyde knew what he was doing.

Paula also says, "Uncle Clyde was so quiet when he worked those dogs. He and Man Rand (the only scout to be elected to the Field Trial Hall of Fame) would be down there in that barn and the other kids and I would try to hear... but even then we couldn't pick out a word they were saying."

Again Paula passes on Uncle Clyde's proven techniques: easy does it. Quiet does it. All of which was taught by Shelley: Clyde's mentor, who I've recounted before was the son of a hotel keeper and was warned by his father he could only have hunting dogs if he kept them quiet 80 as not to disturb the guests. So Er Shelley whispered from an upper floor at the dogs to be quiet. It worked, as Clyde learned, who now hands over this knowledge to us.

Toward the end of Sage's life he had taken so great a liking to Clyde that he offered to sell him Sedgefields Plantation: 8,000 acres and all the out-buildings, dogs, equipment, the whole shebang. But Clyde protested, saying he couldn't afford such a thing.

"Oh yes you can," counseled Sage, "Just cut down and sell all the timber on the place... that'll pay for it."

So the boy who lost his dad at 12, who never finished high school, who walked cross country to become a kennel boy keeping hounds...this boy became owner of one of America's storied plantations. Luck? Yes.

But more than that. Hard work. Always keeping the faith with your employer, employees, and fellow man. And never taking your eye, nor your mind, off the dog before you, and telling yourself, and proving to yourself, you're going to make each and every one of them a champion.

This is the legacy of Clyde Morton: the winningest bird dog handler who ever was—or will ever be. A man who knew if he didn't control himself, he could control nothing.

Category II-J
Yearbook/ **Educational Handbook** /Manual

POSITIVE POTTY TRAINING
by September B. Morn
PAWPRINCE PRESS

Contents

A TASTE OF...
POSITIVE POTTY TRAINING

During the first year of life puppies mature quickly from infancy into adolescence. Each month of Little Fido's first year is roughly equivalent to one year's development for a human child.

At one month of age a puppy is not weaned and isn't yet very mobile. By two months of age he's eating solid food, walking well, and ready to begin potty training. Each individual pup is unique, of course, so some puppies can be potty trained a little earlier, while others may take longer to gain the physical maturity necessary for complete potty training.

If your puppy is at least eight weeks old and you carefully follow the directions in this guide, he or she should be easy to potty train. (If you follow the directions for three weeks without success, it may indicate problems requiring a veterinarian or behaviorist.)

Be patient with your puppy and be as helpful as possible. After all, YOU are the teacher, Little Fido is the student. For the quickest success you must be the best teacher you can be. This booklet is written to help you do just that!

MAMADOG'S JOB

Puppies take their first lessons from the Mamadog (dam). She teaches her infants what constitutes proper canine cleanliness. The dam licks her pups to bathe them as soon as they're born, then at frequent intervals after that. Her insistent yet gentle touch is vital to the newborn pups. In fact, if not cleaned and stimulated by the mother's licking, an infant puppy will be unable to urinate or defecate and will sicken and die.

A good dam licks her pups spotlessly clean of food and debris. She maintains sanitation in the nursery area in the same manner, so there is no buildup of feces or urine around her little pups. The smell of "potty" isn't there, so the puppies learn the den is not a "potty place."

When the pups are a few weeks old they begin to follow their mother around. She may take them several steps away from the den and then urinate. This marks the edge of the "family territory" and by smell and example gives the puppies an indication of where they're supposed to potty.

Once the pups have been weaned to solid food their dam no longer cleans up their body wastes. The dam's owner (the "breeder") must then take over housekeeping chores to maintain sanitation in the puppy area. By that time, however, the pups have become accustomed to toddling away from the sleeping nest to do their potties. Seldom will a weaned and healthy puppy soil his own bed or "den."

A puppy comes to his new family with a few clues about potty rules already, if his dam and the breeder have done their jobs. Little Fido knows not to "mess" in the sleeping and eating areas, however, he may not realize that you expect him to go all the way out to the backyard to potty. He may underestimate the size of your "den" area.

It's not uncommon for a young puppy to seek a potty place just beyond the main activity area of the home. If you spend a lot of time in the kitchen, for example, Little Fido might figure that the livingroom is the "indoor backyard" and far enough away to use as a potty place. Be patient... he's TRYING to be clean. He'll need your help to understand the fine points of good potty behavior.

DON'T PUNISH... TEACH!

Your new puppy's age is an important consideration when potty training him. Puppies younger than ten weeks of age don't get much advance warning from their body's plumbing system and may not make it to the door before they have an "accident."

It's pointless and cruel to punish a young puppy for a potty accident. It's really up to you to anticipate his needs and help him learn where to "go." Success in potty training, especially with a young puppy, is highly dependent upon the vigilance and patience of the humans in the household.

Know When Puppy Needs To Potty

Be consistent! Be prepared! Know your puppy's habits and patterns. Young pups usually need to potty right after: 1) Eating 2) Drinking, 3) Playing, or 4) Waking up.

Also, any time you happen to notice Little Fido walking in a circle while sniffing the floor, or dashing back and forth with a worried look, leaving the room with a backward glance over his shoulder, tippytoeing off behind a piece of furniture, or actually starting to squat... take him IMMEDIATELY to the "Pottying Grounds!"

Observe your puppy and note his normal daily potty cycle. BE READY for your pup at those times and make it easy for him to please you.

Puppies' potty times are mainly dictated by their eating and drinking schedules. It takes a certain amount of time for Little Fido's dogfood to travel the length of his digestive system, then... what went in must come out.

Puppies fed by the free-choice "help-yourself" method usually eat and drink at irregular intervals. This can make it hard for you to anticipate the timing of Little Fido's potty needs because those functions will occur at irregular intervals also. If you experience this problem, you may have quicker success by feeding your puppy at regular scheduled times. (The same holds true if you're attempting to housebreak a recently adopted mature dog.)

Put your pup's food bowl down for him for only twenty to thirty minutes at each meal. Let him eat what he wants in that time, then take the food away until the next mealtime rolls around. Puppies from two to five months of age should be fed three or four times a day. Older pups and adult dogs do well with two meals per day. Pups accustomed to free-choice feeding may take a few days to adapt to the new schedule. They'll soon learn to eat the food when you give it to them. See if this helps your little buddy develop a predictable rhythm for his pottying times.

A puppy from eight to sixteen weeks of age catches on quite readily to potty training. Your job is to make it easy for him to get outside when he needs to. Watchfulness and consistency on your part will have an excellent effect as your pup learns he can rely on you to let him out and praise him for a job well done. He may come to you and whine, or go to the door and sniff or scratch when he needs to relieve himself. If he does, praise him, "Good Fido... Let's GO OUT, GO POTTY." Take him out to the potty place and wait for him to "go". Then praise him in a gentle voice, "Good POTTY, Fido."

When it's time for potty, ask your pup "Want to GO OUT? Want to GO POTTY?... Let's GO OUT, GO POTTY." Call him or carry him to the door, then take him out right away. Take him to the area you've chosen for him to use and tell him "GO POTTY, Fido." Don't stare at him, just be casual. Some dogs prefer a little privacy: turn your back.

The quickest progress will be

> Go outside with your pup and "catch him in the act" of doing the RIGHT thing. This method may require a raincoat and a flashlight, but it's the surest way to get the idea across.

made if you go outside with your pup and wait with him until he goes potty. You'll be able to "catch him in the act" of doing the RIGHT thing. This method sometimes requires a raincoat and a flashlight, but it's the surest way to get the idea across to the pup.

By telling your puppy to "GO POTTY" then praising him "Gooooood POTTY" when he goes, you will be teaching him a command. Yes, your dog CAN learn to do his business ON COMMAND! This is very handy at times, as you can easily imagine. You'll actually be able to stop at a rest area, point to a likely spot, tell Fido to potty there... and he WILL. (Amaze your friends!)

The BORING WALK

A problem might arise if your puppy goes outside for potty and forgets what he went out there for... so he starts to play and explore the yard. If this happens, you can remind Little Fido what he's supposed to be doing by repeating the command "GO POTTY" when he gets sidetracked.

Limit your pup's potty outings to a certain area of the yard. Long walks around the block or romps in the park are often too stimulating for a puppy to "remember" to potty. A dog can get so involved in the myriad of scents, sights, and sounds that he becomes too distracted to think about potty until he's back inside the house. The Boring Walk is very useful to keep a pup's mind on "business."

How To Do The "BORING WALK"

First of all, don't do anything that might "jazz up" your puppy once he's in the potty area. WALK with him to a likely spot then STOP. Stand still. Give Little Fido a low-key command to "GO POTTY." Allow him to sniff around and find a good spot. If he starts to play instead, just mill around a bit to redirect his interest away from the distractions he finds. Take a SLOW step to the side... or backwards... then stop. You could, perhaps, turn your back to the pup and take a small step sideways.

Don't fidget. Be BORING. Then the most interesting thing for your puppy will be his own urge to potty. Praise him calmly when he "goes."

Be Sure He's Finished! Some puppies need to potty several times before they're done. Make a mental note of your pup's potty "pattern" and be sure to give him all the time he needs. A potty outing should take exactly as long as it takes... but a dog in good health who delays more than five minutes may not really have to go.

When your pup "does his duty" praise him SOOTHINGLY, "Gooooooood Potty." Keep this praise low-key or Little Fido may get so happy and excited from your enthusiasm that his muscles will tense up. He'll stop piddling midstream, only to finish after he's back in the house... OOPS!

If your pup is one who has some trouble with potty training, continue to keep an eye on him for a short while after he comes back inside. If he "forgot" to do something, he'll probably "remember" within five minutes of returning indoors. If he looks restless or anxious, take him back out for another few minutes to finish up.

(There's more to "Positive Potty Training" than space here.)

CATEGORY III

CLUB
PUBLICATIONS

Category III-A-1
National Club Publication (Magazine Format)

THE
CAIRN TERRIER CLUB OF AMERICA
NEWSLETTER
Marilyn M. Bumby, Editor

A TASTE OF
THE CAIRN TERRIER CLUB OF AMERICA NEWSLETTER...

Ask The Doctor

Question: Please explain the theory of "dilution" and its misconceptions.

Answer: I am not sure what misconceptions there are about dilution, but whatever they are, I hope this straightens them out.

Dilution as a breeding technique is very straightforward. Lots of people say they use it to correct their problems, but for the most part they do not understand dilution, and, therefore, they misinterpret the results they get. In other words, they really do not dilute traits, they just think they do. Here is why.

Unlike test mating, in which you must know the genotype of one of the dogs in the mating and it has to be either a carrier or be affected with the disease in question, with dilution, you must know the genotype of both dogs. Dilution is a technique you use to get rid of a gene you know is present in an animal you wish to breed. Test mating is a technique you use to determine if a gene is present in an animal you wish to breed.

Here is a situation in which you might want to use dilution.

You have a Cairn male, "Barny," that won Westminster two years in a row. He won 68 best of breeds and was a group winner 42 times. Every time he won group, he won best in show. He is an impressive dog, correct! So far he has bred 86 bitches, producing 344 puppies of which 109 are already champions. Here is the situation, take your pick:

1) You thought you had plenty of time so you haven't kept one of his puppies for yourself yet;

2) You own his son who has already won 12 best in shows, one at Cobo Hall in Detroit in March 1994.

You just found out today that Barny has PRA. He is 4.5 years old. What do you do now? (There are several ethical issues raised here, but I am going to answer only the question of dilution). Barny has to be homozygous (aa), since he is affected and his son has to be heterozygous (Aa) a carrier for the trait. You now know the genotype of Barny and his son. If you want to breed these dogs safely, you have to get rid of the PRA genes. The only way to do that is by dilution.

> If you want to breed these dogs safely, you have to get rid of the PRA genes. The only way to do that is by dilution.

Dilution does work, it is real, you can dilute a gene. That is, you can reduce the chance that the gene is present in the next generation by breeding the dog to a mate that is known to be genetically normal for that trait. That is the caveat, in order to have any meaning you must know the genotype of both dogs. Otherwise, you are just blowing smoke. If you do breed to a known genetically normal dog, you reduce the risk that the gene is present in the next generation by one half each time you do it. A generation time in dogs is 2.5 to 3 years if you are lucky. So, you need to be young when you start the process. Remember, in dilution you always breed the next generation, you do not continue to breed Barny or his son and call it dilution, because if you do, you are blowing smoke. If you continue to breed Barny or his son, you are spreading the gene, not diluting it.

> You only want to fool around with dilution when you have a very good phenotype which needs to be saved.

It takes, at a minimum, 12.5 years to produce animals from an affected dog (Barny) or a defined carrier (his son) which have a relatively low risk of carrying the trait. In this case, they are 93.7% and 96.8% sure to be free of the PRA gene. Notice that dilution does not allow you to bypass the production of carriers. You produce just as many carriers by dilution as you do by test mating, but the time span is longer for dilution. The way to short circuit the time factor is to combine dilution and test mating. Dilute the trait a couple of generations (depending on where you start); then test mate the dog you pick to see if it is a carrier.

> You produce just as many carriers by dilution as you do by test mating, but the time span is longer for dilution.

You only want to fool around with dilution when you have a very good phenotype which needs to be saved. A phenotype like Barny's should be saved (although I probably went a little overboard when I described him), and it is well worth the time it takes, because it is likely to take even longer to produce a dog like Barny from scratch. As they say, don't throw the baby out with the bath water, but know where you are at when you have the tub in your hands.

How about the cost of all of this? Well, it doesn't cost anymore to breed Barny this way than it does any other way, right? The side benefit is that you know where you are genetically and that lets you know what to do with the dogs.

What do you do with all of the puppies? You do what you always do, sell them. Remember, you are breeding a superb dog, and the puppies will be in demand, so you need to require that the puppies be neutered (or you need a non-breeding agreement through AKC), so that the trait is not spread. You don't cut the price on the puppies, and you don't give them away, because with dilution, done correctly, the puppies will always be phenotypically normal, all of their lives, even with PRA as the trait.

What do you do if someone says, "That's a superb puppy, and I want him/her for breeding? I'll give you $4,000.00 (or whatever is a lot of money to you)." For sure this will happen when you have puppies from a dog like Barny. For me, I would not sell a puppy for breeding that had a 50% or higher risk of carrying a gene for a trait as severe as

PRA without an ironclad agreement that the dog would not be offered or used at public stud. I would require that the dog be registered at GDC with the attendant risk attached and to be sure this happened I would do it myself. I would require that offspring of the dog be registered at GDC with the appropriate risk attached so that potential purchasers of the offspring would have an outside accurate source of information about the dogs. I would require that the purchaser sign an agreement stating that he/she understands the risk of PRA which is involved and which clearly defines what that risk is.

Lastly, I would have to be assured that the purchaser understands how to handle the breeding of a dog with a risk like this, and if I was not convinced they knew how, I would not sell them the dog while it was intact, no matter what they offered.

As a rule, all puppies produced in dilutional or test matings that are left intact, for whatever reason, should be registered with GDC with their attendant risk no matter what trait is involved.

How about the dogs with a risk of less than 50%? I picked PRA as the example for this discussion for several reasons, but mainly because it is a severe, permanent, blinding and untreatable disorder. Since it is a severe, nasty disease, I would make the same requirements that I did above. If it was a less severe disease, I would relax a little, requiring that the dog is registered with GDC, that the purchaser understands the disease and how to breed against it, and signs an agreement showing that. Secondly, I picked this disease because, based on the survey, it has a general carrier frequency in the breed of 6.1% which makes it a good illustration of the point I want to make. If the risk of the carrier state in the puppy you sell is equivalent to the general risk in the breed, you are not harming the breed as a whole; of course, you are not helping it either. Even so, we have to function as breeders and the dog we are dealing with is a superb animal, so for me, I would warn the purchaser of the risk, get a signed agreement that he understands and knows the risk, register the dog with the attendant risk at GDC, and sell them the dog.

> What do you do with all of the puppies? You do what you always do, sell them.

> If the risk of the carrier state in the puppy you sell is equivalent to the general risk in the breed, you are not harming the breed as a whole; of course, you are not helping it either.

"Ask The Doctor":
Dr. George Padgett
Rm A19 VCC
College of Veterinary Medicine
Michigan State University
East Lansing, MI 48824

Category III-A-2
National Club Publication (Newsletter Format)

AKC JUDGES NEWSLETTER
Editors:
James W. Edwards and Anne M. Hier

SUMMER 1995 VOL. 9, No. 3   American Kennel Club • 51 Madison Avenue • New York, NY 10010

LISTENING TO THE JUDGES

LISTENING is one of the great virtues that should never be underestimated when searching for advancement of a system involving human interaction. This virtue has been added in a very special way to the system used to advance judges.

Written evaluations of provisional and regular judging assignments are now possible, as the result of recent changes in the judging approval system. Previously, provisional judges and those seeking approval for additional breeds have been observed by members of the Executive Field Staff. These observations have been treated confidentially, and the field staff was not permitted to discuss the observations with the judges. That policy has been changed and—conditions and time permitting—judges now may both provide and receive written evaluations in a specially designed system that features the Judge's Evaluation Form, a complete copy of the document is on page seven of this *Judges Newsletter*.

This new system works as follows. On the morning of a provisional assignment (for example, in English Foxhounds, with an entry of 05-07-03 (YZ), the AKC representative would provide you with a copy of the Judge's Evaluation Form. You would complete the first section of the document, which is based on your activities as the judge of English Foxhounds from 9:20-10:00AM on that day. (Alternately, for breeds with large entries, only a selected class or classes may be examined—as agreed to in advance.) This form provides an opportunity for you to respond to the specific questions about your assignment,

as well as providing reasons to the AKC representative for the placements made. The form is rather simple and brief, and, if completed immediately following foxhound judging, will be easy to implement. The representative observes your judging of English Foxhounds from ringside (admittedly some distance away, or perhaps from within the ring if desirable), and discusses this judging assignment with you at a convenient time. Such a discussion is confidential and begins by the representative LISTENING to your reasons for the placements made. Having listened to your reasons and read your responses on the Judge's Evaluation Form, specific questions on the form are answered by the AKC representative and an opportunity for discussion is provided. Thus, a judge simply states what (with reasons) he or she is doing when judging a breed under actual show conditions, and the representative responds accordingly. A copy of the completed form is given to the judge, one is retained by the representative, and the original is sent to the Judges Department and placed in the judge's file.

In the past, some judges have been denied regular approval for breeds, and have either been required to judge additional provisional assignments or the provisional status has been retracted, based on many factors including the quality of their judging. The written Judges Observation Report on ring procedure and general skills provided some of the reasons, and now the written Judge's Evaluation Form will provide other essential information.

(continued on page 8)

UH OH...PIE CHARTS!

1994 Independent Specialty Shows Held
(1,860 total)

Top Ten Breeds Which Had the Most Independent Specialties in 1994
1. German Shepherd Dogs......181
2. Collies 92
3. Shetland Sheepdogs.............81
4. Doberman Pinschers.............75
5. Cocker Spaniels..................74
6. Great Danes 66
7. Poodles 64
8. Boxers 63
9. Irish Setters 62
10. Bulldogs 57

In 1994 there were 1,860 independent specialty shows. Not included in this total are an additional 367 designated specialty shows held in conjunction with all-breed shows. Let's see...1,860 divided by 136 breeds averages out to almost 14 specialty shows per breed. If we are just looking at numbers, then it appears educational opportunities abound in most breeds. In reality, the top ten specialty breeds listed above represent only four variety groups but were responsible for a whopping 43% of all 1994 independent specialties. German Shepherd Dogs alone

(continued on page 2)

A TASTE OF *THE AKC JUDGES NEWSLETTER...*

LISTENING is one of the great virtues that should never be underestimated when searching for advancement of a system involving human interaction. This virtue has been added in a very special way to the system used to advance judges.

Written evaluations of provisional and regular judging assignments are now possible, as the result of recent changes in the judging approval system. Previously, provisional judges and those seeking approval for additional breeds have been observed by members of the Executive Field Staff. These observations have been treated confidentially, and the field staff was not permitted to discuss the observations with the judges. That policy has been changed and—conditions and time permitting—judges now may both provide and receive written evaluations in a specially designed system that features the Judge's Evaluation Form.

This new system works as follows. On the morning of a provisional assignment (for example, in English Foxhounds, with an entry of 05-07-03-02), the AKC representative would provide you with a copy of the Judge's Evaluation Form. You would complete the first section of the document, which is based on your activities as the judge of English Foxhounds from 9:20 - 10:00 AM on that day. [Alternately, for breeds with large entries, only a selected class or classes may be evaluated—as agreed to in advance.] This form provides an opportunity for you to respond to five specific questions about your assignment, as well as providing reasons to the AKC representative for the placements made. The form is rather simple and brief, and, if completed immediately following Foxhound judging, will be easy to implement. The representative observes your judging of English Foxhounds from ringside (admittedly some distance away, or perhaps from within the ring if desirable), and discusses this judging assignment with you at a convenient time. Such a discussion is confidential and begins by the representative LISTENING to your reasons for the placements made. Having listened to your reasons and read your responses on the Judge's Evaluation Form, specific questions on the form are answered by the AKC representative and an opportunity for discussion is provided. Thus, a judge simply states what (with reasons) he or she is doing when judging a breed under actual show conditions, and the representative responds accordingly. A copy of the completed form is given to the judge, one is retained by the representative, and the original is sent to the Judges Department and placed in the judge's file.

In the past, some judges have been denied regular approval for breeds, and have either been required to judge additional provisional assignments or the provisional status has been retracted, based on many factors including the quality of their judging. The written Judges Observation Report on ring procedure and general skills provided some of the reasons, and now the written Judge's Evaluation Form will provide other essential information.

As one component of the advancement system, written evaluations—based on knowledge, listening, learning, and understanding—represent a step that immediately eliminates some criticism of the previous system. The magnitude of that step deserves to be and will be evaluated in the months ahead.

Category III-B
Local Club Publication

ATTENTION!
Editors:
Sherry Brosnahan and Sue Hunt

Attention!

The Newsletter of the St. Hubert's Dog Training Club

Summer 1995

Any Questions?

From the desk of our editor Sherry Brosnahan

I can't tell you how happy I am to be back in the newsletter business. This winter all of my available "fun writing" hours were gobbled up by Terri's book. Editing "The Book" (three books, actually) has been an enjoyable and memorable experience, but now that I'm done (yes, it *will* be available soon!), it's wonderful to enjoy some free time again.

First, I must apologize for taking so long to finish this long-awaited second issue of **Attention!**. All winter I've longed for this moment, and finally it's here. I'm confident you'll find this issue well worth the wait. Because so much has happened since the first issue, this one is crammed with news about our club and our sport. I hope you'll enjoy reading it as much as I've enjoyed researching, writing, and assembling it.

'Buddy'

Continued on page 2

A TASTE OF *ATTENTION!*...

Any Questions?

I can't tell you how happy I am to be back in the newsletter business. This winter all of my available "fun writing" hours were gobbled up by Terri's book. Editing "The Book" (three books, actually) has been an enjoyable and memorable experience, but now that I'm done (yes, it will be available soon!), it's wonderful to enjoy some free time again.

As we promised in the premier issue, Sue and I will continue to endeavor to make Attention! your newsletter. We've incorporated all of your suggestions in this issue: it includes more training topics, more useful information about our sport, and more "Up Close and Personal" information. Anne's "Train of Thought" column will help you form your personal picture of perfection and "Exercise Finished" offers my tips for motivating the recall. This issue also debuts what I hope will be a popular feature, "Club Member Profile". And what better club member to profile first but Jackie Entwistle, our very first Club Member of the Year!

Regarding your suggestions, I must confess that my favorite was to offer useful information about training, matches, and trials in lieu of the three month calendar. Many of you were quick to realize that compiling the calendar was quite a chore - and most of us read Events and Match Show anyway. So in this issue, you'll find my first reviews of trials and matches. And, at Benita's request, I've included my personal "Are You Ready?" checklist for those of you getting ready to show your dogs at matches and/or trials.

With Spring, our thoughts turn to travel, and for many of us this means traveling with our canine companions. Throughout this issue, travel is a recurring theme. In this issue's special feature, "Paws on the Information Highway", George Collier leads us on a canine-friendly tour of the information highway. Benita Shor reviews the many guides to canine travel in her "Attention Canine Travelers" column. In her first column, our own Miss Canine Manners, Cara Mia, offers her favorite tips for doggie etiquette at dog shows.

"Club News" (and do we have club news!) reviews two of our club's big firsts: our first obedience seminar and our first annual club awards dinner. As if to prove that club members don't rest on their laurels, we already have the beginning of what appears to be a very long list of members' achievements for 1995. And to continue to remind us all that this is our fun sport, I've included "Canine Cuisine" with my promised (and not-so-secret) recipe for dog brownies.

Like most of our Club projects, this issue of Attention! didn't happen without help. Thanks to everyone who took the time to suggest interesting or amusing topics. Thanks to everyone who praised the first issue - Sue and I always respond welt to positive reinforcement (especially food treats)! A special thank you to my guest columnists, Benita Shor and George Collier. And don't miss the special "Thank Yous" in Carol Moran's column, "She Came, She Spoke, She Conquered". Finally, thanks to everyone for their patience while waiting for this issue of Attention!

You've probably heard me say this before, but I'll say it again (and again and again). This may be a dog club, but it's people who will ensure its long term success. Thanks again to everyone who helped make our first year such a success!

Obediently yours,

Sherry Brosnahan

Category III-C-1
Individual Article in National Publication

DEMODICOSIS
by Carole Fry Owen
(THE BAGPIPER)

There are two words mean and nasty enough for a junkyard dog. Demodectic mange.

Is it hereditary? Is it cause for euthanasia? Can it be cured, or controlled?

News from current veterinary texts, recent veterinary periodicals and even from small town general practice veterinarians is good. But be glad you live in 1994/95- in the days of Mitoban®, Interceptor®, ivermectin and modern antibiotics.

Some quick answers about this often dreaded skin disease, before we get technical:

1) Yes, demodectic manage can be transmitted through families. But some cases may not be familial.

2) No, it usually is not cause for euthanasia.

3) Yes, demodectic mange may resolve itself, especially in puppies. Certainly, it can be controlled, and even cured.

Many of us Scottie owners may be living under preconceptions from the past. Perhaps we've heard stories from breeders who dealt with demodectic mange 15 or 20 years ago, with little success.

Speaking scientifically, let's call demodectic mange its proper name, demodicosis. It hasn't been too long since demodicosis might spell the end of the line for a pet.

One Scottie breeder recounted her experience of about 10 years ago with a young male she had purchased and championship titled. Each of his four litters had demodicosis-affected dogs. At that point, he was neutered and placed in a pet home, though he had no demodicosis himself. Of note, three of the four dams were the breeder's own bitches and had never produced demodicosis with other studs. Four of this male's five known affected offspring eventually were put down by their owners.

Today, euthanasia probably would not be the end result. "Prognosis of generalized demodicosis has improved dramatically in the last five years," states the text Small Animal Dermatology, 1989. "To euthanize 6 to 12 month old dogs because they have severe generalized demodicosis is unwarranted since many of them will recover spontaneously."

Though I have never experienced demodectic mange in my dogs, this research assignment has equipped me to handle it should it come. I have skimmed the basics you should know from a number of up-to-date veterinary medicine sources.

This article is not intended to be a research tome with extensive footnotes. Sources are listed at the article's end. If you encounter a difficult case of demodicosis, I urge you to check these references for more in-depth information on treatment options.

WHAT IS IT?

Demodicosis is the most important parasitic skin disease of young dogs. Actually, you'd be less likely to find it in a junkyard dog than in a "fancy animal." It is more common in purebreds. Characterized by hair loss, usually without itching, it may be accompanied by silvery scales and the crusts and infection of seborrhea and pyoderma. A moth-eaten appearance around the eyelids, at the corners of the mouth, and on the front legs is typical of mild cases. Thickened grayish skin is common.

Perpetrator of demodicosis is Demodex canis, a mite which stakes out squatters' rights on almost all dogs — usually as benignly as lichen on a rock. The mites live in hair follicles and are invisible except using a microscope. Like Staphylococcus bacteria are normal inhabitants of a healthy bitch's vaginal vault (within reason), Demodex canis are normal dwellers on a dog's skin (in very small numbers). Problems arise when the parasites proliferate out of harmonious bounds and populate the skin by the thousands.

D. canis is not contagious. Yes, it is true that the mites are transferred to nursing puppies from their mothers during the first two to three days of life. However, a dog with demodicosis does not spread the condition to its housemates. What causes a normal D. canis population to go ballistic seems to be some defect as yet unidentified in a dog's cellular immunity. Factors including stress, estrus, pregnancy and underlying medical problems can play a part.

SCOTTIES AND DEMODICOSIS

What about our own Scotties? Ask around. You won't have any trouble finding breeders who've experienced demodicosis. However, our breed does fare better than many. *Veterinary Pediatrics* (1990) doesn't list the Scottish Terrier as a breed with unusual familial predisposition to develop generalized demodicosis. Those breeds are Old English Sheepdogs, Collies, Afghan Hounds, German Shepherd Dogs, Shih Tzus, Staffordshire and Pit Bull Terriers, Doberman Pinschers, Dalmatians, Great Danes, English Bulldogs, Boston Terriers, Dachshunds, Chihuahuas, Boxers, Pugs, Chinese Shar Peis, Beagles and German Short-Haired Pointers.

How do rescue Scottish Terriers stack up? Do they suffer frequent demodicosis because of original neglect? Probably not. Daphne and Marshall Branzell, San Antonio, TX, have rescued and placed about two dozen Scotties and Westies in the last several years. Some had skin problems, but none demodicosis. They do regret the one Scottie with advanced demodicosis which they had to turn down for rescue since his prognosis was uncertain.

Understanding demodicosis demands knowing the difference between localized demodicosis and generalized demodicosis.

LOCALIZED DEMODICOSIS

Extremely common in puppies is the localized variety. Hoskins' *Veterinary Pediatrics* defines localized demodicosis as "five or fewer lesions affecting no more than one body region (such as head or extremities)." Of interest to breeders, the text notes: "Any dog with more extensive disease is at least suspect for having a disease that may be passed on to offspring." Most localized cases appear before one year of age.

Veterinary Pediatrics also cites research showing that "90 per cent of cases of localized demodicosis in pre-pubertal dogs resolve spontaneously in 3 to 8 weeks" and admonishes that treatment doesn't speed recovery and may not be warranted. The text does advise beginning treatment for generalized demodicosis if the localized problem remains active more than eight weeks in a puppy.

Small Animal Dermatology states, "Most cases of generalized demodicosis start as local lesions in young dogs. If lesions do not undergo spontaneous remission or receive adequate treatment, the patient carries the disease into adulthood. Adult-onset generalized demodicosis is rare."

GENERALIZED DEMODICOSIS

This type is a familial disease, at least when it appears in puppies. It is one of the most severe canine diseases and is difficult to treat. It begins localized, but doesn't get better.

Veterinary Pediatrics quotes research that generalized demodicosis also may resolve without miticidal treatment in 30% to 50% of cases of dogs under one year of age. "Not every case of generalized demodicosis in young puppies should be treated," states the ultra conservative (or ultra liberal) Hoskins' text. Adds *Small Animal Dermatology*, "There is no evidence that treatment of localized demodicosis prevents generalization in cases so destined."

What is an owner to do? Treat or not treat? You and your veterinarian will need to weight the possibilities. It's a Catch-22 situation.

Interestingly, debilitating disease will predispose older dogs to demodicosis. The link is not conclusive, but certain diseases are suspected to cause adult-onset demodicosis. These diseases include hyperadrenocorticism (Cushing's Disease), hypothyroidism, diabetes mellitus, hepatic disease, allergies and neoplasia, according to research reported in the 1994:4 issue of *Journal of the American Veterinary Medicine Association*. Cure rates for demodicosis appear higher in dogs in which an underlying disease is identified and treated.

Veterinary Forum (March, 1994) quotes specifics in a recent study showing "adult-onset canine demodicosis (greater than two years old) to be caused by corticosteroid administration (32%), hypothyroidism (20%), cytotoxic drugs (12%) and hypoadrenocortism (8%). Internal disease or malignant neoplasia also is mentioned as an underlying cause of generalized canine demodicosis. Other sources note that true hypothyroidism is not a cause of demodicosis, but that low T3 and T4 function may accompany demodicosis.

DIAGNOSIS

For diagnosis, skin scrapings are the key. All cases of seborrhea and pyoderma should be scraped. Their primary cause could be demodicosis. Skin scraping would seem simple. However, many mistakes are made either because it is not done, or it is done improperly. Whereas deep scrapings are used to find sarcoptic mites, for demodectic mites the area is squeezed to extrude mites from hair follicles.

To diagnose sarcoptic mange, one mite is sufficient. To diagnose demodicosis, a vet is looking for many adult D. canis mites, or for an increased ratio of immature forms to adults. Presence of an occasional adult D. canis mite is normal. Skin scrapings show D. canis mites readily, so the disease is hard to confuse with others. Texas veterinarian Dr. Neal Tindol points out that if there are typical demodectic lesions, it is wise to treat for the disease even if a scraping shows no mites.

If you suspect demodectic mange, but skin scrapings are negative, ask if a coverslip was used on the slide. States Small Animal Dermatology, "every year the authors continue to receive referred demodicosis cases that were misdiagnosed owing to false-negative skin scrapings." Failure to use a coverslip can cause false negative results.

DECISION

How aggressively should a particular dog be treated? Is the ultimate sacrifice of euthanasia justified? Here are some prime considerations:

1) Does the dog belong to an at-risk breed?

2) Have closely related dogs developed generalized demodicosis?

3) Is there an associated health problem which is not correctable?

4) Is there widespread and/or deep secondary bacterial infection?

5) Is cost of treatment prohibitive to the owner?

6) Is the dog's sole value as a breeding animal, and not as a pet?

If your own veterinarian opts to not immediately treat a puppy showing localized or even generalized demodicosis, don't necessarily panic. However, it's doubtful your family veterinarian will take the academic laissez faire approach to heart.

Hoskins' *Veterinary Pediatrics* makes valuable points, but its condescending comment, "At times the clinician may be forced to treat to appease the concerned owner" rubs this breeder/pet owner/writer the wrong way. I, and perhaps you, might prefer to err on the side of unnecessary treatment. If you're not comfortable waiting for self resolution, look for another vet.

"I'd trash the Hoskins' text," said one veterinarian I interviewed, relative to its "wait and see" advice. "Demodicosis is a difficult disease." He thinks statements about a high frequency of self resolution are dangerous because they may make the disease seem simpler than it is.

The fact that a dog would not be in a vet's office if its owner was not concerned leads veterinarians like ones at the three clinics in my small community to treat most all dogs that present with demodicosis—whether localized or generalized. What vet wants to be blamed for "waiting to see" on a case that eventually blows up? Hoskins' text clearly states that "every case of generalized demodicosis does begin as a localized form."

LOCALIZED TREATMENT

"Benign neglect is a reasonable and rational course of action, or inaction," reminds Small Animal Dermatology. However, if treatment is desired, several sources suggest daily topical therapy locally with one of the following:

•Benzoyl peroxide shampoo, lotion or cream

•Benzoyl peroxide gel (OxyDex® Gel, Pyoban® Gel)

•One part rotenone (Canex®)/three parts mineral oil

•Mild rotenone ointment (Goodwinol®)

•Lindane and benzyl benzoate lotion

•Amitraz (Mitaban®) solution at 0.66ml/cup of water (Note: *Small Animal Dermatology* advises against use of amitraz for localized cases because of risk of developing resistant mites.)

No corticosteroids! Dogs affected by demodicosis are immunosuppressed animals, and corticosteroids increase immunosuppression.

GENERALIZED TREATMENT

The only Food and Drug Administration-approved method of treatment for generalized demodicosis is the miticide amitraz (U.S. trademark Mitaban®). Amitraz treatment has no apparent side effects except mild sedation for 12 to 24 hours. Before Mitaban®, the organophosphate ronnel or trichlorfon were used.

Graphic success is noted by *Small Animal Dermatology* author George H. Muller, D.V.M. Muller has investigated amitraz since 1977. He has used it in more than 400 dogs with generalized demodicosis: "Over 86% of all cases completely recovered with only four to eight treatments. The remaining 14% were kept in good condition by periodic maintenance treatments every 2, 4, or 8 weeks. Many of these dogs, also, may eventually achieve permanent cure."

The good news claims *Small Animal Dermatology* is "Euthanasia, commonly resorted to in the past, is rarely necessary if a dedicated owner will use modern remedies. This does not mean that treatment is easy or foolproof. Many owners accept this regimen as an acceptable price for salvaging their pets' lives."

When a prominent Scottie breeder noted demodicosis in a puppy a few years back, a professional handler cautioned her about the quality of life the puppy might have. She put the puppy down. Fortunately, times have changed.

AMITRAZ THERAPY

Procedure as outlined in *Small Animal Dermatology* and other sources is:

1) Clip dog's coat—all of it!

2) Remove all crusts.

3) Shampoo with produce which will kill bacteria and remove scales and exudates. Protective ointment to eyes is suggested. Towel dry before amitraz application, or shampoo dog day before treatment. Dog should be dry, or almost dry to prevent dilution of amitraz.

4) Apply amitraz (Mitaban®, FDA-approved concentration is 250 parts per million (ppm) by wetting and sponging the entire body, not just affected areas).

5) Blow dry (or others say, drip dry) dog. No swimming or bathing before next treatment.

6) Repeat shampoos and amitraz treatments every two weeks until there are two clear scrapings two weeks apart.

7) Reevaluate four weeks after last treatment (multiple scrapings from most severely affected areas).

One source advises treating ear canals every two to three days with amitraz in mineral oil (1 ml/10-20 ml mineral oil).

Dogs with pododemodicosis (paw involvement) may need special more frequent antibiotic and/or amitraz soaks of the feet.

Certain adjuncts to antibacterial shampoos and amitraz dips may be warranted. Possibilities recommended by *Small Animal Dermatology* include: Cephalosporins, erythromycin, lincomycin, oxacillin, chloramphenicol, gentamicin, or injectable carbenicillin have proven most effective.

Daily whirlpool baths during early treatment: povidone-iodine (Betadine®), chlorine, or chlorhexidine (Nolvasan®)

Oral Vitamin E, 200 mg per dog, five times daily for six weeks (Study quoted showing improvement in 141 of 143 dogs with generalized demodicosis).

A cure often is defined as complete eradication of mites with no relapse in the following 12 months. The truth is, some dogs respond to treatment, but are never clear of the mites. They may need regular treatment for the rest of their lives. It's trouble, but still a happier choice than euthanasia for many pet owners.

Extra Label Successes

There is worldwide debate about the best use of amitraz. You should be aware that many veterinarians utilize amitraz even more successfully in a non-licensed manner; or use other pharmaceuticals not licensed at all for treatment of demodicosis.

Extra label usage of amitraz includes weekly (or even more frequent) application, instead of bi-weekly use. Extra label usage also may include higher concentrations (500 to 1000 ppm, instead of 250 ppm). Daily half body treatments at five times the recommended solution have recorded a high resolution rate in difficult cases. Though these frequencies and concentrations of Mitaban˜® are not FDA approved, they have proven more effective than the licensed protocol in certain dogs.

Drugs not licensed for treatment of demodicosis, but successful in treatment of tough cases, are the heartworm preventative milbemycin oxime (Interceptor®) and invermectin. Especially when conventional therapy is not successful, these extra label therapies may be helpful. Veterinary dermatologists caution that these drugs should not be the first choice of treatment.

Interceptor® has been used successfully once or twice daily at a dosage of 0.5 to 1.0 mg/kg daily. The treatment is quite expensive, but one study in *Veterinary Forum* (March, 1994)

noted that in 80 dogs classified as conventional treatment failures, results showed "96% achieved negative skin scrapings within 90 days; 42% have remained negative for over one year." The going rate in my community to treat a Scottie with Interceptor® would be about $60 per month, if dosed with one tab of 5.75 mg Interceptor® daily.

Ivermectin, a cattle and horse product, has been used effectively orally or by injection. *Veterinary Dermatology* (1993,4) relates successful extra label daily oral treatments with 0.6 mg/kg of the cattle product Ivomect® or the oral horse product Eqvalan®. Texas veterinarian Dr. Scott Burt mentions there have been numerous deaths reported with Eqvalan® because it is hard to dose it accurately.

Ivermectin is contraindicated in some herding breeds, notably Collies, Shetland Sheepdogs, Old English Sheepdogs and Australian Shepherds. All dogs must be evaluated for heartworm disease before ivermectin treatment is initiated. A tip to mask the unpleasant taste of ivermectin: oral dosages may be mixed with the canine vitamin supplement PetTinic® to make ivermectin more palatable.

LIFE WITH DEMODECTIC MANGE

Breeder X lives with demodicosis. What she deals with in her one affected Scottish Terrier is as bad as it gets. Breeder X's young champion male developed it at four years of age. The local vet first diagnosed the condition as canine acne. He prescribed prednisone, and things got worse.

"I finally told my vet, 'Somehow, we're not doing something right,'" remembers Breeder X. She headed for her state's veterinary teaching facility. Clinicians there found generalized demodectic mange. A skin scraping diagnosed it in short order. Her original veterinarian later said he would never have thought of a skin scraping. For five months, the dog had been misdiagnosed and treated with corticosteroids, the ultimate in mistreatment for demodicosis.

Two years into intensive treatment, the dog does have clear times. But he has suffered half a dozen flare-ups, some serious enough to start treatment all over. Sometimes the spot treatment will do. Specialists at the state's vet school call his case the worst demodicosis they have seen.

"We'll go through the whole process, get three squeaky clean scrapings, and the vets say, 'He's clear.' There is no 'clear.'" emphasizes Breeder X. "It has been a go-away and come-back sort of thing. In fact, he's going through it right now."

Treatment is rigorous, and Breeder X is religious about it. Her process is: Pyoban® benzoyl peroxide shampoo every other day. Mitaban® amitraz dip once weekly. Ivermectin orally once daily. Oral Baytril® antibiotic for Staph infection. Topical gentamicin antibiotic for ears. Nolvasan® antibiotic soak for feet twice daily. Vitamin E at 200 I.U. every eight hours.

Tough for this breeder was the new look for her would-be special, something akin to a Chinese Crested, only no crest. When treatment is needed, the dog is shaved down. "The first time I did it, I bawled and bawled. All of it went—eyebrows, beard, everything. If you want to see what's under there, try a #10-blade clip." On the bright side, her husband brags, "Look at his muscles ripple."

"I don't want to use him at stud now," emphasizes Breeder X. However, she hasn't forced herself to neuter the dog yet. The stress of a bitch in season seems to fuel his condition, but "if I start him on ivermectin the day the bitch starts, I can keep the Demodex from flaring. Ivermectin must taste absolutely atrocious. He will cough, sputter, gag and then want a cookie RIGHT NOW to wash that stuff down."

Before his own problems, the dog sired several totally clear litters. However, significant to the breeder was the litter with three out of four affected pups by puberty - this from a dam that had been bred previously to three different males with no demodectic offspring.

What's it like living with severe demodicosis? Not bad enough that Breeder X would put her dog down. "He's a happy, healthy dog that loves to go camping and fishing. No fisherman is safe. A fish is a fish. They have it on the fishing line, and he's got it in his mouth."

"Now that he's clipped down and has no hair again, he's back to sleeping in bed, between the pillows and closest to the mattress. He'll stay there like a lizard until it warms up in the morning." Living with demodicosis: "You have to love the animal," concludes Breeder X. "You have to do the treatment like they say."

REMEMBER

Some landmark points to remember are the following, "down from Mt. Sinai" remarks from *Small Animal Dermatology.*

•Adult-onset demodicosis is often followed by cancer or internal disease.

•A skin scraping for demodectic mites MUST be made in all skin disease of the feet and in all pyoderma and seborrheas.

•Examining material from skin scraping without a coverslip can cause false negative results.

•The tendency to develop generalized demodicosis seems to be hereditary.

•Advise breeders not to use previously infected or carrier animals for breeding.

•Many drugs receive credit for demodicosis cures that in reality are spontaneous recoveries.

•Corticosteroids are contraindicated in patients with demodicosis, since these dogs are immunosuppressed. Under no circumstances should systemic corticosteroids be used in cases of generalized demodicosis.

TO BREED OR NOT TO BREED

Let's end this discussion of demodicosis with what you're really wondering about: breeding considerations.

The recommendation on breeding couldn't be stated more emphatically in *Small Animal Dermatology:* "It is strongly recommended not to breed dogs that have recovered from general demodicosis or those that have produced affected pups. It is clear that the tendency to develop this disease is inherited. The American Academy of Veterinary Dermatology recommends neutering all dogs who have generalized demodicosis, so that the incidence of the disease is decreased and not perpetuated."

The above decree does not mention mild, localized cases of demodicosis. They may not fall under the above breeding ban. It is possible some of those dogs might be safe candidates for breeding, but nowhere in my review of literature is that actually stated. I would imagine most veterinarians would advise the most careful consideration before a breeder includes any such animals in a breeding program.

We may be living in the best of times for treatment of demodicosis. However, we can't treat the genes that may predispose a dog to it. Take care.

REFERENCES TEXTS:

1) Small Animal Dermatology (Fourth Edition): by George H. Muller, DVM, Robert W. Kirk, DVM, and Danny W. Scott, DVM. W.B. Saunders Co./Harcourt Brace Jovanovich, Inc., Philadelphia, 1989, pp. 126-127, pp. 376-394.
2) Veterinary Pediatrics, Dogs and Cats from Birth to Six Months: by Johnny D. Hoskins, DVM, PhD. W.B. Saunders Co./Harcourt Brace Jovanovich, Inc., Phil., 1990, pp. 382- 385.

JOURNAL ARTICLES:

1) Duclos, DD, James GJ, Shanley, DJ: "Prognosis for treatment of adult onset demodicosis in dogs: 34 cases (1979-1990)." *Journal of the Am. Vet. Med. Assoc.* '94, 4: 616-619.
2) Medleau, LM: "Using ivermectin to treat parasitic dermatoses in small animals." *Vet. Med.*, Aug. 94: 770-774.
3) Medleau, L. Ristic, Z: 'Treating chronic refractory demodicosis in dogs." *Vet. Medicine*, August, 1994: 775-777.
4) Reedy, LM: "Canine demodicosis, research and treatment." *Vet. Forum.* March, 1994: 48.
5) Ristic, Z: "Ivermectin in the treatment of generalized demodicosis in the dog." *Vet. Dermatology.* 1993, 4:40-41.
6) Sosna, CB, Medleau, L: "Treating parasitic skin conditions." Veterinary Medicine. June, 1992: 573-586.

CONFERENCE PRESENTATION:

1) Miller, WH Jr.: "How I treat generalized demodicosis." Eastern States Veterinary Conference 67. Jan. 17, 1991.

PERSONAL INTERVIEWS:

1) Burt, Dr. Scott: Highland Animal Hosp., Big Spring, TX.
2) Hill, Dr. Debra: Western Hills Animal Clinic, Big Spring, TX.
3) Tindol, Dr. Neal: Sierra Animal Clinic, Big Spring, TX.

Category III-C-2
Individual Article in Local Club Publication

* This article was also winner of THE ELLSWORTH S. HOWELL AWARD as the best article on judging, exhibiting, dog show reporting or any other aspect of conformation showing.

FOR THE LOVE OF DOGS:

A LOOK AT THE HISTORY OF DOG SHOWS

by Tibby Chase

(THE CORGI CRYER)

Late on a Friday afternoon, just as you are about to leave work, an officemate casually asks, "What are your plans for this weekend — beaches, boating, a barbecue?" Stuffing the last folder in your briefcase, you reply as casually as you can, "I'm leaving early tomorrow morning for Timbuktu (or some similarly obscure place) for a weekend of dog shows." Then, hurrying to avoid any further comments, you race for the door. From the background comes, "But why drive all that way, when there are so many other things to do closer to home?"

Why indeed? One answer is that dog sports are a very popular American pastime. In 1993, the AKC sanctioned over 10,000 events involving 1.7 million entries. Fifty percent of the events were dog shows and/or obedience trials, and the other fifty percent included field trials, lure coursing, tracking, herding, hunting tests and matches. This translates into over 190 events every weekend of the year and these are only

AKC events. Moreover, organized dog shows have been held for over 120 years — longer than organized golf, basketball, tennis or professional baseball. The premier dog show of the year, the Westminster Kennel Club Show, first held in 1877, is second only to the Kentucky Derby in being the oldest continuously held sporting event in America.

Such longevity confirms the continued popularity of dog events, but does not really answer the question, "why participate?" One way to gain insight into this question is to go back to the "roots" of dog showing. A trip back in time, examining the origins and actual accounts of nineteenth century American dog shows, is not only fun but sheds light on the concerns that motivated our "foundation" breeders, exhibitors and show organizers. While much has changed, that which has stayed the same helps explain why generation after generation, Americans have enjoyed their dog shows.

ORIGINS OF AMERICAN DOG SHOWS

In the aftermath of the Civil War, Americans increasingly looked across the Atlantic, to England, for models of social, cultural and leisure activities. The growing middle class and the wealthy industrial entrepreneurs saw emulation of British mores as one way to bring order to the chaotic conditions following war.

Among the more popular "Anglo" trends adopted by these groups were an admiration for pure bred dogs and the social status associated with them; a desire to participate in regulated sporting events; and an intense interest in the "art" of animal breeding.

The pure bred dog found a warm welcome in the Victorian cultural milieu that characterized mid to late nineteenth century America. Like their English counterparts, Americans considered the dog a special animal, " the friend of man and faithful and vigilant protector of his property." Pure bred dogs in particular were characterized as "noble" and "beautiful", and endowed with high moral character. Writing in 1881, George Romanes, a noted zoologist and close friend of Darwin, celebrated the "high intelligence" and "gregarious instincts" of the pure bred dog. In his theoretical 50-step ladder of intellectual development, he included both dogs and apes on step 28 as the most intelligent of animal species (steps 29-50 were reserved for humans). (1)

In America, articles appeared regularly in popular publications such as Harper's Weekly, the Illustrated American and Gleason's extolling the deeds of heroic dogs. In most cases, whether true or not, the dogs were identified as a specific breed or breed type, with the most popular being Newfoundlands, Mastiffs, Bulldogs and assorted terriers. Books appeared with clearly identifiable pictures and the "newest" official standards for specific breeds. One of the most influential books, The Classic Encyclopedia of the Dog, by Vero Shaw, was published in England from 1879-1881. It was the first book to include color plates of outstanding specimens of pure bred dogs. These color illustrations were quickly reproduced in America by the Goodwin Tobacco company as insert cards for chewing tobacco. The first baseball cards in America were actually dog cards! In addition to tobacco products, pure bred dogs appeared regularly on

advertising cards for various businesses and products. Vegetine, a popular New England tonic or "blood purifier", adopted as its symbol a "pure blood" Newfoundland named Major. The advertising card proudly boasted that, "Major is six years old, is very intelligent, sagacious, and faithful." Other companies used images of Mastiffs, Great Danes (known as German Boar Hounds), Greyhounds, Pugs, toy spaniels, and hunting dogs to enhance the social status associated with their products.

The social desirability of pure breds was further heightened by the popularization of the expense and effort associated with obtaining such dogs. The sporting press regularly reported owners valuing dogs at prices from $500 to as ridiculously high as $10,000. This at a time when a loaf of bread was five cents. The impression was that only the wealthy or aspiring middle class could afford the time and money to import, buy and/or raise such special pets or sporting companions. The English influence seen in Queen Victoria's lavish displays of her pet dogs, along with her patronage of early English shows, provided status-seeking Americans with the ultimate in social endorsement for pure bred dogs and dog shows.

THE GROWTH OF ORGANIZED SPORTING EVENTS

In 1895, journalist E. H. Morris wrote, "the increasing interest in sport of all kinds brings out an equally marked appreciation of whatever is noble, beautiful or useful in the animal world and hence the growth in public favor of the annual dog shows." (2) From the beginning, dog shows were viewed as sporting contests. Americans had traditionally enjoyed outdoor sporting activities. The fields and woods of rural America provided ample opportunity for all types of hunting activities involving dogs including grouse hunting, woodcock shooting, waterfowling, deer stalking, rabbit hunting, coursing with greyhounds and fox hunting with horses and hounds. In the American psyche, dogs and sport were closely aligned.

In the later part of the nineteenth century these sporting pastimes expanded to include organized competitive events. In a span of thirty years from 1870 - 1900, America witnessed an explosion in competitive sporting events and the formation of regulatory sports organizations as diverse as the American Kennel Club, The US Lawn Tennis Association, The US Golf Association, yachting clubs and the American Baseball Association. Thus the scene was set for the first American dog shows as competitive sports. They combined America's fascination with pure bred dogs and its traditional affinity for dogs and sporting pastimes.

DOG BREEDING
AND DOG SHOWS

The American interest in animal breeding provides the final key to the rise in popularity of American dog shows. Once again, Americans followed the lead of their English counterparts. From the early eighteen hundreds on, the English prided themselves on their success in perfecting the art of animal breeding. First with domestic farm animals and in the later part of the century, dogs. Breeding was considered both an art and a science.

English sportsmen devoted much time and effort to creating documented varieties of sporting dogs for specific uses. Walsh's comprehensive 1868 Encyclopedia of Rural Sports, published about the time of the first dog shows, devotes pages to listing pedigrees and names of outstanding sporting dogs, es-

pecially Greyhounds with pedigrees going back twenty generations. The pinnacle of nineteenth century English dog breeding was reached with the previously mentioned publication of Shaw's Encyclopedia of the Dog. Shaw described over 60 native English breeds and included extensive pedigrees along with some of the first written standards. He devoted an entire section to the principles of selecting and breeding dogs, of which much is as valid today as it was over 120 years ago.

Americans entering the sport of pure bred dogs took a similar pride in adopting these dog breeding principles. Walsh's 1885 book, The Dogs of Great Britain and America, devotes extensive chapters to the need for careful selection of breeding stock. Evidence of this concern with breeding surfaces in the extensive coverage sporting papers gave to the American Bred class at early dog shows. Unlike today, winning from the American Bred class was quite prestigious as it signified the coming of age of American breeders versus English breeders.

VIGNETTES FROM
A NINETEENTH CENTURY
AMERICAN SHOW

What was it like to exhibit at these early dog shows? Accounts from several of the pre-American Kennel Club regulated shows (1874 - 1884) provide a montage of how such shows operated. The first organized American dog show was held in Chicago in 1874, followed by others in Springfield, IL, Manchester, NH, and Memphis, TN. By 1884, eleven shows were held annually, all benched and all "profit making" enterprises. Average duration was three to four days, and judging was held in only one or two rings with four to five judges for the whole show. Entries ran from 500 at the smaller shows to over 1,500 at Westminster. A typical entry fee was $3.00.

While most shows offered from one hundred to two hundred classes, only twenty-six to thirty breeds were represented. Sporting breeds predominated with numerous classes for setters (all three modern breeds) along with "Russian Setters", Pointers, Cockers, Field, and Irish Water Spaniels. Amongst the hounds were Greyhounds, Fox Hounds, Harriers, Beagles, and Deerhounds. Non Sporting (all other breeds) featured Mastiffs, St. Bernards, Newfoundlands, Berghunds, Leonburgers, Ulm dogs (our Great Danes), Collies, Dalmatians, and a variety of terriers. Among the more unusual breeds were the Chinese Edible Dog (1878) and the Pekin Spaniel (1884). In 1882, there was even a special class for "wooden or glass dogs." Dogs were judged in classes by breed, but there was no formal "Best of Breed" designation nor were there group or Best in Show judging. Championship classes were offered for dogs that had won at previous shows, and winners of these classes seemed to

The First Dog Show on Landing

An Enthusiast in Dogs

be equivalent to Best of Breed.

Aside from breed judging, a big draw was the separate judging for special prizes. The first Westminster had over 30 special prizes worth over $5000, ranging from a silver cup valued at $150 for the best pair of setters, to a silver-mounted Fly Book and Flies valued at $50 for the best red Irish Setter brood bitch and her get. The best Pug could win a silver collar, and a Gordon Setter puppy a Colt revolver. An intriguing special prize was offered for the best "Trick dog" — won by Fritz (no breed given). Breeders also offered cash awards for the best display of dogs sired by their stud dogs.

Being profit-making enterprises, attracting spectators to shows was as critical as attracting exhibitors. Special attractions included Greyhound racing, leaping contests for Greyhounds, and a distinctly unsuccessful fox hunt at the 1878 Westminster, where the fox took refuge amongst the benching causing "no end of chaos." At times it appeared that the press coverage was more concerned with the social status of the spectators themselves, than with the merits of the dogs with comments such as, "the majority of those attending wear fashionable garments, and have much to boast socially (1884)." A female spectator at the

114

1878 Massachusetts Kennel club lamented that the admission fee of fifty cents, "was more than a poor person can well afford... they should have a people's day to allow the working man to see everything that is noble and graceful and commendable in caninedom."

Show dogs suffered innumerable indignities at these early shows, beginning with the journey to and from the show in drafty baggage cars or carriages. Describing the arrival of dogs at the 1877 Westminster, a columnist noted, "they came in all sorts of conveyances, some packed in huge coops, others on stout chains, and still others carried in baskets on their owner's arms." Once at the show, benching for the large dogs was straw-filled wooden stalls and for smaller dogs, "delicately upholstered cages decked with satin and point lace." Sickness was a constant threat, especially from distemper. And more than anything the dogs were constantly subjected to "throngs of utter strangers chucking them under the chin or pointing fingers and saying 'Dowgy, Dowgy'." Food and "mucking out" was provided by the show organizers, twice a day unless an owner made special arrangements for a dog keeper.

Despite these limitations and drawbacks, the sport of dog showing grew at a rapid pace, especially towards the end of the nineteenth century. With the advent of the American Kennel Club in 1884, more consistent rules for organizing and managing shows emerged. The first stud book appeared in 1887. In 1893, the AKC took steps to protect the health of show dogs by requiring a veterinary exam for each dog before benching, and limiting the age of entries to dogs over six months. Judging protocol was standardized using 100 point scales for each breed, and a championship point system was established with shows rated based on entries. The first AKC recognized championships were offered soon after 1884. Simple items such as numbered armbands were introduced along with show catalogs and judging schedules. By the turn of the century, the rough framework of our modern day shows was well in place.

LESSONS LEARNED FROM EARLY DOG SHOWS

It is tempting to view nineteenth century shows as quaint events with little to teach the modern dog show exhibitor. Yet many of these pioneer exhibitors and breeders were as devoted to the "progress" of their breeds as any modern specialists.

To these individuals we owe a debt of thanks for persevering through the initial unorganized stage of dog exhibitions, and taking the initiative to formulate the basic rules and regulations that make our modern shows possible. Moreover, their love of dogs, desire for honest competitive sport, and sincere interest in dog breeding are as valid reasons for being involved in dog shows today as they were over a hundred years ago.

BIBLIOGRAPHY

1. Harriet Ritvo, *The Animal Estate*. Cambridge, MA: Harvard University Press, 1987, p. 35.

2. E. L. Morris, "Notes On the Annual Bench Show", *The Illustrated American*, May 1895, p. 30.

Category III-D
Subject Related Series Or Regular Column

HERD AND SEEN
by Karen Martinac

(THE CORGI CRYER)

THE CORGI CRYER - VOL 17, NO 3

Joe Kapelos doesn't pull his punches. A lifetime of working with dogs -- and people -- has given him a keen eye for both. His strong and direct opinions are informed by his vast experience, a kindly heart, and a serious sense of fair play.

A recent trip to the Pacific Northwest provided an opportunity to spend an evening with Joe and his wife Linda Leeman, full partners in an enterprise called "Ewetopia", and truly it seems to be. Their house looks out on ten acres of paddocks and pastureland outside the town of Roy, Washington, surrounded by horse farms and blessed by a view of regal Mt. Rainier to the southeast. In the two years since they bought the property, Joe and Linda have built "Ewetopia" into a center for herding training in the Northwest. Scrap lumber and many hours of labor much of it volunteered by dedicated students -

Joe Kapelos (left) instructs at Ewetopia

have transformed an empty field into a series of arenas where dogs and handlers are challenged to develop a wide range of herding skills. A "beginners" arena contains rounded corners cleverly designed by Joe to both shield and shade stock for easy and quick intake and exhaust from the working area. A "Sheep Shed" provides a sheltered view in case of rain (always a possibility in Western Washington), and is a center for notices about herding events and information about all types of herding. A bound booklet put together by Joe and Linda covers basic herding techniques and terminology, and contains copies of Joe's regular herding column for Front and Finish. Joe professes not to really like trialing at this stage of his life, but recently took to the field of competition after being challenged that he had "lost his touch". A row of blue ribbons and High In Trial rosettes proves he has not.

I first met Joe during the summer of 1990, when the AKC herding program was new and the PWCCA was about to hold its first National Specialty AKC Herding Test at Joe's old place in Graham, Washington. A few of us worked with him to prepare our Corgis for the (then) mysterious Herding Test. Our dogs were enthusiastic: we knew squat. Joe not only seemed to know everything, he was willing to educate us - - to correct our odd assumptions, laugh at our naivete, and encourage our every step. He's a good teacher, and he always holds uppermost the welfare of the stock and the dog. Joe has a list of credentials as long as your arm (AKC, CKC, and AHBA judge, member of the original committee that put together the AKC program, owned and trialed German Shepherds, Aussies, Kelpies, Australian Cattle Dogs, Shelties, Pulis and Border Collies, students who have earned AKC, ASCA, and AHBA titles and even become judges, etc.) but it's his love of dogs and his gift for working with both dogs and their owners that make him stand out. His outlook on approaching training is simple: "let the dog tell you where he is". He always works each dog as an individual, but stresses the importance of a dog's relationship with its owner and how that impacts the dog's behavior and its response to stock work and training.

Four years ago, Joe told us that if enough Corgis started herding it would change the breed. Asked to explain his prophecy, Joe applied it to all herding breeds: "Temperaments will change first, and quickly, because when herding a dog has to be controlled and confident." As a breeder of Australian Cattle Dogs, Joe had witnessed this kind of change firsthand. He continued, "Mindless animation wins in the breed

ring, but this kind of dog can't work. Some of these dogs are plugged into 220 when they should be connected to 110." Taking dogs out to work makes the importance of good temperament and what good herding breed temperament is - readily apparent. Likewise, movement will improve, because a herding dog "must be able to turn and always remain balanced. You'll see much better fronts being developed if the dogs are required to work". Commenting specifically on the many Corgis he has seen, Joe has both criticism and praise: "Corgis need more workmanlike coats, and some dogs are far too low to the ground for any kind of practical work. From a working point of view, some Corgis are too long, and this length makes them subject to back injuries. But temperaments are some of the best, most have properly set eyes that are wonderful for working, and most have lots of instinct and drive".

For changes in the breed to be noticeable, Joe says, time and numbers will be required, and it will happen faster if the "name" dogs in a breed take up herding. Here we can see that the Mayflower and

PWCCA versatility awards offer incentive by showcasing conformation dogs who can work - and working dogs who well-represent the breed standard. Some Border Collie people who would like to see their breed recognized in the AKC Herding Group have suggested that a dog be required to earn a working title before it could be awarded a breed championship. Applied to the entire Herding Group, wouldn't this challenge our image of the Corgi as a herding dog?!

I inquired how more "breed" dogs

(and their owners) might be lured into herding, and Joe had a ready answer, describing the activities of the "Ewetopia Demo Team", which takes herding to the breeders instead of waiting for the breeders to come to herding. The team, variously constituted but always representing at least five different breeds, puts on demonstrations at all-breed shows in Washington and Oregon, and is designed to give all the herding breeds recognition for their herding abilities. At a recent show in Puyallup, Joe plucked the winning Corgi (a student) from the conformation ring and put it on stock, producing an unmistakable image of the marriage between form and function. To encourage breeders to work their dogs, he recommends that both all-breed shows and specialties get all events in one place so that more breeders will see the dogs working, and suggests that breed judges be strongly encouraged (AKC could help here) to watch performance events to form an indelible impression of how conformation relates to work.

Joe was "present at the creation" of the AKC herding program, playing a major part in designing its rules and courses, and I asked him how he would assess its impact to date: "In general the program is contributing to the betterment of breeds. It gets people out working their dogs and paying attention to their dogs, which is always a good thing, and the program deserves credit for reaching hundreds of people not being reached before." He has a few well-considered criticisms accompanied by constructive suggestions to make competitions a fairer test for dog and handler. At the top of his list is consistency in judging. As any of you who are trialing know, interpretation of the rules varies widely, and Joe suggests that the AKC hold fewer but more thorough seminars so that all judges will be educated to interpret all the rules in similar fashion. Second is the necessity of providing appropriate sheep for tests and trials: not "velcro" sheep, or those so flighty that they hit the opposite fence when they see a dog (where have we seen this?), but sheep that will move when the dog moves them and are reasonable for everybody, providing a fair test of the abilities of dogs at each level. He cautioned that constantly running the "A" course can ruin a dog, as the dog is out of balance 90% of the time, and suggested putting a gate on the Hold/Exam pen and turning the center gate 90 degrees to give the dog more options and freedom of movement. You Corgis please try this and report on the results! And he believes that "a judge should be judging the sheep: a dog's style is an individual thing and should not be standardized".

The AKC herding program is contributing to the betterment of breeds.

It was hours after dark when I took leave of Joe and Linda's warm hospitality, having absorbed as much as I could for one evening. A herding enthusiast could hang out for years in this place working dogs, listening, watching, and learning, having found "Ewetopia".

* The booklet A Flock of Information Ewe Ought to Know Wether You Herd It or Not is available for $13.00 (includes postage) from Joe Kapelos, 6311 - 288th Street South, Roy, WA 98580-9726.

THE CORGI CRYER - VOL 17, NO. 4
CORGIS HERD IN HOLLAND

Nutmeg Farm's Lynnette Milleville made her annual trek to Europe in September, combining education and training, fellowship and fun. She started with an enviable ten days in Austria, visiting friends in Vienna and meeting with shepherds in the countryside. Some Austrian shepherds, who have very small flocks, are using dogs in the German style - as "living fences" - and some have gone to using fences and no dogs at all.

Taking the train to Stuttgart, Lynnette met up with Sarah Sawyer of the Belgian Sheepdog Club of America, and attended the German Shepherd National Trial, which she describes as "three days of bliss." Perfect fall weather prevailed, and Lynnette had permission to go anywhere on the course and to take pictures for her forthcoming book about training tending dogs, titled Hear My Voice. The German course is very similar to the AKC Advanced "C" course, but is about three times larger than the "C" course at Nutmeg Farm. Each dog has 300 - yes, three hundred - sheep per run, and while a run generally takes 45 minutes to an hour, there is no time limit. The welfare of the stock is always considered first, so, for example, sheep will be allowed to graze longer if need be. Each handler works two dogs: the sec-ond backs up the first and helps the handler, but is not judged and does not have to be a German Shepherd. Reminiscent of "Arnie's Army" in golf, thousands of spectators follow the sheep around the course. Judging is excellent, says Lynnette, because the Germans "have a clear definition of the 'perfect' performance." The trial was won by Carl Fuller "with a spectacular run on very

A Dutch shepherd with his dog

difficult and spooky sheep."

On a high from the German trials, Lynnette drove to Leersum, outside Amsterdam (there was something here about the thrills of the Autobahn which I was cautioned not to print), where she gave herding lessons for several days and spent a day observing and talking with working shepherds. There are thirty shepherds in Holland who still tend flocks daily, but only three use the native Dutch Shepherd Dog (similar to an old-fashioned German Shepherd), as the rest have gone to Border Collies. With Lynnette's encouragement during her visit a year ago, Dutch shepherds this year have formed the first all-breed herding club in Holland, named simply and appropriately "Sheep". Its goal is to develop a national herding breed, and

Lynnette was the guest speaker at its first annual meeting, where she used the 23rd Psalm as the basis for talking about the meaning and importance of "shepherding" the flock.

Finally, Lynnette gave a three-day seminar which covered driving, fetching, and tending. Thirty dogs participated, representing a variety of European breeds from Switzerland, Germany, Holland and England And there was one Corgi from Holland, who "was a gutsy little dog and worked up a storm!"

Somewhere in the midst of all the herding activities, Lynnette, who plays alto and soprano sax in church, took time out for a saxophone lesson. Throughout the three-week journey, she relates, "People were wonderful they fed me incredible food - and went out of their way to be helpful. I was able to work with European styles and be educated by working shepherds. People really know their dogs abilities, and they're very open about bringing in other people to help them learn more."

It seems clear to me that Lynnette will need a press attache, possibly from The Cryer, to accompany her on next year's trip.

Corgis Are Far Out ...

While it is as yet uncertain what coming AKC rules changes will include, it appears likely that a short outrun will be added to the Started level on the "A" course. Since an outrun is already a requirement for Intermediate and Advanced dogs (which we see Mayflower Corgis are rapidly becoming), what is an outrun and how do you teach it to a Corgi?

Joe Kapelos defines an outrun as "the semicircular run the dog makes to get to the far side by going out behind the stock." Under current AKC rules, a Started dog is simply required to "lift" the stock, approaching from any position directed by the handler, and move the stock to marker #1, then proceeding directly to the "Y" chute. The handler is allowed to take any position, and may accompany the dog on its approach to the stock. An outrun requires that the handler remain in a specified position on the course. The dog begins at the handler's side, and is sent out - by himself - away from the handler and out around the stock. The dog may go either to the left or right, but once started must continue on the same side. The dog must go out to the side, not up the middle. The object is to quietly lift the stock preparatory to moving it in any direction the handle may request

Carol Weigand, whose Corgi students have been posting notable qualifying scores at local trials, explains how she teaches the outrun:

"I think it's important to break down any new exercise into small parts. I teach the 'out' first, similar to training a Utility go-out, either pushing the dog out away from me, having it go out after food, or taking it out to a point on the field. The dog must learn to turn and go away from the handler. When the dog gets 'out' there, I can then give it a 'way' or 'bye' to go on around the stock, which is held in one place with grain during this early training." As training progresses, Carol keeps widening the circle the dog traverses around the stock, and stresses that it's important to work in a big field and in different locations so the dog does not become "course trained" by going to the same spot every time.

Lynnette Milleville starts by teaching circles around the sheep (both "go bye", clockwise, and "away", counterclockwise), as she wants the dog to get used to long, arced flanks. She teaches "out" separately, away from stock, making the dog go "out" against a fence. Then she introduces "out" with stock, pushing the dog away from the stock on the flank, working up to wider and wider circles. With the dog now used to wide half circles, she starts doing "little gathers", sending the dog on a "way" or "bye", stopping it at the balance point, then bringing the sheep a few feet, gradually extending the distance. She teaches the outrun rather late in training, after the dog has learned to drive. Then when the dog gets to the other side of the stock, she knows it can push the stock and will be focused on the stock, not on the handler.

There has been some trepidation among Corgi people over the outrun, since Corgis tend to like to work in close and are obviously not built for the very wide, swift outruns so exciting to watch in a Border Collie. Would Corgis be able to compete in the more advanced trial classes? But as usual, Corgis find ways to generate excitement of their own. Mayfly Sharon Grous, whose trial successes are chronicled below, is exuberant about how quickly her "dwarf dogs" are getting the idea. "They can do it," she enthuses. "It's so great to watch them! I don't see any limits any more."

On course at the German National Trial

Category III-E
Yearbk./Educ. Handbk./ **Manual** /Breed Book/Special Volume

AKC JUDGES' INSTITUTE WORKBOOK
by James W. Edwards and Anne M. Hier

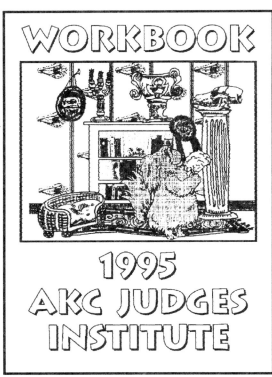

CONTENTS

"It is first necessary for a judge to know dogs generally before he can know any single breed of dogs in particular. He must be able to differentiate between sound, honest animals and unsound, crippled weeds, be they Saint Bernard, Pekingese, or plain mongrels.

Many specialists or one-breed judges are too narrow in their specialties. While such persons are assumed to know more about their own particular breeds than the all-rounder knows, the very fact that they do not know canine structure in general prevents them from knowing thoroughly any single breed of dog.

When one has learned a good deal of the anatomy of dogs in general, whether it apply to a dog of some accepted breed or to a gutter dog of no breed at all, it is time to specialize in the requirements of more specific breed or breeds."

"You Can Judge Dogs"
Irving C. Ackerman and Kyle Onstott
Pure-Bred Dogs/American Kennel Gazette, July 1, 1939

Moving Matching

Match the description of gait to the correct breed.

(a) unrestrained, free and vigorous	____ Poodle
(b) unique stilted action	____ Dachshund
(c) light, quick and agile	____ Lhasa Apso
(d) no description of gait	____ Irish Setter
(e) there is no wasted action	____ Puli
(f) impression of effortless power	____ Komondor
(g) takes long strides	____ Shiba Inu
(h) should trot, not pace	____ Miniature Pinscher
(i) unique lightness of movement	____ Bulldog
(j) typical jaunty air	____ Old English Sheepdog
(k) normal for an active dog	____ Bloodhound
(l) light springy action	____ Samoyed
(m) high stepping and free	____ Newfoundland
(n) hackney-like action	____ Bull Terrier
(o) may amble or pace	____ Chow Chow
(p) lively, acrobatic dog	____ Field Spaniel
(q) long, low and majestic stride	____ Italian Greyhound
(r) big, very lively, graceful and efficient	____ Bernese Mt. Dog
(s) fluid and smooth	____ Bedlington Terrier
(t) elastic, swinging and free	____ Norwegian Elkhound

On the Ethics of Conformation Judging -- Quiz

1. If you were employed to judge for five days a week, fifty weeks a year, with an average entry fee of $17, and judged approximately 165 dogs per show, the total annual revenue generated to the show giving clubs by you would be approximately: *(a)* $70,000 *(b)* $270,000 *(c)* $500,000 *(d)* $700,000

2. Which of the following can be equated with ethical behavior for all judges? *(a)* honesty *(b)* common sense *(c)* breed knowledge *(d)* all of these

3. An internationally renowned judge of bloodhounds, Mr. Ickeringill, adjudicated on Saturday and, you are judging bloodhounds on Sunday. At the judges' dinner on Saturday evening you inadvertently hear that Mr. Ickeringill selected the special shown by Handler Houdini for BOB. As you judge bloodhounds on Sunday, which of the following statements best describes your actions?
(a) in respect for Mr. Ickeringill, you award BOB to Handler Houdini's special
(b) in respect for Mr. Ickeringill, you pay particular attention to the special shown by Handler Houdini
(c) knowing that Handler Houdini's special won on Saturday, you select another special for BOB because no bloodhound is perfect and it is nice to pass the wins around
(d) you simply award BOB to the best bloodhound in the ring
(e) more than one of these

4. As an AKC approved judge, which of the following best describes the relationship between AKC events and canine events not sanctioned by the AKC. Specifically, assume that you are judging Boxers on Sunday at an AKC member club championship show and you accept an invitation to judge Boxers for the All High and Mighty HighFour Championship Show—a non-AKC event—to be held in another state (although only 5 miles away, just across the river) on Saturday. According to AKC Constitution and By-Laws the Board of Directors has the authority (and ethical obligation) to do what in reference to your assignment at the All High and Mighty HighFour Championship Show?
(a) to charge you with conduct alleged to be prejudicial to the best interest of the AKC
(b) to understand that it has no jurisdiction in regard to a non-AKC event
(c) to quietly ignore your Sunday assignment *(d)* to cancel both judging assignments

5. The AKC policy that stresses the importance of the perception that dog shows be well judged and that fairness prevails under all circumstances is in the best interest of: *(a)* exhibitors *(b)* judges *(c)* AKC Board of Directors *(d)* AKC *(e)* all of these

Meditation

"Finally, brethren, whatever things are true, whatever things are honest, whatever things are just, whatever things are pure, whatever things are lovely, whatever things are of good report; if there be any virtue, and if there be any praise, think on these things." -- *Philippians 4:8*

Category IV

BOOKS

A taste of...
THE AUSTRALIAN SHEPHERD
by Liz Palika

"I don't care if my dogs are pretty," the rancher said as his work-callused hand rested on the head of a blue merle Australian Shepherd, "I need a dog that has the instincts to work stock. He needs to be gentle with the lambs and rough with the steers. He needs to think for himself but still take direction."

Keith Talbert works a ranch that his great-grandfather originally homesteaded. He and his wife raise working Australian Shepherds, sheep, dairy cows and horses, as well as three young sons. "I need a dog that will be good with my boys, yet have the stamina to work with me all day and I'm out here from sunup to sunset. He's got to be healthy—I can't be babying a dog, you know." Keith's expression contradicted the toughness of his words but his next comment reflected the opinion of most Australian Shepherd breeders and fanciers, "I want a sound mind in a sound body."

The Australian Shepherd today is an attractive dog as well as a sound, healthy dog. Known for its bobbed tail and beautiful merle coloring, the Aussie is medium-sized, eighteen to twenty-three inches tall at the shoulder, averaging between forty-five and sixty pounds, with the bitches smaller than the dogs. Coat colors include black, red (liver), blue merle (black, gray and silver) and red merle (brown, red, rust and sorrel) any of which can be offset by copper and white trim.

With its smoothly flowing trot and natural athletic ability, as well as its strong guardian and herding instincts, the Aussie has excelled as a working stockdog. Known for its ability to work a variety of livestock, from ducks, sheep and cattle, to geese, goats and pigs, the Aussie is also a versatile stockdog. Although not normally recommended because of the danger to the dog, Aussies have even worked horses and American bison.

The Aussie is more than just a stockdog; it is also very much a companion dog. An Aussie is happiest when doing something— anything—with its owner. No matter whether it is going for a walk, playing Frisbee, riding in the car, playing with the kids, running alongside a horse, or simply lying by its owner's feet, Australian Shepherds need to be with their people.

Australian Shepherds have strong guardian instincts which were originally developed to guard livestock from predators or thieves, but are easily transferred to people. Because of these strong instincts, Aussies feel a need to be close to and protect their family and can be quite formidable protectors. Many Aussies have put themselves in danger to protect their owners from raging bulls, goats in rut and protective mother cows, as well as bears and other predators. Aussies haven't hesitated to protect their owners from human predators, either. Muggers, purse snatchers and burglars have been sent on their way by protective Aussies.

One of the traits that appeals to many people is the Aussie's versatility. The breed's trainability is so important it is mentioned prominently in the breed standard. This trainability, coupled with its natural intelligence, allows Australian Shepherd owners to try new avenues for the breed to excel in. Aussie's capabilities are limited only by the imaginations of the people who own them.

Category IV-A — Single Breed

THE AUSTRALIAN SHEPHERD

CHAMPION OF VERSATILITY

by Liz Palika

Illustrated by Gail Trower

The Australian Shepherd is truly a champion of versatility. With an intense desire to please and do the job right, the Aussie excels at any task he's given—including best friend. But there's adventure beyond the hearth for owners of Australian Shepherds. You can show your Aussie, herd with your Aussie, compete in obedience trials or agility with your Aussie. This once-favorite of rodeo performers is now starring in all of these arenas, though the one he still takes center stage in is his owner's heart.

The Australian Shepherd: Champion of Versatility tells all about this ultimate companion. With chapters on choosing your dog, bringing her home, training, showing, herding, and health care. This book covers all the aspects of caring for an Australian Shepherd. Color photo insert brings the breed to life.

Liz Palika and her Australian Shepherds have been involved in a number of dog activities. Perhaps most notable is the outstanding work she has done in organizing her Therapy Dog Program, "Love on a Leash".

CONTENTS

HOWELL BOOK HOUSE

A taste of...
OWNER'S GUIDE TO DOG HEALTH
by Lowell Ackerman, DVM

from Chapter 8
ENDOCRINE DISORDERS

HYPOADRENOCORTICISM (ADDISON'S DISEASE)

Just as Cushing's disease occurs from an overabundance of adrenal hormones, Addison's disease or hypoadrenocorticism is due to a deficiency of these compounds. However, Addison's disease involves more than just a deficiency of cortisol. The adrenal gland also produces other hormones, such as aldosterone, which regulates the amounts of sodium, potassium and water in the bloodstream. This family of hormones are referred to as the mineralocorticoids, just as cortisone is a member of the corticosteroid or glucocorticoid family.

Most cases of Addison's disease in the dog are due to atrophy of the adrenal gland and an autoimmune nature is suspected.

One of the most common blood abnormalities seen in dogs with Addison's disease is electrolyte imbalances. Sodium levels have a tendency to be lower than normal and potassium levels have a tendency to be higher than normal. This is because the adrenal hormone aldosterone is responsible for electrolyte regulation. If potassium levels get high enough, they can be toxic to the heart, which might be evident on electrocardiograms (EKG) and radiographs (x-rays). The ratio of sodium to potassium is therefore an important indicator of electrolyte balance, and indirectly reflects adrenal gland function. This is a helpful clue but not absolute in all cases.

The diagnosis of Addison's disease is made by utilizing the ACTH stimulation test, the same one used in the diagnosis of Cushing's syndrome. With Cushing's disease, the cortisol level in the blood tends to markedly increase after an injection of ACTH. On the other hand, with Addison's disease, the cortisol level fails to stimulate after the ACTH injection. This is because the adrenal glands can't make enough cortisol to respond to the injection in dogs with Addison's disease.

Since Addison's disease is potentially fatal, it is sometimes necessary to start therapy before the results of the ACTH stimulation test are available. If this is necessary, a rough guide to the likelihood of the diagnosis being correct can be made by looking at white blood cell counts before and after the injection. Normal dogs tend to increase their eosinophil counts and decrease their neutrophil-to-lymphocyte ratio after the injection. Evaluating these changes and any important electrolyte imbalances may allow for a presumptive diagnosis while awaiting confirmation.

Category IV-B — Care and Health

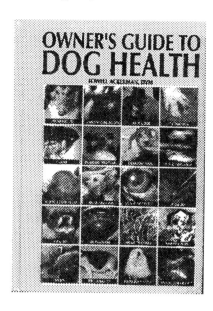

OWNER'S GUIDE TO DOG HEALTH
Lowell Ackerman, DVM

CONTENTS

• Are vaccinations always safe? • Do dogs need vitamin supplements?
• What's the significance of low-thyroid level? • Can hip dysplasia be prevented?
• How do you recognize allergic reactions? • When should you feed lamb?
• Do ticks bite? • Are dogs color-blind? • Do doggie pacemakers work?
• How effective is frozen sperm? • How can you select a better dog food?
• How can you prevent early tooth loss and gum disease?
• Can dogs wear braces or hearing aids? • When should you visit a specialist?

Veterinary medicine makes significant advances every day, and with these advances arise new questions and concerns. Owner's Guide to Dog Health provides a reliable way for dog owners to understand how new veterinary procedures can promise a longer life for their pet.

Written by internationally respected veterinarian Dr. Lowell Ackerman, this illustrated guide discusses in layperson's terms signs of illness and disease, diagnosis, treatment and therapy options as well as preventative measures. Owner's Guide to Dog Health provides readers with current, accurate information about new procedures and technological advances in all areas of canine care, including nutrition, skin and haircoat care, vaccinations, and more.

Hundreds of color photographs and illustrations throughout the text help the reader to visualize signs of illness, different stages of infection, procedures and treatment.

TFH PUBLICATIONS, INC., NEW JERSEY

A taste of...
CANINE GOOD CITIZEN
by Jack and Wendy Volhard

from Chapter 1
Why a Canine Good Citizen?

As A GIFT to yourself, your dog and your neighbors, train your dog to become a Canine Good Citizen. It will mean sanity for you, safety for your dog and compliments from your neighbors. Canine Good Citizens are close to being perfect pets. They are welcome almost anywhere because they behave themselves around people and other dogs. They are a pleasure to take for a walk and can be taken on trips and family outings. They are members of the family in every sense of the word.

Untrained dogs have few, if any, privileges. When guests come, unruly dogs are locked in the basement because they are too unruly. When the family sits down to eat, dogs are put outside because they beg at the table. Nobody wants to take them for a walk because they pull, and these dogs never get to go on family outings because they are such a nuisance.

Dogs have a life expectancy of eight to sixteen years. Now is the time to ensure these years are going to be mutually rewarding. Teach your dog to be that perfect pet you always wanted — a Canine Good Citizen.

This book describes an eight-week training program to turn Max from an exuberant lout into a Canine Good Citizen in just a few minutes a day. It will take considerably fewer than eight weeks, if Max is a willing pupil. Much of what you will teach can be and should be combined with your regular routine of feeding, walking and grooming Max. After you have gone through the program and passed the Canine Good Citizen test, frequent reviews of the lessons will keep Max on the straight and narrow. Think of Max's lessons as you would of memorizing a poem—if it is not periodically recited, it will be forgotten.

One of the commands you will want your dog to learn is to come when called. To be successful, remember this principle: Whenever your dog comes to you, be nice. Reward the dog for coming to you.

No matter what, be pleasant and greet your dog with a kind word, a pat on the head and a smile. Teach your dog to trust you by being a safe place for him. When he is with you, follows you or comes to you, make your dog feel wanted. When you call Max to you and then punish him, you undermine his trust in you. When Max comes to you on his own and you punish him, he thinks he is being punished for coming to you.

You may ask, "How can I be nice to my dog when he brings me the remains of one of my brand new shoes, or when he wants to jump on me with muddy paws, or when I just discovered an unwanted present on the carpet?"

The answers are not rooted in discipline, but are found in training, prevention and understanding your dog.

Category IV-C — Training and Behavior

THE CANINE GOOD CITIZEN

Every Dog Can Be One

Jack & Wendy Volhard

Illustrated by Melissa Bartlett

CONTENTS
1. Why a Canine Good Citizen?
2. What Is a Canine Good Citizen?
3. What Happens When?
4. Understanding Your Dog
5. Stress and Your Dog
6. Sit! Down! Stand! Stay!
7. Out for a Walk
8. Training with Distractions
9. Coming When Called
10. Taking the Test
11. Summary of Exercises
plus Glossary, Bibliography,
References for Motivational Method and Index

THE VOLHARDS for the past twenty-five years have taught over 10,000 people how to communicate effectively with their pets. They conduct weekend seminars in various parts of the United States, Canada and England, as well as five-day training camps, which have been attended by individuals from almost every state, Argentina, Australia, Canada, England, Germany, Mexico, the Netherlands, Puerto Rico, the Republic of Singapore and the West Indies. Over the years they have served different dog organizations in a variety of capacities, and are internationally known as "trainers of trainers."

Jack has authored over 100 articles for various dog publications and is the recipient of five awards from the Dog Writers' Association of America (DWAA). He is the senior author of four books and four videotapes. He has been an AKC judge since 1973, is approved for all Obedience classes and is a member of the Association of Dog Obedience Clubs and Judges.

Wendy is the recipient of three awards from the DWAA and developed the most widely used system for evaluating and selecting puppies. Her film "Puppy Aptitude Testing" was named Best Film on Dogs for 1980 by the DWAA. She also devised a Personality Profile for dogs to help owners gain a better understanding of why their pets do what they do. Her article "Drives—A New Look at an Old Concept" was named Best Article in a Specialty Magazine for 1991 by the DWAA.

HOWELL BOOK HOUSE, MACMILLAN, USA

A taste of...
THE GREAT NEW YORK DOG BOOK
by Deborah Loven

from Chapter 1
So, You Want To Get A Dog

There are as many reasons to share your life in New York with a dog as there are opening nights on Broadway. Do you see happy pairs of dogs and owners parading around your neighborhood and feel a little left out? Does the memory of your own wonderful childhood pet haunt you? Are your kids lobbying hard for a dog? Do you catch yourself gushing over new puppies you meet, and only smiling vaguely at a friend's new baby? Just last night, after the Chinese food deliveryman brought your usual order of General Tso's Chicken, did you suddenly notice that *nobody barked* when he buzzed your intercom?

For companionship, affection, protection, involvement, and fun, opening your life to a dog can be a joy. So, after careful deliberation, you decided to get a(nother) dog. Now what do you do?

Well, what kind of a dog do you want? Do you have misty fantasies of running around the reservoir with a flashy Irish Setter, your collective hairs blowing in the wind? Do you picture yourself, scotch in hand, seated by a fireplace in an English manor house, your spaniel flopped adoringly at your feet? Does the image of yourself window-shopping on Madison Avenue with a bright-eyed, beribboned Yorkie cradled in your arm appeal to you? Whatever you envision, the key is to discover what kind of a dog would suit *you* and *your* lifestyle.

from Chapter 5
Someone to Watch Over... Your Dog

At some point in your dog-owning career, you won't be able to get home in time to take care of your pet. You'll work late, you'll need to go out of the city for a few days, or you'll plan a vacation. After you've exhausted imposing on friends or relatives, you'll need to seek professional help.

Your dog has *lots* of options in your absence. He can be cared for by a professional pet-sitter or dog walker, who will cater to his needs in your home. He can while away the hours merrily playing with pals at a doggie day care center. He can pack a little bag and go off to a dog bed and breakfast with posh accommodations. Or he can spend the time in the country at a traditional boarding kennel. As usual, your New York City dog's options are practically as interesting and varied as your own.

Category IV-D — General Reference
THE GREAT NEW YORK DOG BOOK
by Deborah Loven

CONTENTS
1. So You Want to Get a Dog
2. Walking the New York Dog
3. The Canine Gourmand & Snappy Dresser In New York
4. "Style Me, Baby!": Groomers
5. Someone to Watch Over... Your Dog Dog-Walkers, -Sitters, & Boarding
6. Training: The Manners Of Your Dog
7. Go For It! Training Beyond Basics
8. "Does His Nose Feel Hot To You?"
9. "Come Fly With Me": Traveling
10. "Hey, I Know My Rights!": The Law and Your Dog
11. When That Time Comes: A Dog's Passing
12. New York's A Wonderful Town For Dogs And People Who Love Them.

EVERYTHING YOU NEED TO KNOW ABOUT KEEPING AND CARING FOR A DOG IN NEW YORK CITY

Among the subjects covered in The Great New York Dog Book:

• Should you keep a dog in New York City at all?
• Where to find that dog of your dreams
• Designing your dog's day to suit both of your needs
• Accessing support services for both of you—from groomers to grief counselors
• Finding a training program for your dog's safety and your sanity
• Working out with your dog
• Selecting a veterinarian, acupuncturist, chiropractor, or holistic doctor for your pet
• Understanding the legal and housing issues of New York City dog ownership
• Discovering the city and the world with your canine pal
• Where to go for that shopping spree, Barkmitzvah, or doggie birthday bash
• The best therapists, interior decorators, artists, and photographers catering to city dog lovers

Cover photograph © by Petography
HARPER PERENNIAL, A DIVISION OF HARPER COLLINS PUBLISHERS

A taste of... PICK OF THE LITTER
by Bill Tarrant

There's a mist in the hollow behind the place tonight and, up above, the moon has that glow of muted light seen through soft whiskers. Like a snowman who needs a shave. It's a wet moon announcing a wet tomorrow. I'll trudge to the woodpile in the morning to come back laden and huffing—and see my footprints in mud or snow.

There's a comfort to backtracking, you know? For one thing, it means you ain't lost. For another, it means you're going back to maybe someplace better than what you left to find.

Sometimes when you backtrack, you see and feel and smell things and times and places that were good, and the mind faintly forms them — you know it can't hold them — as they slip away like the mist that rolls past my window. But that one moment of holding is golden and warm and beyond that bully capability of muscle or wealth.

Which sets me thinking. Why don't you and I backtrack twenty years of *Field & Stream*? Say we revive and relive some twenty tales of dogs and men and the things they chase (if nothing but pictures in their heads), the follies they fall into, and the empty bag they usually bring home. Or that rare day — that one in two million — where the light is right, the tree limbs are missing, the gun is swift, the dog calls the flush, and you'll never forget the soft wonder of that feathered lump in your palm.

Let's do it! For as I recall, and we'll check this as we go, there was laughter, gentleness, simplicity, God. There was downright stupidity and heroism and sharing and denial and defeat and love. Oh yes, love. That pooch-bellied pup with last-night's-ice-cream-carton smell. The four-year-old John Wayne of the bird patch with fullbored nose, banjo-strung pelvic-drive muscles, a great quiver of ruff above his neck when he slams to point. Or the tottering old warrior with locked hips, gimp legs, opaque eyes, matted hair, and watery eyes that says, "I tried boss and missed, but you know... I love you."

And men. The ones you go to field with. There ain't many. For that's the rarest of all loves. The way they flinch when you throw the safety, that red in the back of their neck when they miss. The thoughtful surprise of finding he brought a slab of ribs to heat on the truck's manifold. Or maybe just a PayDay candy bar he's carried all day. Or that other thing that happens—he put blanks in your gun when you laid it down to go see Miss Jones. That relentlessly dull hour when nothing flies and the sun comes high and piercing and you know the ducks will never leave the reservoir, but he... he begins, begins softly, a poem. And you thought he only read the classifieds for used guns. And here comes this poem of man and place and field and bird, and a heat comes through you the way raw whiskey sears your innards. You hush, "I'll be damned." But only to yourself — for you want to hear the end of that poem.

It's all there, you know. Down the backtrack. The finest dogs and the best men God ever put to earth. They made us giggle or gasp once, let's have them do it again. Come on, time's a runnin'. Oh, forget your damned compass. I know the way. Let's go!

Category IV-E — Anthology

PICK OF THE LITTER
by Bill Tarrant

Illustrations by Eldridge Hardie

CONTENTS

Here in PICK OF THE LITTER are the very Best of Bill Tarrant's dog stories plucked by him from his well loved column in *Field & Stream*. The stories are bold, heartwarming and born of long experience.

Among the twenty stories included are: "Of Miracles and Memories" - the moving story of the death of a favorite dog; "The Mechanical Dog" - the article that sparked the first hunting retriever test-hunt ever held in America; "Let's Not Forget" - the piece of advocacy journalism that helped to elect Man Rand, the first African American to be in the Field Trial Hall of Fame; and "Somewhere Near Olympus" a profile on a (then) future Olympian.

BILL TARRANT has raised trained and hunted great dogs all his life and has written seven highly praised books on bird dogs and his days afield with them.

LYONS & BORFORD, PUBLISHERS; NEW YORK

A taste of...
A PEDIGREE TO DIE FOR
by Laurien Berenson
A Melanie Travis Mystery

There's a lot to be said for dying in the midst of something you love. But fond as Uncle Max was of his Poodles, I doubt that he'd ever envisioned himself being found dead on the cold, hard kennel floor, his curled fingers grasping at the open door of an empty pen.

For their part, the Poodles didn't seem to think much of the idea either. All seven of the big black dogs were scratching at their doors and whining when Aunt Peg came out the next morning looking for Max, who was inexplicably missing from her bed when she woke up. The moment she saw him, she knew what had happened. The Turnbull men weren't known for their strong hearts; the doctor had warned Max more than once to slow down. But in the end, all the things they'd done together—giving up smoking, taking up walking, watching their cholesterol—hadn't made the slightest bit of difference.

Not one to panic when composure served better, Aunt Peg had closed her husband's eyes, then covered him with a blanket before picking up the phone and calling for an ambulance.

I learned all this from my brother Frank, whose name she'd supplied when asked by the police if there was someone they could call. One look at Aunt Peg and they must have realized that the sedatives the paramedics had so thoughtfully left behind were going to go to waste. That's when they started making comforting noises about next of kin.

We've never been the type of family to advertise our emotions. Aunt Peg would no sooner keen and wail than join the chorus line of the Rockettes. Nevertheless Frank had arrived prepared to offer whatever support was needed. That none was soon became apparent when Aunt Peg declared that his hovering was making her nervous and sent him home.

Now, three days later, Frank was kneeling beside me in the front pew of Saint Mary's Church in Greenwich. He looked every bit as uncomfortable as I felt when the rest of the funeral party trooped up to the altar to receive communion. It was painfully obvious that we were the only two to remain behind.

Thanks to my Aunt Rose, Max's sister and a member of the order of the Sisters of Divine Mercy, the church was full. As the priest began dispensing hosts from the golden chalice, I pushed aside the missals that littered the pew, sat back, and resigned myself to a long wait. Two by two, the sisters glided by, their rubber-soled shoes noiseless on the church floor. Many, I noted absently, were of the old school, which meant that they still wore the dark habits and crisp white wimples I remembered so vividly from my youth.

Category IV-F — Fiction

A PEDIGREE TO DIE FOR
by Laurien Berenson

Melanie Travis's life is going to the dogs. With school out for the summer, a stint as a camp counselor falling through, and her sometime boyfriend dumping her for a Las Vegas chorus girl, the thirty-something Connecticut teacher and single mother figures that things can't get any worse.

She figures wrong...

Everyone knew that Melanie's Uncle Max had a weak heart. When Aunt Peg finds him dead on the cold floor of their championship kennel, surrounded by eleven whining, prize-winning Standard poodles, she isn't shocked... and doesn't panic. But Melanie is surprised when, three days after the funeral, Peg shows up seeking her help. One of her prize pooches is missing—and it's beginning to look like Max's sudden demise is more a matter of... murder.

With her four-year-old son Davey happily ensconced in day camp, Melanie manages to maneuver herself into Connecticut's elite canine circles. Posing as a poodle breeder in search of the perfect stud, she mingles with sophisticated exhibitors and professional handlers... and soon starts feeling a little out of her class. Until she meets Sam Driver. Although the irresistibly attractive breeder is soon wooing her with seductive candle lit dinners, Melanie resolves to be wary.

Then the killer strikes again, and Melanie realizes that she has been barking up the wrong tree. Suddenly she finds herself on a long leash of intrigue and greed... hot on the scent of a chilling secret to die for.

The first mystery in a sleek and classy new series, A PEDIGREE TO DIE FOR introduces a warm and winning heroine with an unerring nose for detection.

Laurien Berenson is also a breeder and exhibitor of Miniature Poodles.

KENSINGTON PUBLISHING CORP., NEW YORK, NEW YORK

A taste of...

PET OWNER'S GUIDE TO
PUPPY CARE AND TRAINING
by John and Mary Holmes

from Chapter 1 **TAKING ON A PUPPY**

Taking on a puppy is a major responsibility and commitment, and it is something that should never be rushed into. With luck, you are looking forward to a relationship that will last twelve to fourteen years, so your choice of dog should never be decided on a whim or on an impulse. There is little doubt that the majority of dog problems arise because so many people buy the wrong puppy or dog. It is like marrying the wrong person - you either have to make the best of a bad job, or make a break and start again. However, the difference with owning a dog is that you have taken on an animal that is totally dependent on you for all its needs. This relationship should never be abused. The responsible dog owner must appreciate that if you take on a dog - it is for life.

The first responsibility is to the dog, who in return for the love and devotion he so willingly gives deserves to enjoy a reasonable quality of life. To some people this means feeding the dog well, going for a daily walk, which is often on a lead, and giving a lot of love. In many ways, this type of existence does not sound unreasonable, but there are hidden dangers. It is the so-called love, provided in abundance, which leads some owners into over-pampering and overfeeding their dogs, slowly but surely shortening a dog's life.

In order to enjoy life to the full, your puppy needs mental as well as physical exercise. He needs to live like a dog, not like a human—rolling in the grass, and, in permitted areas, allowed to gallop freely without the restriction of a lead. It is becoming increasingly difficult to find open space where a dog can run free, but it is important to be able to provide suitable exercise for a young, healthy dog.

Your second responsibility is to other members of the community. The responsible dog owner must appreciate that there are people who do not like dogs, and sadly, there are people who are frightened of them. You may be confident that your big, friendly, bouncy puppy means no harm when he goes rushing up to a stranger - but to the person who does not understand dogs, this could be seen as threatening behavior. Increasingly, legislation is being introduced to protect the non-dog owning public, and more than ever before, dog owners must ensure that their dog is under control at all times.

You must also be prepared to clean up after your dog. This may not be the most pleasant aspect of dog-ownership, but it is deeply antisocial to leave dog mess in public places—and you may well face a heavy fine if you are found to be negligent.

Category IV-G — Short Book Under 100 Pages

PET OWNER'S GUIDE TO
PUPPY CARE AND TRAINING
by John and Mary Holmes

CONTENTS
1. Taking On A Puppy
2. The New Puppy
3. Family Life
4. Caring For Your Puppy
5. Health Matters
6. Understanding Your Puppy
7. Training Exercises
8. Growing Up

PUPPIES—the very word makes people smile. It's easy to love puppies and it's true that baby dogs need the security that comes with a loving home. But puppies also need good care to grow up healthy and sensible training to reach their full potential as cherished adults. Big or small, purebred or mixed, long-coated or short-haired, serious or silly, puppies are all pretty much alike, and the good care and training you give a new puppy now will make an important difference all its life.

JOHN and MARY HOLMES are lifelong breeders and trainers. They are expert problem solvers and have helped many novice owners overcome behavioral snags with their dogs. Here they advise on every side of raising a puppy, including Selection, Advance Preparation, Feeding and Exercise, Basic Behavior, Socialization, Training for Good Behavior, Problem Solving, Health Care, and more. The Holmeses are well known for their training abilities and also for their prolific writing on many subjects of interest to dog lovers.

From those first days when the puppy arrives home to the pleasures of living with a happy, healthy, well-behaved dog, the Pet Owner's Guides offer easy-to-follow advice and information so you can get the best from your dog.

Cover photograph © Carol Ann Johnson
HOWELL BOOK HOUSE, MACMILLAN • USA

139

THE DOG WRITERS EDUCATIONAL TRUST

In 1975, the Dog Writers' Association of America (DWAA) assumed responsibility for the Foley Trust, which had been operating since 1962. Renamed the Dog Writers' Educational Trust (DWET), it was established as a not-for-profit trust to provide scholarships for young people "desiring a college education who are interested in the world of dogs or who have participated in the junior handling classes at dog shows in the United States or Canada."

Almost 95% of the Trust's income goes to scholarships and to the Trust's endowment fund. Over 200 grants totaling more than $170,000 have been awarded since 1975. Annual scholarships are available in any field of study with designated scholarships for students of mass communications and journalism.

The Trust offers financial assistance in the form of scholarships to those who are enrolled in or about to enter college. Students who are seniors in high school or those already in college or graduate school may apply for the following year. (Deadline is December 1.)

Applicants whose parents or other close relatives have been active as dog breeders, exhibitors, judges, or club officers are considered. Preference is given to those students who are active in the sport of dogs.

THE SCHOLARSHIPS: Allocation of the annual scholarships is based on four principal factors:
1. Involvement with dog-related activities
2. Scholastic ability: the student should be in the top third of the class
3. Financial need
4. Character: humane attitude, all around ability, and the potential to contribute meaningfully to society

The Trustees are seeking young people whose potential promises they can contribute to society as well as benefit from a college education.

When the recipient of an award is chosen and notified by the Trustees, he or she must accept in writing within thirty days and furnish the name and address of the college or university where the check should be sent. The check will be remitted to the school's financial aid officer, to be used for tuition and fees for the school year.

Grants are renewable, but a new application and current transcript must be tiled each year for the scholarship winner to be reconsidered.

The scholarships awarded by the trust are outright awards. Voluntary repayment is welcome at any time, however, so the Trust can continue to expand its aid. The amount and number of awards vary each year according to funds available.

A current application form may be obtained by sending an SASE (#10 business size) to:

Mary Ellen Tarman
Exec. Sec., Dog Writers Educ. Trust
P.O. Box E
Hummelstown, PA 17036-0199

CATEGORY V

GRAPHIC ARTS
SHORT FICTION
PAMPHLETS
POETRY

Category V-A-1 — Photography: Color

BIG NOSE -- WARM HEART
Jeff Chevrier
(DOGS IN CANADA 1995 ANNUAL)

Category V-A-2 — Photography: Black and White

PET WALK '95
Jane Lidz
(OUR ANIMALS)

Category V-B — Illustration

THE AMERICAN ESKIMO DOG
Chet Jezierski
(THE AKC GAZETTE)

Category V-C — Series of Photographs/Illustrations

DOG SHOW
Chet Jezierski
(D: THE DOG NEWS ANNUAL)

Category V-D — Short Fiction

SECOND TIME AROUND
by Boyd Wright
(THE AKC GAZETTE)

The letter wiped out half my life. Reading it stripped away my flimsy veneer of adulthood and made me feel as angry and ashamed as I had 13 years ago at the age of 14. Struggling for control, I tried to sort out my emotions. Who was I angry at now? Myself. Why? Because at 14, in my selfishness, I had wasted an opportunity that could never come again. Or could it? I reread the letter.

Dear Mr. Prentice,

I lost my husband Tony last year. He was a Corporal in the Marines and was killed April 17, 1945, on Okinawa. He died a hero and they gave him a medal.

Before Tony left he said if he did not come back and I could not take care of his dog Gold I should write to you. He said you gave the dog to him and you were very kind.

I am getting married again and moving to the city and cannot take the dog. He is 13 years old and is never any trouble. People stop on the street to say how beautiful he is. I have his papers and they are in your name. Tony never changed them, so the dog still belongs to you.

Respectfully,
Maria Corvallaro

> I promised to feed him and groom him and keep up his training. And so I did. For about a week.

I had never given the dog to Tony and I certainly had never been kind to him. What really happened was almost too painful to remember, but I forced myself.

It was 1933 and my parents had promised me a present for getting on the honor role at Buckley School. In June, when we moved from New York to our summer home on Long Island, my father took me to the kennel that trained hunting dogs for his Sportsman's Club. Puppies that didn't make the grade could be sold to members. Right away I saw the one I wanted, the only Golden Retriever among all the black Labradors. The trainer was reluctant to let the pup go for a pet because at 6 months his early field work shore promise. But my father was a good persuader.

I was big on Albert Payson Terhune that year and I wanted to name my dog Lad, but he already answered to the uninspired name of Gold, and the trainer urged us to keep it. "It's not too bad," my father assured me. "In a few years you can call him Old Gold."

I loved that dog, his glorious golden beauty and his happy, playful puppiness. I promised to feed him and groom him and keep up his training. And so I did. For about a week.

That summer I took golf lessons and riding lessons and I sailed my very own dinghy — a gift from the year before — to the yacht club junior championship. But more important, it was the summer I discovered girls. First it was Paula Jennings and I spent every chance I could hanging around the bathing beach to be with her. Later it was Sally Underwood and for her I put in hours on the tennis court. There were picnics and movie parties to the Cove Theatre in Oyster Bay, and on Saturday nights we danced to big-band records under Japanese lanterns.

When my mother or the chauffeur drove me home from all this, Gold would usually be hanging around the servants' back porch and I would find that our cook had fed him. Sure, I used to play with him, but there was never enough time.

Tony was two years younger and lived down the road. I think he was the oldest of six.

His mother took in our washing. His father drove a broken down Model T and used to lean on a shovel for W.P.A. My family hired him by the day when our regular gardener needed help.

While his father worked, Tony would stay back in the shade, playing by himself or just watching. He was so quiet you hardly knew he was there. But Gold knew. The kid started throwing sticks for the dog, laughing with him and making up silly games. Before I realized it, the had become best friends.

> On that Saturday evening, somewhere amid the maze of Manhattan cross-streets, I came suddenly to realize that there were other creatures in the world beside myself.

Often Gold would disappear and somebody would have to go down to Tony's house to fetch him. Tony meant no harm. It was just kid nature and dog nature taking its course. And all this time I was too busy, too wrapped up in me, too sure of myself, to care.

Come September and we packed up to move back to the city and school. The chauffeur had the station wagon loaded and we couldn't find Gold. He wasn't at Tony's house but Tony wasn't there either, so we went off without the dog.

That night Tony's mother called to say Gold was with them. My mother told her to keep the dog until the chauffeur could go get him. Later I was surprised when my father came home from his office to our apartment at Park and 79th with other ideas. "I'll drive out there myself on Saturday," he told me, "and I want you with me."

I was too dumb to notice as the big gray LaSalle purred out the parkway that my father drove with grim attention and paid little heed to my prattling about Buckley's varsity football squad.

Tony's house was a chaos of wet clothes and dirty kids. Gold welcomed us politely, then retired into a corner with Tony. My father and I sat uncomfortably as Tony's flustered mother cleared a space at the kitchen table. Then my father began to speak and what he said makes me cringe to this day.

DWAA Best of the Best 1995

He told these people, almost complete strangers, that he was disappointed in his son, that I had behaved selfishly and irresponsibly by neglecting my dog, that the dog was obviously attached to Tony, that Tony had earned the right to keep him, and that it was his decision that I should learn a lesson by giving my dog away.

Even now I can feel how my fists clenched and the tears started to my eyes. In the silence that followed there was a clatter of feet and Gold sat at my side. He knew something was wrong. His right paw jabbed at my clenched hand and his head ducked just for a moment to give me a single sympathetic lick across the knuckle. Then he was gone, back to Tony, scrunching close to his new master.

I grew up that day. Driving back through the late summer afternoon, my father explained why he had to do it. But I already knew. I knew whose fault it was and I bore him no anger. If anything, that sad trip brought us closer together. As we neared the city and lights flickered on, his right arm came out to envelop me and I put my head on his shoulder and my pride gave way and the tears came. I cried not so much for what I had lost but because in a way I felt released. On that Saturday evening, somewhere amid the maze of Manhattan cross-streets, I came suddenly to realize that there were other creatures in the world beside myself.

> For a moment he sniffed my hand as if hoping to find someone, then realizing I was not the one he sought, he turned away, courteously and with dignity.

I never saw Tony again. My father's business shifted west and we moved the next spring to Pittsburgh. I went to boarding school and college, then, as war drums began to beat, to Officer Candidate School. My Army career was brief. Right after pinning on my second-lieutenant's bars we started to play war games around the bayous of Louisiana. We had just begun to taste the heat and muck and bugs when some fool ignited an ammo dump. I was one of the lucky ones to survive and was sent home with a medical discharge.

I went to work for my father contracting for the War Department. Sure we made money, but we also worked like blazes for the war effort and put most of our profits into war bonds. My mother died the month our troops landed in Normandy and my father just after V.J. Day. I took over the business and I've done well switching to the peacetime economy. When I got the letter about Gold I hadn't even had time to look for a new place to live and had been rattling about the family's big house with only the housekeeper for company.

I arranged to take time off from the office and drove 400 miles to Long Island. Gold greeted me with a cautious wag of the tail. My boyhood memories had not romanticized him. He cut a splendid figure. Age had whitened his muzzle and thickened the massive shoulders and the great barrel of a chest. For a moment he sniffed my hand as if

150

hoping to find someone, then realizing I was not the one he sought, he turned away, courteously and with dignity.

He did not seem unhappy to leave Marie or her intended, who was introduced to me as Vincent. I got the feeling that the move to the city was a pretext and that Vincent objected to starting marriage while the ghost of his wife's ex-husband stalked the home in the form of a faithful dog.

For a month Gold lived with me in Pittsburgh, unfailingly obedient and polite — and unfailingly aloof. He took little interest in his surroundings. His sad eyes seemed to say that he might as well live here as anywhere.

Yesterday saw a crisis at my office. I ate supper at my desk and came home weary. Gold lay in his favorite spot, the living room fireplace, cool and cleaned for the summer. As usual he did not get up and as usual I went to him to pet him, repeating his name and saying the things people say to dogs.

Not a flicker. I might as well have spoken to a stone. Gold lay there, head between his paws. He just didn't care.

Maybe it was the heat or the tension from the office or maybe I was only feeling sorry for myself, but suddenly I didn't care much either. My life seemed empty, as if I had worked forever and gained nothing. I went into the kitchen, got a beer from the refrigerator and walked down the hall to my father's old study. The room was filled with his things and I seldom entered it. But tonight I threw myself into the desk chair and sat with arms dangling in a fit of nostalgia and depression.

I don't know how long I sat. Suddenly Gold was at my side. He had padded down the long carpeted hall without my hearing him. The right paw jabbed at me exactly the way it did when he recognized my distress 13 years before. Then the head ducked quickly and the tongue flashed once again across my knuckle. But this time it didn't stop. The tongue lapped on and on, caressing me and pouring out love.

We sat there into the small hours, an old dog and a young man who ought to know better. When finally I went up to bed, he leaped the stairs ahead of me. This morning we raced out to the lawn and romped while the dew was still fresh. When I left for the office I assured him I would be back soon, and when I returned this afternoon he was on the steps. I hardly had the car door open before he reached me with a joyful bound.

Tonight, as I write, he lies curled under the desk, on my feet, as close to me as he can get.

I have won my second chance.

Boyd Wright was in the newspaper business for 35 years. Now retired, he is a freelance writer for religious publications.

Category V-E — Pamphlet

THE NATIONAL ASSOCIATION OF DOG OBEDIENCE GOOD PUPPY HANDBOOK
by *Lonnie Olson, Terry Ryan, Herb Morrison and Anita Fahrenwald*

The
NADOI
"GOOD PUPPY"
HANDBOOK

National Association of Dog
Obedience Instructors, Inc.

A TASTE OF *THE NADOI GOOD PUPPY HANDBOOK...*

Bringing a new puppy home - what an exciting time! Will he live up to your expectations? Will he become your treasured companion or the neighborhood terror? What he becomes is largely up to you.

Puppies go through many changes in the first 12 months of life. You can make this an easier time for both you and your puppy by being aware of these changes and understanding what to expect as normal puppy behavior. You will want to encourage those activities which will make your puppy a better companion and discourage those which you would not want to see when the dog is fully grown.

Bringing thge New Puppy Home

The ideal time to bring your carefully selected puppy to its new home is 7 weeks of age. By this age he has had the opportunity to interact with other dogs and begin to understand how to be a dog. If taken from the litter much younger, he may not have learned to get along with other dogs. If the puppy is much older than 12 weeks and has not received adequate socialization, he may have already formed a stronger bond with dogs and be more difficult to socialize with humans. The dog is a social animal and his social group is his pack. Taking him from his natural pack and placing him in a new, human pack does not change his social nature. He must learn to be a follower and respect the human members of his new family as the pack leaders. Simple obedience training and discouraging unwanted behavior in the pup will help to show him you are "worthy" of his respect and help establish the owners as pack leaders.

7 - 12 WEEKS
Positive First Impressions

From age 7 to 12 weeks, the puppy is beginning to learn what the world is all about and his first impressions will be lasting ones. Spend the first several days getting to know each other and encouraging appropriate toilet habits. It is important that the pup be allowed to investigate his new environment under supervision, experiencing all the sights and sounds. If he becomes fearful of a slippery floor or an unusual object, don't coddle him. Allow him to regain composure and let him continue exploring on his own. It is especially important during this time for him to meet a variety of people: men with beards, children, mail carriers. Introduce your pup to as many new experiences as possible: car rides, household and other strange noises, other animals, water, and traffic. It is very important to create positive experiences with all the situations he will be dealing with later in life (like the Vet's office). Rough play and frightening experiences should be avoided. If the pup learns that humans are fun, he will probably not be fearful of people as an adult. The puppy should also learn to socialize with other dogs. Encourage supervised play with other puppies. If possible, enroll in a puppy training class designed especially for puppies less than five months of age.

In the past, people held the misconception that training should be postponed until the dog reached the age of 6 to 12 months. Modern research has shown, however, that puppies are very capable of learning at a young age. Their brain is completely developed at age 7 weeks and they can begin learning basic obedience at that age. The "maturity" factor is something else to consider. A puppy has a very short attention span; therefore, training sessions should be frequent and brief.

What About Housetraining?

Housetraining is usually begun as soon as the puppy arrives in his new home. Dogs are naturally clean animals and will try not to soil their living area if they can avoid it. The key in housetraining your puppy is to take him out (that's right, go WITH him) frequently. The Pup's bladder is small and he is just beginning to gain control of the muscles that operate it. If the puppy is fed on a regular schedule, it will be easier for you to predict when he needs to be taken outdoors. Take him out regularly. Always give him a chance to eliminate immediately after waking, eating or playing. Praise the puppy for going in the appropriate place. Monitor his every move when in the house roaming at will. If you are unable to keep him in your sight, place him in his portable puppy playpen (crate) in the middle of the room in which you are working.

Shy or Exuberant

Puppies are usually curious and outgoing. If your puppy seems shy, try to expose him to new people and situations, praising him for any outgoing response. Be careful not to push the puppy beyond what he can handle. Coaxing the puppy into new situations can actually cause him to be more timid. Reassuring him with attention and petting might make him think you are rewarding him for being shy.

> If your puppy is too outgoing or exuberant, you will want to gently but firmly calm this behavior.

Let him set his own pace and ignore shy behavior.

If your puppy is too outgoing or exuberant, you will want to gently but firmly calm this behavior. It will become more difficult to correct as he matures. Do not try to 'talk him out of' aggressive behavior by cooing, "now, now — be a good puppy". This sounds like praise to the pup and will encourage him to repeat the behavior. Up until now, the puppy's mother and littermates have helped to teach the pup to inhibit his bite. When he bites too hard in play his littermates bite back. Older dogs will growl and pin him to the floor. They do not tolerate this nipping and biting, and you should not tolerate it either. Do not excuse it as playbiting or teething! Teach your pup to gnaw only on acceptable dog toys.

Accepting Restraint

Puppies should learn to be restrained while still very young. It is one of the best ways to establish pack leadership. It is also a good way to calm the excitable pup. Roll him gently onto his side and hold him in place with one hand on his neck and one on his side. At first, he may struggle and whine. Remain quiet and hold him in position. When he relaxes (he's saying "Uncle"), let him up. This is a gentle, natural, and positive way of disciplining rebellious behavior and your puppy must learn to accept it. This is the way the mother dog would discipline her pup, and it is in a "language" your pup already understands.

While you are teaching your puppy to accept restraint, you should also get him used to having all parts of his body handled; including ears, eyes, mouth, tail, and toes. (If he is used to having his toes touched, it will be easier for you to trim his toenails.) When grooming is introduced early in life, it makes grooming and veterinary exams much easier for everyone, including the dog. Make these sessions pleasant - give him a treat when he lets you handle him without a fuss. If the puppy's first grooming sessions are pleasant, he is more likely to enjoy grooming when he is grown. Even dogs with short coats need to be brushed. Grooming is another good way to help you establish the leadership you need.

Early Training

The ideal time to begin teaching your puppy to come when called is when his following instinct is at its strongest, about 7 to 10 weeks of age. Owners often unintentionally train their dogs not to come: when the puppy comes to them, they do something the puppy thinks is unpleasant (such as punishment for an "accident" on the rug). He will remember this, and will probably start to balk when you call him. Instead, call him to you frequently just to praise him and pop a treat into his mouth. Then let him go off and play again. You can easily practice this whenever you play with the puppy, both indoors and out. When it is time to put him in his pen, cuddle him for 20 or 30 seconds before doing anything else. If the puppy associates pleasant things with coming to you, he will be less likely to run away from you later on.

While you are teaching your puppy to accept restraint, you should also get him used to having all parts of his body handled; including ears, eyes, mouth, tail, and toes.

A Puppy's Social Needs

It is not unusual for a puppy to bark and cry when left in a room by himself. Dogs are social animals and enjoy the company of people. That's why they are treasured as family pets. If his first nights in his new home are spent banished to the garage or bathroom, he will cry his little heart out. If you intend for your new companion to live in the house with you, you should use a portable puppy playpen and move it into the bedroom with you at night. If he can see, smell and hear you, he will not feel alone. Putting a puppy into a crate is neither cruel nor harmful. Most dogs seem to enjoy having their own 'space' in which to relax. When the trauma of leaving his littermates and moving to a new home has passed, the puppy's crate can be moved to another location at bedtime without upsetting the little guy. Even if the puppy is to eventually live outside, you can make the transition easier on both of you if you do not leave him locked up alone the first few nights. Get him used to spending time in his kennel or yard during the day. Then gradually make the transition to staying out overnight as well. In the meantime, use his crate to maximize your puppy's contact with you during this extrememly critical socialization period.

(There's more to The NADOI Good Puppy Handbook than space here.)

155

Category V-B — Poster/ **Calendar** /Special Publication

1996 SAMOYED CALENDAR
Kent and Donna Dannen

Category V-G — Poetry

I NEVER WAS A MOTHER
by Terry Albert
(SPDR SPEAKS!)

I NEVER WAS A MOTHER

I never was a mother,
With children of my own,
But small creatures needing loving hands
Found their way into my home.

My brother's cat, the neighbor's dog,
An AIDS victim's last request,
To each and every one of them,
I promised to do my best.

Sad eyes behind the shelter bars,
A beloved pet was lost.
I vowed that I must get him out,
no matter what the cost.

This type of work fills my heart
As each I get to know.
They stay to rest, grow healthy, strong,
Then I must let them go.

To new homes and new lives,
With my prayer for love-filled years.
I watch my charges leave one day
As I hold back my tears.

Some One assigns us each a part
To play in life's great game.
No, I never was a mother
But the role was near the same.

— Terry Albert

CATEGORY VI

NON-PRINT MEDIA

Category VI-A — Videotape

BREAKING THE CYCLES OF VIOLENCE
The Latham Foundation

Breaking The Cycles of Violence

Every day, animal protection officers observe neglected and abused children and battered spouses. Simultaneously, human services caseworkers encounter maltreated animals in the course of their work. Although the child protection movement originated in animal protection, officials today are largely uninformed as to what constitutes reportable abuse in each other's field and rarely receive cross-training from each other. Meanwhile, society clamors to halt the violence enveloping our communities.

Child abuse, domestic violence, and cruelty to animals are interrelated crimes, symptomatic of disturbed individuals and dysfunctional families, and predictors of repetitive violence that may escalate in range and severity. To date, compartmentalized intervention strategies have not worked.

Despite historic tradition and research linking common concerns in human and animal services, crosstraining is a recent occurrence. Several national and numerous local conferences have been held in the past few years, bringing together leaders from child and animal protection, family violence prevention, and veterinary medicine. Participants at these meetings have had much in common and had previously not seen the relevancy of collaborating. However, it is apparent that communications gaps still exist among the disciplines due to terminologies, procedures and protocols.

The Latham Foundation established a Child and Animal Abuse Prevention Project to identify key issues and to coordinate community coalitions in response to violence. As part of this process, the Latham Foundation conducted a national needs assessment of 582 child protection, domestic violence, animal welfare, animal control, and veterinary professionals. 90% of respondents believed there is a connection between cruelty to animals and family violence; 88% felt learning more about this link would benefit their work. The survey confirmed the need for crosstraining professionals in the concept that all violence directed against vulnerable members of the family—whether two- or four-legged—is a human health concern and part of the same "tangled web."

This Video and written Guide are designed to introduce caseworkers in three disciplines to this concept, and to provide them with tangible tools to assist in identifying, reporting, investigating, validating, and managing cases of abuse, neglect and cruelty. The goal is:

> To help agencies fulfill their intervention and prevention missions better by recognizing related forms of victimization.

> To mobilize community forces in a collaborative, multidisciplinary attack against family violence in its various forms.

> To educate officials regarding each other's philosophies, systems responses, and case management techniques to stimulate coordinated community responses to violence.

The Latham Foundation believes a multidisciplinary response to child abuse, domestic violence, and cruelty to animals will be most efficient when the three disciplines respect and preserve their distinct roles, while they forge a functional team addressing complex challenges too great for any one of them to solve individually. It is hoped that this collaboration will gradually filter down to community leaders in related fields such as law enforcement, juvenile justice, probation, mental health, medicine, educators, and parents.

Ultimately, the true beneficiaries of this project will be the victims of abuse themselves. Working together, we can begin to reweave the fabric of the community; without coordinated responses, a new generation of productive, nurturing individuals will be lost.

-- Phil Arkow (Author of booklet which accompanies Videotape)

What does the research show?

23% of battered women seeking shelter at the domestic violence safehouse in Colorado Springs, Colo., and 11% of the women seeking restraining orders, counseling or support services, reported animals had been abused or killed in their homes.

Specific abuses included:
• shooting dogs in front of the children
• kicking and beating dogs and cats
• not feeding horses and sheep for days
• throwing dogs and cats across the room, down the stairs, or at the wall
• not letting a puppy out and beating it when it messed in the house
• hitting a dog with a closed fist

A New Jersey study of families involved with the Division of Youth and Family Services for reasons of child abuse revealed that pets had been abused or neglected in 60% of these families. In 88% of families in which physical abuse occurred, animal abuse was also observed. (Interestingly, levels of basic pet care, use of veterinary services, and rates of pet sterilization did not differ significantly from general norms.) A British study by the Royal SPCA found that of 23 families with histories of animal abuse, 83% had been identified by social service agencies

as at risk for child abuse or neglect.

Why should human services care about animal problems?

Social scientists and law enforcement agencies are beginning to see cruelty to animals as a serious human problem, closely linked to other violent crimes. Several factors have prompted this new concern:

Dramatic case histories that have attracted public and professional attention, where serial killers and mass murderers had committed acts of animal cruelty in their childhood. These incidents were largely ignored by law enforcement and social service agencies at the time and their predictive nature was not recognized.

Social scientists are paying more attention to all forms of family violence. Since pets are present in more than half of American households, and are even more prevalent in homes with children, including animal cruelty as another form of family violence is appropriate.

Investigators of serious or organized cruelty to animals, such as dogfighting or ritual sacrifices, have found many other criminal offenses or social concerns which coexist with these activities.

CRUELTY TO ANIMALS ...
Another Form of Family Violence

Cruelty to animals takes numerous forms in the context of family violence:

• Parents kill a child's pet to punish the child.

• Parents threaten to kill a child's pet to secure acquiescence or silence for sexual abuse.

• Children kill pets to rehearse their own suicide.

• Children kill animals before a dominant adult can do so.

• Children torture animals as gang initiation rites or to gain status from their peers.

• Batterers force partners to engage in sex with the family pet.

• Children identify with their abuser and begin to abuse animals themselves.

• Children create a fiercely loyal bond with an animal and escape to an imaginary world where the abuser cannot hurt either of them.

SPECIAL
AWARDS

THE ALPINE/DENLINGER AWARD

SPONSORED BY: ALPINE PUBLICATIONS

To the most outstanding
individual article in a magazine
or canine newspaper.

A BOND OF TRUST
Jan Mahood

(THE AKC GAZETTE)

*This article was also winner of Category II-F-2,
Best Individual Feature in an All Breed Magazine.
(Article on page 43.)*

THE CYCLE NEWSPAPER OF THE YEAR
SPONSORED BY: CYCLE DOG FOOD

To the newspaper and writer that have done the most to promote the health and proper care of dogs.

RANNY GREEN
THE SEATTLE TIMES

I LOVE YOU, PEGGY SUE, PRETTY, PRETTY, PRETTY...
Seattle Times -- 2/26/95

It was a Shootout at the OK Corral with a new twist. The giants fell early, leaving two small females to take their best shots to determine which stands alone.

There were seven gunslingers of all shapes and sizes trying to impress one discerning judge with a distinct familiarity and natural partiality toward two of them.

But another robust, flamboyant stylist with a penchant for flair, who answers to Peggy Sue, catapulted into the national spotlight by being named best-in-show at the prestigious Westminster Kennel Club Dog Show Feb. 14 at Madison Square Garden in New York City.

For owners Vandra Huber of Woodinville and Dr. Joe Kinnarney of Reidsville, N. C., Champion Gaelforce Postscript's triumph was a dream come true.

As I exited the press area to interview the judge, Dr. Jacklyn Hungerford of Carmel, Calif. and the smooth handler, Maripi Wooldridge of Apex, N.C., I caught a glimpse of Huber heading for the ring. I whirled around as she headed toward me, arms outstretched ready to give me a big hug. "We did it! Seattle did it!" she said with tears of joy streaming down her cheeks.

An hour earlier at the nearby Southgate Hotel, I greeted her in the fourth-floor lobby as she was returning from a dress-hunting expedition for Wooldridge. "We found her a nice white dress," said Huber. "She's gonna look great. It's a striking contrast to Peggy Sue! (a jet black 4-year-old Scottish terrier)."

I wished her luck and told her to bring one home for Seattle.

The rest is history.

The word in the press room and grooming area all day was "look out for that miniature poodle" (Champion Surrey Sweet Capsicum, owned by New York real-estate attorney Robert Koeppel) and winner of the nonsporting group. The red-hot, 3-year-old Pepper (its call name) piled up 28 top awards and 109 group titles and figured to get a good look from Hungerland, a poodle fancier.

But keep in mind, this is a show known for upsets, and once again the group outcomes held true to form.

The first night, America's top show dog of all time, Champion Altana's Mystique, a German shepherd, bowed out unceremoniously in the herding group, to a virtual unknown Bouvier des Flandres that had been exhibited only three months and owned only one best-in-show.

Earlier, Champion Hi-Tech's Arbitrage, a boxer named Biff, the nation's No. 4 show dog last year and owner of 50 bests-in-show, was defeated by a 8-year-old gray muzzled Akita called Ben, who had been shown only twice the past year and had pretty well resigned itself to a life of leisure

Westminster is a show known for upsets, and once again the group outcomes held true to form.

at home. A few days earlier, the owners opted to see if it could win a record eighth breed championship and capture a fourth group placing. Bingo, on both scores!

Other Select Seven finalists included a white toy poodle, a Norwegian elkhound and a black cocker spaniel. The latter was the nation's No. 2 show dog last year.

After examining each closely, in gait and stationary, Hungerland centered her attention on Peggy Sue and Pepper, which were positioned alongside each other in the lineup. Finally, after 15 minutes, she walked back to the judges table, filled out her catalogue with the winner's name and returned to the floor with a Westminster Kennel Club official on each arm.

She gave the lineup one more courtesy look and pointed to Wooldridge and Peggy Sue as the Garden crowd rose and applauded.

For the third time, since 1978, America's top dog was from Washington.

"She looks every part a terrier," said Hungerland. "She looks as though she can challenge the world. She's in excellent condition and she's just a lovely, lovely bitch. She moved well and seemed to be asking, 'Pick me.'

"Two things had to happen. She had to ask for it and I had to fall in love with her. She delivered on both counts."

"We would have been happy with the breed title," exclaimed Huber. "The group and best-in-show, that's frosting on the cake."

"She gave her typical 105 percent," said Wooldridge. "This dog's tank never runs empty. Whenever you think she might be tired, she comes up with a burst of added energy. She's a phenomenal little dog who has given me a memory for a lifetime."

A handler's worst nightmares, those invisible foes called stress and nerves, were never apparent as the workmanlike Wooldridge coaxed maximum mileage out of Peggy Sue's tank. "That's exactly why I selected her to show this dog," said Huber. "Their chemistry is perfect. She knows Peggy Sue's limits and maximizes her strong points every time out. That dog just loves to perform for her."

To relive "a dream of a lifetime," Huber has viewed the videotape telecast of the best-in-show proceedings several times.

"Her gait was perfect. She really had fun and seemed to feed off the crowd's enthusiasm. She turned into a star.

"When all the cameras began popping off afterward, she didn't miss a beat in Maripi's arms. She seemed to give the photographers every look they wanted."

It was Huber, a University of Washington School of Business professor, who guided Peggy Sue to her first BIS when she was only 18 months

At the Dog Fanciers Club luncheon at Sardi's Restaurant, the top dog is served ground sirloin steak on a silver platter by the eatery's owner, Vincent Sardi.

old. "She didn't show well at first," recalled the owner. "But suddenly, one day she said to herself, 'This is fun,' and since then there's been no stopping her."

A Westminster best-in-show creates an instant celebrity status. For Huber, her husband, Mike, Kinnarney and Wooldridge, the celebrating continued into

the early morning hours, enjoying New York bagels back at the hotel and relaxing. A few hours later they appeared on CBS' "This Morning".

At noon, they were honored guests at the traditional Westminster windup event, the Dog Fanciers Club luncheon at Sardi's Restaurant, where the top dog is served ground sirloin steak on a silver platter by the eatery's owner, Vincent Sardi after all seven group judges and the best-in-show arbiter comment on their selections.

"As we ate, she was very ladylike throughout the luncheon," said Huber. "But when Mr. Sardi brought that steak to her, she woofed it down in about three bites."

The most gratifying return for Huber has been "the kindness shown by everyone. That goes for people from all breeds. Of course, my Scotty friends are beaming with pride."

A maxed-out telephone answering machine, flowers and letters awaited her upon returning home.

And she was presented with a license-plate holder from the Washington All Terrier Club, that read: "I Love Peggy Sue, Best in Show (BIS), Westminster Kennel Club, 1995."

Asked why she's attracted to Scottish terriers, Huber says, "Because they're fiery, spunky and independent. Yet at the same time they're quick to jump on your lap and give you a kiss. They greet you at the door with unabandoned joy. Where else can you find that today?"

OTHER AREA WINNERS

Three other area entries were breed winners at Westminster. They were Champion Kallista Christian Dior, a Petit Basset Griffon Vendeen, owned by Jan and John Schreiber of Graham, Pierce County; Champion Rendition Triple Play, a parti-colored cocker spaniel, owned by Brigitte Berg, Issaquah; and Champion Lajosmegyi Patent Pending, a Komondor, owned by Anna Quigley and Patricia Turner, Chehalis.

THESE SENIOR CANINES DRAMATIZE COMMITMENT

(*Seattle Times* -- 4/2/95)

"Don't ever lose your compassion for animals," my father, Walter Green, once told me. "When you do, a part of your heart and soul goes with it."

As a pet columnist, you hear it all. Calls from sobbing readers pleading for a story about their lost pet. Publicists asking for a mention about their new product that's "guaranteed" to provide your pet quick relief from fleas. Or a club official promoting an upcoming show or seminar. (That's what the Dog and Cat events classified columns nearby in this section are designed for.)

Over two decades, many of you have become detectives and called with story tips or planted seeds for others.

A couple of weeks ago, two readers phoned within hours, detailing the plight of four older dogs in local shelters. Neither packed the ingredients needed for a col-

umn but together they seemed to capture the gutwrenching persona of the human-animal companion bond.

I was tempted to dismiss both potential stories until I went home and pondered them more thoroughly, They nagged at me, and begged to be written.

TOTAL OPPOSITES

What follows is the wingspan of pet

Placing a geriatric canine (for large breeds we're talking 10 and older) is a monumental assignment

ownership. One tip reflects total dedication to three living creatures, the other dramatizes the disposable society syndrome, where one pet can easily be replaced by another.

Placing a geriatric canine— for large breeds

we're talking 10 and older—is a monumental assignment fraught with frustration and resignation by kennel staffers. Usually, these sweet, beleaguered creatures don't realize what hit them when they find themselves dispatched from the security and warmth of a carpeted bedroom or linoleum laundry room floor to the cold concrete confines of a shelter kennel on Death Row.

The fragility of life is staring them in the face. Fright and bewilderment is reflected in their eyes and body language. Their safety net of owner and home is gone. And yet that's what makes the four underdogs in these two stories so captivating.

Take Jennifer, for example, a charismatic 10-year-old German shepherd who endeared herself to the Seattle Animal Control staff after she was released there last month by an owner, who "acquired a new pet." Keep in mind there are dozens of exiled Jennifers in area shelters, clinging to hope of getting an almost sure death sentence commuted by a compassionate, committed new owner.

"She acted like she was picking and choosing who she wanted to be with," says Mary Felix-Klenk, shelter animal-care supervisor. "She captured everyone's heart here. Because the shelter wasn't overflowing, we kept her longer than normal. She had a mellow, subdued personality. Yet she was a regal, classy gal.

"Don't ever lose your compassion for animals," my father once told me. "When you do, a part of your heart and soul goes with it."

DOG SHOWCASED

Jennifer was featured late last month as the Pet of the Week in both the Queen Anne and Magnolia News. But before the profile ran, she was adopted.

Because she hadn't been spayed, a date was set at the Seattle Animal Control Municipal Spay-Neuter Clinic with Dr.

Mary Ellen Zoulas for surgery.

Everyone was all smiles, recalls Felix-Klenk. "It's these kind of success stories we need more often in a business like this."

During the routine surgery, Zoulas discovered a large invasive tumor on each ovary. The new owner was contacted and Zoulas recommended euthanizing the dog while it was anesthetized.

Fortunately, the owner hadn't established a deep bond with the dog. "It was bad enough losing her, but it would have been much worse had the two been longtime friends," Zoulas emphasizes.

"It took all of us from a giant high to a monumental low," says Felix-Klenk. "We were feeling good and Jennifer's adoption validated our commitment to her. It was like someone pricked our party balloon."

If Jennifer's ill-fated journey has left you exasperated and downcast, too, all that's about to change.

Meet Apollo, a 10-year-old, Doberman pinscher; Kelly, an 11-year-old German shepherd and Lucky, a 6- or 7-year-old large black dog of un-known parentage.

The three were brought to a humane-shelter in Bellevue last month after their owner, Karen: (not her real name), died in her 40s of complications from HIV-AIDS.

VERY IMPORTANT

"These dogs were the most important thing in our daughter's life," says Karen's mother, Jennifer (a fictitious name). "Her life revolved around them, and her biggest worry to the end was finding suitable homes for each after she died.

"They slept on her bed or curled up around it during her ,final months," says Jennifer. "They gave her kisses and were her best friends. Her No. 1 wish was to die at home in dignity with her dogs alongside."

Lucky was her pro-tector, according to Karen's mother. "Not in a snarling, growling way, just letting you know not to bother her (Karen) unless she wanted you there."

All three dogs were very subdued the day Karen died (March 2), says Jennifer. "They sensed we were losing

her," she recalls.

After Karen's death, the trio was cared for in the home for several days before being taken to the humane-society shelter.

> "These dogs were the most important thing in our daughter's life,"

Apollo was featured on a local television news program and was quickly placed. A few days later, Kelly and Lucky went to new homes as well.

> "Her life revolved around them, and her biggest worry to the end was finding suitable homes for each after she died."

We're thrilled," says Sylvia Feder, coordinator of the agency's Pet

Project, which provides free pet food, litter and care services for animals belonging to owners suf-fering from HIV-AIDS.

"The three had two strikes against them with their ages, but it's grati-fying these people saw something special in each of them. It's a big lift to all of us, and I'm sure (Karen) is smiling down with a big sigh of relief."

HUGE SUCCESS

Spay Day King County, a new campaign to reduce companion animal overpopulation, resulted in 832 steril-ized pets -362 dogs and 470 cats.

The Feb 28 promo-tion was underwritten by the county for all surger-ies of animals owned by those residing in the ser-vice area of King County Animal Control.

Pet owners were re-quired to have a valid li-cense for their animal at the time of surgery. More than 100 veterinarians in 80 clinics participated.

The license fee for a sterilized pet in King County is $10 per year. Unaltered pet licenses are $55, which includes a $25 spay-neuter voucher.

THE ELLSWORTH S. HOWELL AWARD

SPONSORED BY: HOWELL BOOK HOUSE

For the best article on judging, exhibiting, dog-show
reporting or any other aspect of conformation showing.

A LOOK AT THE

HISTORY OF DOG SHOWS
by Tibby Chase

(THE CORGI CRYER)

*This article was also winner in Category III-C-2:
Best Individual Article in Local Club Publication.*
(Article on page 110.)

THE EUKANUBA CANINE HEALTH AWARD

SPONSORED BY: THE IAMS COMPANY

For the article that with a strong, interesting presentation best promotes the health and well-being of dogs.

COACHING THE CANINE ATHLETE
by M. Christine Zink, DVM, PhD

(THE AKC GAZETTE)

The fitness boom of the '9Os is not just for humans. While more people are biking, hiking, skating, running and walking, more dogs participate in athletic events now than at any other time in history. People are rediscovering their dogs' roots, and dogs and owners alike enjoy preparing for and participating in a variety of new performance events.

In the past several years the AKC has more than doubled the number of events it sponsors. Retrievers, pointers, setters and spaniels can now enter non-competitive hunting tests at a variety of levels of difficulty, sighthounds can try their paws at lure coursing, herding breeds can work sheep in herding tests, terriers can test their mettle by going to ground and dogs of all breeds can participate in obedience and agility, an exciting sport that tests the timing, coordination and athleticism of dog and handler alike. Additional organized canine performance events include flyball, sledding, draft dog tests, coonhound trials, free-style heeling, weight-pulling competitions, water rescue and more.

In addition to this explosion of events there has been an exponential increase in the level of performance in the more traditional endeavors. Dogs campaigned in conformation have been trained to place each foot on command when free-stacking, obedience performances have improved so much that many dogs have obtained several perfect scores and retrievers commonly mark the falls of three birds at distances of 200 yards or more.

With these exciting changes comes a responsibility on the part of the dog trainer to understand canine structure and locomotion, to learn how to condition dogs for specific performance events and to feed nutritionally balanced diets—in essence, to view and respect the dog as an athlete.

In this matter the dog fancy lags behind the horse fancy. Horses have been recognized as athletic animals for centuries. There is an abundance of information on exercise and nutrition for the equine athlete and on lameness and medical conditions that affect equine performance. Only now are we beginning to understand and appreciate the dog as an athlete.

A coach for humans must select the

best potential athletes, train them in the skills of the game, provide them with appropriate conditioning exercises and diet, make sure they receive expert medical care and give them emotional support and encouragement

when needed. Those of us involved in canine performance events must be the coach for our dogs.

Janice deMello, one of the top obedience instructors and competitors in the country, agrees. "Because most people participate in canine performance events as a hobby, many give little conscious thought to conditioning their dogs," she says. "This can lead to serious, career-ending injuries, often when the dog is in its prime."

Olympic competition represents the pinnacle of human athleticism. Much can be learned about our dogs by studying the conformation of the humans participating in the Olympics. A case in point is gymnastics. Those who are successful in women's gymnastics at the Olympic level are not, in fact, women, but girls. This may be because the degree of balance and flexibility required for the balance beam and floor exercises is difficult for a mature woman with hips, breasts and the elevated ratio of body fat that puberty brings. In contrast, the participants in men's gymnastics are all post pubertal. This is because exercises such as the pommel horse and the rings require upper body strength that can only be achieved by men after puberty.

Although Olympic gymnastics may be an extreme, there are numerous other examples of sports in which individuals with specific physical characteristics are more likely to succeed. These extremes in size and shape do not

begin to compare with the variation in the size and conformation of dogs. Humans have taken advantage of the plastic genetic makeup, short gestation period and large litter size of the dog to mold their best friend into a variety of shapes and sizes. Therefore, before beginning a program of conditioning and skill-training, it is necessary to objectively evaluate the dog's structure.

Consideration should first be given to whether the dog is a heavy-set breed such as the Clumber Spaniel or the St. Bernard, a light-boned breed such as the Afghan Hound or the Whippet, or a breed with medium structure such as the Labrador Retriever or the Border Terrier.

The heavier a dog is in relation to its height the more effort will be required in performance events, particularly those that involve jumping, and the more stress will be exerted on the musculoskeletal system. Thus, although a Clumber Spaniel and an Afghan Hound may weigh the same, the Clumber Spaniel carries that weight on a smaller frame and will therefore create more stress on its musculoskeletal system while jumping, an exercise that involves resisting the effects of gravity to become airborne and then succumbing to the effects of gravity while landing.

The ratio of body weight to height is even greater in dogs of breeds such as the Basset Hound, the Dachshund and the Corgis. These breeds are achondroplastic dwarfs — they have shortened legs attached to a normally proportioned body. Because they are longer in body than they are tall, these dogs must drive themselves forward more in order to clear a jump.

Although dogs with certain body

types will be handicapped in some performance events, proper conditioning and modifications in training can provide significant compensation.

Julie Daniels, one of the top agility competitors in the country, spends a great deal of time conditioning her dogs before entering competition. She says, "The further removed a dog's body is from the ideal for a sport, the more attention should be paid to increasing strength and flexibility in that part of the body.

"My Rottweiler Jessy is an excellent specimen of a breed that is too large and heavy set to be ideal for agility. When she won her first major in the conformation ring she weighed 95 pounds. To prepare for agility competition I reduced her weight to 76 pounds and conditioned her by following a program of roadwork, swimming, weight pulling, flexibility exercises and jumping. She went on to become the top-winning Rottweiler in agility. I credit this conditioning program with keeping her injury-free throughout her career. At the age of 9 she is still in fantastic shape."

Whether a dog is being prepared for the conformation ring or the Iditarod, it is essential that canine athletes be maintained at a correct weight. There is no breed standard that says the ideal dog of that breed should be "flabby, moderately overweight and with a pendulous abdomen!" Instead, many standards expressly state that the dog should be shown at peak fitness.

George Alston, a professional handler renowned for showing dogs in peak physical condition, emphasizes, "Level of fitness is usually what separates the Best-in-Show dogs from the also-rans." Excess weight also increases the stresses on the musculoskeletal system regardless of the performance event.

How can one determine whether a dog has excess fat? While palpating the rib cage and the loin, one should be able to feel the bones of the vertebrae and the ribs under the skin. How can one judge whether a dog is fit? Stand behind the dog and, with your right hand, push on the outside of the dog's right hind leg, thereby causing the dog's center of gravity to shift to the left. With your left hand, feel the muscles of the left hind leg. The muscles should be firm and well-defined. Repeat this process for the other legs.

In addition to understanding the dog's overall shape and level of fitness, the owner/handler of a performance dog should evaluate the dog's conformation. Such an evaluation should look at the dog while stacked and gaiting. It is essential that this be done by someone familiar with canine conformation and with the standard for that breed. As the dog's structure and gait are examined, keep in mind the performance event the dog is to be conditioned for. Make a list of the dog's strengths and weaknesses (no dog is without both). This list is then used to create a conditioning program unique to that individual.

For example, while evaluating a Doberman Pinscher to be trained in agility, you may discover the dog has minimal shoulder layback and a short upper arm. This dog will put more stress on the front assembly when it lands from a jump, and should therefore be trained using jumps at full height only when excellent footing and a soft landing surface can be provided.

Before beginning a conditioning program, every dog should have a thorough veterinary exam to make sure it has no preexisting medical problems. The dog's hips should also be x-rayed and evaluated for hip dysplasia. Although hip dysplasia is commonly thought to affect only larger dogs, there are enough smaller dogs with the problem to warrant evaluating them, too. In breeds that have a significant incidence of elbow dysplasia, elbow x-rays should also be evaluated. In some breeds a cardiac examination is recommended. Finally, the dog's eyes should be examined by a veterinary ophthalmologist.

Once the dog has been evaluated, a conditioning program can be established. What exactly does conditioning mean? The dictionary defines it as "developing a state of health, readiness or physical fitness." The implication is that conditioning is an essential prerequisite for readiness to compete.

Simply stated, conditioning consists of a planned program of exercise and nutrition. When designing an exercise pro-

gram, consideration should be given to the dog's age and current level of fitness, to any preexisting medical conditions or injuries, to the performance event(s) the dog will compete in and to the handler's time and physical constraints.

Although young puppies can be introduced to some of the skills and tools of their future trade, conditioning exercises should not begin in earnest until well after a dog's growth plates have closed (at approximately 10 months in small dogs and 14 months in the larger breeds). The growth plates are the locations in each bone where new bone forms, and damage to the growth plates can result in serious limb deformities.

Alston cautions, "I frequently see people overdoing roadwork. Dogs should not begin roadwork until at least 2 1/2 years of age and a dog should not do roadwork two days in a row. The muscles need a chance to repair and regenerate after the intense exercise that

CONDITIONING EXERCISES

• Swimming: Continuous swimming is better than having the dog retrieve a ball or bumper. Try having the dog swim behind a rowboat.

• Roadwork: It is essential to keep the dog at a trot. You can run, ride a bicycle, sit in the back of a station wagon or use in-line skates to keep up.

• Retrieving: Avoid Frisbees. Throw the object low so the dog does not have to leap to catch it.

• Mechanical trotters: Use trotters designed for dogs. Those designed for humans frequently are too short and do not have safeguards to prevent a dog's foot from getting caught.

• Conditioning jumps: Use four or five jumps set at a distance that allows the dog to take two strides between each jump. Gradually increase the height of the jumps and the distance between them so that the dog always takes two strides between jumps.

• Cavaletti: These are very low jumps or poles on the ground through which the dog trots.

• Agility exercises: The weave poles, A-frame, teeter-totter, dog walk and tunnel can improve a dog's strength and coordination.

• Flexibility exercises: Lateral bends and quick turns are excellent.

• Stationary exercises: Try stretching exercises, begging, play-bowing and others.

roadwork provides."

Dogs that are overweight must be trimmed down and exercised more gently in the initial stages of the program. Swimming is the best exercise for overweight dogs. If it's not possible for the dog to swim each day, it may be exercised initially by trotting on lead for five minutes every other day. The length of the walk should be increased gradually over a period of eight to 12 weeks until the dog is trotting for 30 minutes at a time. At the same time, cavaletti (low jumps, often no more than poles on the ground), agility exercises and stationary exercises should be used to improve strength and flexibility. Overweight dogs should not do roadwork; the handler must walk with the dog so that they can take into consideration the level of effort exerted by the dog and the environmental conditions such as temperature and humidity.

> Swimming is so superior as an exercise for dogs of all ages, that everyone should train their dogs to swim

Dogs with physical conditions such as hip dysplasia that can result in arthritis should be given only moderate exercise throughout their lives. The best exercise for these dogs is swimming, because it is a non-weightbearing exercise. The dog should train and compete only in ideal conditions, and should be carefully monitored for signs of fatigue or pain.

In all cases, an exercise program should start gradually, should be consistently applied, should provide variety and should progress toward a specific goal. Conditioning is not just a weekend activity. The owner must make a commitment to exercise the dog regularly throughout the week.

For example, a Golden Retriever that is being prepared for its national specialty two months away may be taken swimming on Saturday when there is more time for travel, and on Sunday it may have skill training (practice stacking, free baiting and gaiting) in the morning and a 30-minute trot in the evening. During the week the dog may be trotted for 30 minutes on Tuesday and Thursday. On Monday and Wednesday it may be worked on cavaletti and conditioning jumps, and on Friday it gets to watch a movie on HBO.

Exercises should cover both general conditioning and specific skill training. Some examples of general conditioning exercises are swimming, retrieving, walking or running, mechanical trotters, conditioning jumps, canine cavaletti, specific agility exercises and stationary exercises.

Swimming is so superior to the others as an exercise for dogs of all ages, that everyone should train their dogs to swim as young puppies if at all possible. Most 7-week-old puppies are natural swimmers and can be encouraged to swim by walking with them in a creek with shallow areas they can trot through and slightly deeper areas where they can swim to catch up.

Retrieving is a popular way to exercise a dog, but it has the highest potential for injury. Frisbees should be avoided if at all possible, or thrown low to the ground to prevent the dog from twisting on landing. The rear legs of a dog are not stable enough to support the dog's weight on landing, and injuries of the spine and rear legs are common in Frisbee-catching dogs.

Mechanical trotters can be useful, particularly in the winter when it may be difficult or unsafe to exercise outdoors. However, they can be exceedingly boring for owners and dogs alike. Canine cavaletti, low jumps placed so that as the dog trots it places one foot between each jump, can be more interesting. The cavaletti force the dog to concentrate on its gait to prevent tripping over the bars.

Certain agility obstacles can be very helpful in strengthening specific muscle groups and improving coordination. For example, the weave poles can help to strengthen the muscles of the spine. Likewise, stationary exercises can be used to strengthen specific groups of muscles. For example, teaching a dog to sit up or beg can help cure a young dog of puppy-sitting by strengthening the back muscles. Teaching the dog to pat a forepaw against your hand while sitting up (a high five) teaches the dog balance and improves coordination.

Stretching is another form of stationary exercise and should always be used to warm a dog up before competition. Many competitors use the play bow as a stretching exercise. In the play bow, the dog stands with its front legs stretched out in front, close to the ground, and its hindquarters up in the air (often wagging its tail).

In contrast to general condition-

ing exercises, skill training involves teaching the dog how to perform the specifics of each event. For conformation, that means the dog is taught to stack itself foursquare with its head up and weight centered. For hunting tests, this means the dog is taught to run in a straight line in the direction the handler indicates. For obedience, this means the dog is taught to sit straight in front of the handler.

Skill training is most successful when the exercises are broken down into smaller components and each component is trained separately. For example, the obedience recall actually consists of four exercises: staying while the handler leaves, coming to the handler, sitting in front of the handler, and then returning to the heel position on command. Dogs that are taught the skills in smaller bites develop more confidence and are less likely to injure themselves.

Although physical conditioning is important, mental conditioning is also essential.

Although physical conditioning is important, mental conditioning is also essential. deMello says, "As important as physical conditioning is the fact that even the most physically fit dog may tire easily if not mentally conditioned." The best way to mentally condition a dog is to provide frequent periods of play and to incorporate play into the skill-training exercises. Play is an essential part of a dog's emotional makeup. Games such as tug-of-war and chase-the-owner are a way to relieve the dog's stress through play, while at the same increasing the dog's focus on the owner and strengthening the dog-human bond.

In addition, it is important to be careful not to overtrain, in physical conditioning or in skill training. A journal should be kept of the dog's training activities and it should be used often to adjust the frequency, duration and intensity of training. And remember, just like you, every dog needs one day off a week!

The other component of conditioning is diet. Although canine nutrition is of great interest to those competing in performance events, we know relatively little about what constitutes the ideal diet for dogs involved in specific events. There are, however, two generalizations that can be made.

First, the most serious nutritional disorder in dogs is obesity. Although it is a much greater problem in pets, many performance dogs are also overweight. There is no magic formula to find the correct amount of food a dog should eat. Weight gain or loss is determined not only by the amount of food ingested, but also by the quality and digestibility of the food, the activity level of the dog and the dog's rate of metabolism. As in humans, the correct amount of food is best arrived at empirically. Barring certain medical conditions such as hypothyroidism, if a healthy dog is gaining weight, it is either eating too much or not exercising enough.

Second, there is substantial research showing that overfeeding puppies, especially those of the larger, fast growing breeds, can increase the incidence of a number of musculoskeletal conditions, particularly hip dysplasia. A

Play is an essential part of a dog's emotional makeup.

collaborative study between several veterinary schools and a dog food manufacturer recently showed that growing puppies fed 25 percent less food than littermates fed as much as they wanted had a significantly reduced incidence of hip dysplasia. This finding has led many veterinarians to recommend changing from puppy food to a quality adult dog food at 4 months of age—something many breeders of large dogs have been doing for years.

Certainly, most premium dog foods are adequate for animals involved in most performance events. More research needs to be done to determine the optimal diet for dogs involved in endurance events such as mushing.

This decade's explosion of interest in canine performance events will have many positive effects on dog and owner alike. Training a dog is one of the best ways to strengthen the human-canine bond. By learning as much as we can about canine structure and its relationship to performance, we can contribute to our dogs' general health and ensure success in our chosen performance events.

Let's make sure the '90s are remembered as a decade in which we learned to appreciate our dogs' marvelous athletic abilities and to understand new ways to keep our dogs fit and healthy throughout their lives.

Christine Zink is a veterinarian who has trained dogs from three groups to more than 30 obedience, field, conformation and agility titles. She is author of "Peak Performance: Coaching the Canine Athlete".

THE GERALDINE R. DODGE AWARD
PRESENTED BY: ST. HUBERT'S GIRALDA

To the article that best promotes a positive approach to
the problem of animal overpopulation,
or encourages cooperation between the dog fancy
and the animal welfare community
in reducing the number of unwanted animals.

WORKING TOGETHER WITH SHELTERS
Gina Spadafori
(THE AKC GAZETTE)

While it's true the breed rescue movement has grown to the point where there's hardly a shelter director alive who isn't familiar with it, it's also true that misunderstandings and conflicts of interest have made cooperation difficult at times.

Rescuers chafe at what they see as hard-line shelter policies, and shelter administrators complain about rescuers they feel aren't prepared for the reality of living on the front lines of the war against animal overpopulation. Add to this mix high stress levels and high turnover on both sides, and a hodgepodge of goals and policies, and it's a wonder breed rescuers and shelters can work together at all.

But they do.

Led by stable, levelheaded rescuers and open-minded, flexible shelter administrators, breed rescue has gained a foothold in many of the nation's private and municipal shelters. "I think a lot of shelters see rescue groups as an asset," said Joni Peterson of the American Humane Association.

"It's important for both sides to make a real effort in keeping the lines of communication open," said Nina Schaefer of Huntingdon Valley, Pa., president of the Pennsylvania Federation of Dog Clubs and an AKC delegate from the Back Mountain Kennel Club. "I think it's important in the sense that rescue defines us as part of the solution. And that happens when we go in there; we're saying, 'We care about these animals just as you do.' "

So if everyone's agreed that breed rescue and shelters should and could work better together, what are some of the ways to make that possible? Here are a few tips from the front lines.

STRUCTURE FIRST

Put together your rescue program before going public. Rescuers who are all enthusiasm and no experience are the bane of shelter directors, who know from experience those groups that are ill-prepared will not be able to hold their program together long.

Before your group takes its first rescue call, determine the kind of program you're capable of running and the limits you must set. Those in the fancy differ widely — and sometimes angrily — over the format of rescue programs, but only your club can decide what is realistic and possible in your area, based on the popularity of the breed as well as the human and financial resources available to you.

Will you be a referral service only, steering prospective adopters to shelters and private individuals with dogs to place? Will you take any dog of your breed, or just those you consider adoptable? Do you want first crack at any representative of your breed, or do you want to be called by a shelter only when the animal's time is up?

If you decide to take in the animals, what will you do to prepare them for a successful adoption? Groom them? Provide basic vaccinations and tests such as heartworm? Alter them? Perform necessary veterinary treatments? Send them out with collars and I.D. tags? Put them through a basic obedience course or work on the behavioral problems that contributed to their homeless status? What will you charge per dog placed to offset costs, and what other ways will you locate funds to keep the program viable? All these things must be decided before you approach a shelter; those who've been through it say chances are

you not only have to explain your program, but also in some cases defend it.

Once you've determined your policies, pull together the necessary paperwork that supports it and sets your group apart as serious and dedicated. For a professional look, have letterhead made up for your rescue group and use it to prepare mission statements, adoption application forms, information on the breed for prospective adopters and all the contracts and other legal necessities to protect rescuers and the club from liability (see Legal Agenda on page 24 for more about rescue and liability). The good news here is it's not necessary to reinvent the wheel. Ask successful programs for their materials and adapt them to fit your own needs.

DEFINE YOUR GOALS

Clearly define and communicate the goals of your rescue group to the shelters you work with. There are those in shelters who flat out don't trust anyone who has anything to do with the purebred dog fancy, and only education over time is going to build the trust necessary to break through that wall.

The first step is an introductory visit. When Anne McGuire was setting up the rescue program for the Greater Houston Golden Retriever Club, her group prepared fliers and other informational material and made an effort to introduce the program personally to all

"If we're going to work with a group, we need to be sure that sterilizations are performed as promised..."

"That's a bottom line with us."

the shelter directors in her area.

'We had to prove to them we were doing it right," said McGuire, a professor of geology at the University of Houston and a competitor in ANC events. We went out of our way to prove to them we weren't crackpots."

All sides agree the most important point to make is that your group will be as diligent—or preferably more—than the shelters in not placing an animal that hasn't been spayed or neutered. While this is a moot point with those shelters that alter all animals before release, it's a touchy point for those that don't, especially if they've bent rules to let a rescue group have an intact dog, such as waiving a spay-neuter deposit.

Municipal shelters generally do not consider the placement of adoptable animals to be their primary purpose.

"If we're going to work with a group, we need to be sure that sterilizations are performed as promised", said Pat Miller, director of operations at the Marin Humane Society in Northern California. That's a bottom line with us." She said she had come close to striking one breed rescue group off the contact list because of uncertainties over whether the dogs released to them were being altered.

UNDERSTAND THE SHELTERS

Make an effort to understand shelter policies and be careful to work within them. Shelters come in three basic varieties: municipal, private nonprofit and private shelters that are also under contract to perform animal-control duties in a given municipality. The goals of each type vary by definition,

but even within each group you'll find a large range of policies concerning rescue.

"The problem here is that each individual shelter is different, and over the years each shelter changes," said Sandra Paraday, rescue chair for Lone Cypress Vizsla Club in Northern California and a board member of the Santa Cruz SPCA. "Find out what the policies and procedures are, and know what your rights and obligations are."

Municipal shelters generally do not consider the placement of adoptable animals to be their primary purpose. They were formed and continue to serve to protect people and property from animal-people conflicts such as nuisance barking, rabies or predation. Many feel these operations are the hardest nuts to crack when it comes to working with rescue. They are often too busy with government mandated programs to make rescue calls, and may be too restricted by local ordinances to make any accommodations for breed rescue.

While there are many progressive municipal animal-control agencies and many open-minded administrators, it's imperative to understand the underlying motives of such organizations before formulating a plan for working effectively with them. "In those instances, you really need to get to know the people in charge", said Paraday, who has been involved in rescue for 15 years. "Instead of talking to the person at the front desk, talk to the executive director."

Nonprofit shelters and nonprofits that contract with a municipality for animal-control work see things from a different angle. They were formed to protect animals from cruelty, and work to educate the public, to investigate cruelty and to find new homes for homeless animals.

Because their emphasis is on helping all animals, however, rescuers say many shelter workers don't understand or don't agree with the underlying principle of breed rescue and become bitter about why a less adoptable purebred dog is taken by a rescue group while a nicer random-bred dog in the cage next door will eventually be euthanized for lack of a home. Paradoxically, other shelter workers complain that rescuers take the cream — young, healthy purebreds.

While it's possible to change both policies and misimpressions over time through hard work and education, shelter sources and successful rescuers say it's a bad idea to start out a relationship fighting against an organization's policies. "Sometimes all you can do is hold your nose, go in there and get what they'll give you," said

Ann Hurley, a schoolteacher, writer and frequent rescuer at the animal-control shelter in Oakland, Calif.

WORK TOGETHER

Band together with other rescue groups to present a united front and make it easier for shelters to locate individual breed contacts. "Every time things get more complicated it takes up time, and shelters don't have that much of it to spare," said Miller of Marin Humane Society.

Marin, like many shelters in the greater San Francisco Bay Area, works from a rescue list compiled and updated regularly by volunteers with the Ohlone Humane Society in Fremont. The Ohlone List, as it's called, keeps up with changes in rescue contacts and policies and provides area shelters with a reliable resource for quickly locating the appropriate group.

"If we had to generate and develop our own list we wouldn't have the breadth of resources available to us that we do currently," said Miller.

BE FLEXIBLE WITH EDUCATION

Be open to ways to educate shelter staffers both on identifying your breed and on understanding any special care requirements.

"Bulldogs aren't for everybody, and they have special needs," said Lynda Pelovsky, rescue chairwoman for the Bulldog Club of America, Division III. "When we place them, we spend a great deal of time with the adopters. Anyone going in and adopting from a shelter won't have that network to turn to.

"We feel the service we offer will provide a better match, a better chance that the dog won't come back. And some shelters are starting to agree with us."

While a breed such as the Bulldog

> Be open to ways to educate shelter staffers on identifying your breed and on understanding any special care requirements.

is pretty easily identified by shelter workers, other breeds will slip through as mixes, rescuer and shelter workers agree. The American Belgian Tervuren Club recognizes this problem with a pamphlet on how to tell a Tervuren from another breed, according to Alicia Marcinczyk of Cornish, Maine, rescue chair of the Mainely Tervuren Belgian Club.

Other breeds are likewise a challenge. "Goldens are not a problem," said McGuire of the Houston Golden Retriever Club. "But it's a little unusual for someone to recognize an Otterhound."

McGuire and other rescuers suggest providing area shelters with a breed-identification poster, such as the one produced by the Cycle dog food company, or, even better, a copy of the AKC's " The Complete Dog Book."

Support your local shelters, both in words and actions. Pelovsky's Bulldog club uses money from its rescue fund to contribute to area shelters. Other rescuers refer people to the shelters, either in search of a particular promising dog or just on general principle, and then make sure shelter workers know rescue is trying to help all dogs as much as possible.

Hurley, the Oakland volunteer, suggests taking in an obvious mix of your target breed when there's space in your program. Although she knows it's a controversial issue, she said it does wonders to build credibility with shelter staff.

We're all on the same side. We need to support each other, recognize each other's limits and lack of resources and work together.

VOLUNTEER TIME

Even better is to have rescue workers—who are often more knowledgeable then shelter staff in identifying breeds—put in volunteer time in shelters. Rescuers are natural at counseling adopters, and while they're inside they can also be on the lookout for their breed and others, calling other contacts when needed and relieving the shelter staff of this chore. Inside volunteers are often the most effective of all, able to get rules bent and finding a more receptive ear to prospective changes in shelter policy that are beneficial to rescue programs.

If that's not possible, insiders say it's important to let shelters know you're there—often. Leave a business card or informational flier each and every visit, and maybe even pop your head in to the director's office for an informal hello. The goodwill builds up over time, say shelter staffers, and that can pay off handsomely for your program and others, as well as for the entire fancy.

"We're all on the same side," Miller of Marin Humane Society said about shelters and breed rescue groups. "We need to support each other, recognize each other's limits and lack of resources and work with them."

(Gina Spadafori writes a nationally syndicated newspaper column on pets and is involved in Shetland Sheep dog rescue efforts.)

THE JOB MICHAEL EVANS AWARD
OFFERED BY: EILEEN M. EVANS

To the best non-fiction work in a print medium that addresses the subject of the dog in the human environment (i.e. training, working dogs, assistance dogs, etc.)

HIS POWERFUL HAND
by Suzi Kraft
(FETCH THE PAPER)

The Nebraska State Fair was in full swing but a distant thirty-three miles from my wildlife habitat and peacock farm. I accepted an invitation from my friend Portia to make a full day at the fair with her and my German Shepherd guide dog, Hunter.

Two miles beyond Bennet, Nebraska a terrible sound emanated from under her truck. One mile further and a thud made the vehicle shudder. "Portia, turn us around and head back immediately. The valves are going," I said. Six miles later the third tremble forced us to turn off Highway 43 onto Stagecoach Road. Alas, the truck died as the turn was made.

The truck sat right in the middle of a gravel road at the bottom of a very steep grade. Vehicles coming from the opposite direction wouldn't even have time to slow down before hitting us head on! Hunter, Portia and I immediately stationed ourselves away from the truck.

The nearest home was a bit over a mile away and Portia returned with no luck. It was deserted. Todd, a neighbor, happened along and offered Hunter and I a lift to Bennet Corner in a double-sized cement truck. Portia stayed to alert oncoming traffic at the top of the hill.

Good-byes were said to Todd and I thanked him for the lift after a telephone call was made to Bruce at Straube Repair in my home town of Burr. I told him where Portia's truck rested but, in my haste, I forgot to tell him where I was calling from.

I decided to walk up a small grade to the highway intersection. Halfway there, an older vehicle with a dragging muffler approached. We were "shore-lining" the gravel road when the automobile stopped in front of us. Hunter immediately blocked my stride for safety.

The driver put the car in park, left it running, opened the door and advanced toward me. Hunter circled and returned to Heel. A very tall man, over six-foot-four judging by the height of his voice, said, "Ya want a ride?" Before I could answer, his powerful hand grabbed my left shoulder with extreme force. I felt myself being dragged toward the sputtering car.

My shoulder muscle began to tear from his force. Groaning in pain, I quickly dropped to the ground, trying to break his grip. My guide dog understood. Suddenly I felt her legs and leash flying... not away from me, but straight up the man's body.

There was no bark of warning.

Growls... ripping and tearing sounds made my legs quiver. From the man's throat came gargling sounds as he fell against the vehicle. Thoughts of a gun or knife and him hurting Hunter paralyzed my soul. His faltering steps dragged to the car door and the loud car sped away.

I possessed no sense of reality at that moment. The gas station did not exist. Directions were lost. The gentle German Shepherd licked my tears and we stood strong together. I gave the command, "Hunter, find Portia."

Shock and survival molded us into a smooth running machine. I felt God guide my shaking hand to the security of Hunter's smooth metal harness and followed her lead. I do not remember the two and one-half mile journey.

A loud motor once again approached. Sweat began to run down my back. A woman's voice yelled, "Susi, Susi." My will forced Hunter to walk faster. The words sounded familiar... the voice soft and friendly... Portia's hand gently took my arm. Hunter's tail wagged.

Sounds became entangled. Doors slamming. Voices talking. My body was shaking. Hunter's ears lay flat and her body grew taut with my anticipation. Someone said the sheriff must be called at once. An hour elapsed.

Three sheriffs from two counties met our tow truck team in Burr. Hunter and I were led to the baseball bleachers across the street from The Family Pub. There the questions began in earnest.

The questioning sheriff did not believe a blind victim could know how tall the attempted abductor was. To test, he asked if I could tell how tall he himself was. Softly I said, "Your voice tells me you are five foot seven or eight." One of the other sheriffs chuckled and told the first one I was better at judging heights than a sighted person. I was not in the mood to play their games.

My shoulder had begun to throb. Portia secured another van and took me to my physician in a neighboring town. Hunter voiced discontent with soft groans when I was led into the x-ray room without her. Released from the leash, she ran under my chair. No one tried to remove my companion from that moment on.

All reporters love a rescue story. Two newspapers in Lincoln, Nebraska printed the sheriff's report on the front page. UPI sent it over the wires. Our story appeared in the Omaha World-Herald and Nebraska City's KNCY radio station aired it every hour the following day. I turned the phone off. My husband was livid with anger because the newspapers printed our address in the articles. What if that disturbed man tried to find me again?

I needed time away from reality. Peacocks were the answer. Hunter and I spent a lot of time in the large barn and outdoor pens. I felt safe there. The sun was warm and the talkative creatures ate fresh picked tomatoes and overripe muskmelon from my hand.

A month later, there was a surprise at the Lion's Club meeting. President Carol Doeden announced, "We would like to present Hunter a Lion-Hearted Medal of Merit for her courage." The back of the medal was engraved: "Cook Lion's Lion Heart Award To Guide Dog Hunter". I could not respond. Tears and gentle hugs expressed my love and gratitude to the gentle companion that saved my life.

**This true story happened
September 7, 1993.*

THE JUNIOR WRITER AWARD

OFFERED BY: THE DOG WRITERS ASSOCIATION OF AMERICA
To writers under 18 years of age.

The award recognizes and encourages yopung writers who exhibit talent, resourcefulness, dedication, and integrity in their writing about dogs and dog-related topics.

*This year two young writers tied for this award:
Amanda Kelly - "Stamp Of Approval" - Dogs In Canada
Jennifer Bell - "Galahad" - Fetch The Paper

GALAHAD
by Jennifer Bell
(Age 13)
(FETCH THE PAPER)

The Early Years:

I would like to share with you my feelings about my and my family's dog, Galahad. He is a purebred Lhasa Apso and is light brown, furry, sweet and very cute! He weighs only around sixteen pounds. Lhasa Apsos used to rule the old city of Tibet and are very smart.

> I guess my parents couldn't resist him, because they left the place with him in their arms.

First, I want to explain what he was like as a puppy. My parents decided that they wanted a dog, and their next door neighbor recommended to get one at her mother's house, because she bred Lhasa Apsos. When they got there, there were only two puppies left. Galahad (our future dog) and the runt of the litter. Galahad and he came running into their arms. I guess they couldn't resist him, because they left the place with him in their arms. My parents chose Galahad, because they knew runts were known to be sickly, and now, I'm really glad they picked Galahad, because he has been with us for such a long time.

I'm not all that experienced with him at that young of an age, because I wasn't born yet, when he was just a little, lively pup. But I do know a little, from what my parents have told me.

First of all, Galahad always was into some sort of mischief. One Christmas, he got into the Christmas tree and tore it apart. That is quite strange to me, considering when I think of destruction of Christmas trees, the name "cat" always comes to mind. But, he does many things that cats do: drinks milk, licks himself, is very petty, etc. He used to have a lot of accidents around the house, so my parents gave him piddle paper. That helped. Also, as a puppy, he got into my dad's books and tore them up when Dad was gone. That seems kinda cute to me now, but I suppose my dad was pretty angry at the time. That basically covers what he was like as a puppy. I sometimes wish that I could have known the adorable puppy he once was, but that's okay, because I love him no matter what.

> I sometimes wish that I could have known the adorable puppy he once was, but that's okay, because I love him no matter what.

The Middle Years:

The middle years, ahh, a time that I can't remember that clearly either. I would be in the age range of probably 4 - 6. So, once again, my parents have had to remind me of a lot of the memorable stuff he did. In the middle years, he was getting older, more bored and restless. He didn't get into too much trouble and did not play as much when he reached the higher ages. I was born near that time, and Galahad really loved me. He guarded me at all times. When I was on the baby swing, he laid under it and was always caring towards me.

As I watch my baby videos, it's such a riot! Galahad was right next to me, when I was practicing to sit up on a mattress. Then, he was even with me while I was taking a bath! It feels kind of neat to know that Galahad loved me so much as I was a baby. I wonder, as I've grown, if he knows I'm the same person as that baby I once was. He treats me as an adult now, as if he knows I am beginning to look like my parents' size. Now, as I conclude my thoughts on Galahad, I want to tell you about how he has changed as he got older. Much older.

The Later Years:

Now, this is one subject that I can talk about from experience. Galahad now is very spoiled (as if he wasn't before!) We have a separate water bowl for him in the bedroom. Actually, it's a bowl of cool water we used to use as a humidifier, but he started to drink it. Now we're just in the habit of filling it up every time he lies next to it (that means he wants water.)

He also has minor seizures now (just a bob of the head.) He does this either when you accidentally make a loud noise that startles him, or even sometimes just out of the blue, like the time he was on the stairs and had a seizure. He must have lost his balance, because my mom heard a loud thumping sound. She raced over to the head of the stairs and flew down them, to catch Galahad. Thankfully she did. At his old age, if Mom hadn't caught him, then he could have broken who knows how many bones!

He had a lot of strange habits. Notice I said "had". Because, now he's fifteen and doesn't care. He used to bark like crazy when anyone hung up the telephone. He hasn't done that in a long time. Now, for some unknown reason, he barks when you pick up the phone! If it's at his reach, he'll roll on it too! Like I said, he has cat's habits, and he loves to chomp on ice cubes! He will lie by the fridge, and that usually means, "I want an ice cube, please." That is, unless there is something better around. He also used to howl at the monthly emergency drill. You know, the one on the first Wednesday of every month. He doesn't do it anymore. Either he doesn't care or his hearing

He is loyal, loving, and friendly, and no dog could ever replace him or be as wonderful as he is.

has deteriorated. His other strange habits include lying on a pile of fresh laundry, especially at the peak of them, and on us! And, he is so picky! If something isn't exactly right, then forget it. He won't do it. And, he is a terrific guard dog for his size. His bark sounds like one of a Rottweiler, and anytime you make a motion to playfully sneak up on him, he barks and bites at your hand. He does this very playfully and then licks it, to show you he is just playing. He is lazy now, and doesn't care that much about anything, except sleep or dinner.

But I don't mind, because I love him very much and I'm thankful that he has lived so long. I hope he lives forever. The Vet has prescribed vitamins for Galahad, because he was getting so skinny. He's doing better now, and I think, thanks to our vet, this has added a few more years to Galahad's life.

My parents and I think of Galahad as a member of our family and all love him very much! I am proud to have him as a pet. He is loyal, loving, and friendly, and no dog could ever replace him or be as wonderful as he is.

"In memory of Galahad.
July 4, 1979 - May 3, 1995.
We will always love him."

STAMP OF APPROVAL
by Amanda Kelly
(Age 16)
(DOGS IN CANADA)

A while ago I read an article in an American dog magazine that caught my eye. According to this article, junior showmanship judges in the United States had to apply to the American Kennel Club and be approved. I investigated and learned that prospective judges must fill out a Provisional Junior Showmanship Application, which ensures that the applicant is not in any way violating the rules and regulations of the AKC. The application also asks for basic showing experience, such as the number of shows the applicant attends, clubs in which they are a member and the "addresses of 2 persons (unrelated) in the sport who could attest to your knowledge of ring procedure and handling procedures."

I was surprised by this wording, which indicates the two references do not even have to serve in any official capacity with the AKC.

That the applicant's knowledge is not tested or verified could be cause for concern; relying on the opinion of two people does not seem the most efficient way to choose a judge.

The article did, however, make me ask a rather important question: why aren't junior handling judges in Canada subject to approval? Conformation and obedience judges are subject to many sets of applications and tests and must possess certain qualifications before they are certified for even one breed, let alone a whole group. Why should junior handling judging be any different?

Are juniors themselves not judged on the basis of skill and knowledge, in the same way that dogs are judged for their beauty? Exhibitors wouldn't allow a novice to judge their dogs, so why are novices permitted to judge their children?

In 1992, specific rules and guidelines were mapped out by the CKC directors of junior handling for each region of the country. The result was a comprehensive guide that set forth suggested rules and regulations for juniors, the show-giving clubs and the proposed judges. These guidelines were to be distributed to the host clubs and then, in turn, to the judges themselves to make use of.

Because there had been no restrictions on who could judge and what their qualifications were to be, it was hoped that the new guidelines would standardize the judging process across the country. This has not really happened. Whether judges have not received the guidelines from their clubs or are simply not reading them, in many cases unprepared judges are still in the ring.

While it's understandable that junior handling is not a priority during the planning of a show, it should be remembered that junior handling is more than a privilege or reward for the children competing. Ideally, clubs should recognize that juniors are the club members and dogshow stalwarts of tomorrow.

Running a show is made all the more difficult when organizers are expected to find knowledgeable and varied judges for junior handling, so could we not devise a system that provides show-giving clubs with a list of the approved and tested judges who are interested and available in their area? This would undoubtedly take some of the strain off the organizers because they will already be assured, to some extent, that available judges will be qualified for the assignment.

Although establishing such a system would require considerable planning and work, and it would initially be difficult to implement, I think it's plausible, and that juniors must get involved in putting it in place. It is not up to our parents or strangers to organize the things we want; we must take responsibility for ourselves. That is not to say that we will be able to do it all on our own, but it is our sport -- we must put some work into it.

There are many junior handling organizations and clubs across the country; it is through these bodies we can best express ourselves. This proposal may not be perfect, but it gives us all something to think about.

Clubs should recognize that juniors are the club members and dogshow stalwarts of tomorrow.

Amanda Kelly is 16 years old and is in grade 11. She is the secretary for the Nova Scotia Junior Handlers Association.

THE PET-CARE FORUM
ETHICAL ISSUES AWARD
OFFERED BY: THE VETERINARY INFORMATION NETWORK

For the most outstanding work with a strong ethical position in relation to dogs.

THE PERFECT PUPPY --
THE BREEDER'S JOB
by Marjorie Hudson
(SOUTHERN CALIFORNIA DOG)

A call came in to local dog trainer and consultant. "I sold an eight-week-old puppy to a family nine months ago. Now they want to return him and get their money back. They say he's defective. I need an objective evaluation of him. Will you do it?"

The first thing the consultant did was gather some history.

The Breeder: Fran

Although new to breeding, Fran admired the working Doberman and had decided that temperament was her first concern, followed by health and then conformation. This first litter was the result of painstaking research and soul searching decisions. She had certificates and test results saying all the dogs in both parents' pedigrees were clear of major health problems for two generations. Most of the dogs on each parent's pedigree had titles to attest to their working temperament.

The whelping had gone well. The dam had been a wonderful mother and disciplined the puppies appropriately.

The puppies had taken walks with Fran in the large yard and had enjoyed a variety of stimulating toys. They had been gently handled, held and cuddled.

"It's important for them to realize they are individuals," Fran said, "and I wanted to be sure they enjoyed close contact with people."

She said the puppies were outgoing like their dam and handled unexpected noises very well. That steadiness of nerve was what she had wanted from the sire, along with his high von Willebrand's ratings and strong hips.

"The puppies were just what Dobermans should be," Fran said with pride, "particularly the big black male. The other puppies were a bit milder. Both parents have advanced obedience titles so I'm sure they will be trainable," she concluded confidently.

The Buyers: Carl and Josie

Carl works long hours. His wife, Josie, is busy with the house and the schedules of three daughters aged seven through thirteen. Their first dog, a female Mastiff named Bertha, was inherited when she was two from a Hawaiibound brother. Carl and Josie described Bertha as a great "rug" dog, agreeable and relaxed. Because of her bark and size, they felt safe with her around. When Bertha died of old age at ten, the family wanted another dog.

They liked having a dog that made them feel safe. They also liked short hair. But with the children still growing, another 180-pound Mastiff seemed too much. They liked the idea of a Doberman.

An ad in the newspaper brought them to see Fran's puppies. The big, bold, black male caught Carl's eye right away. Carl said he was tired of being the only male in his family. He said they knew about a local training class and talked about their big back yard. The pup would have lots of company. He could sleep on a rug in the kitchen where Bertha had slept. Carl and Josie bought the puppy, and the girls named him Knight.

> He was so destructive he couldn't be in the house and so wild the girls wouldn't go in the yard.

The Problem

Fran did not hear from Carl and Josie until they called saying they wanted to return the eleven-month-old puppy. Knight, they claimed, was defective. He was so destructive he couldn't be in the house and so wild the girls wouldn't go in the yard. He was disobedient and had begun growling when they tried to discipline him. The family wanted Fran to take him back and "deal with him for a week." Then, they were sure, she would return their money. Fran decided to get an independent evaluation while the dog was with her.

Now the consultant had the history. It was time to meet the puppy.

The Puppy: Knight

Fran brought Knight back to her house to be evaluated. Knight leaped and bumped about with friendly enthusiasm. After a thorough investigation of the consultant, Knight seemed to be everywhere in the yard at once. For an hour, Fran and the consultant observed the youngster.

He jumped on the picnic table, barking at a person he saw beyond the board fence. Jumping off, he marked each fence post and tree in turn. Discovering a forgotten tug toy, he grabbed it and ran to Fran, nearly knocking her down. He shook it at her and pawed her legs trying to get her to play Tug of War. Fran told him to "sit." Knight looked directly at her, but instead of sitting he dropped the toy and ran off. He picked up a stick and shook that. He returned with the stick, and this time went to the consultant and sat.

The Evaluation

The consultant found Knight to be high spirited, assertive, sound and very energetic. He was definitely unruly, but he was in no way "defective." He was, in fact, everything the breed standard called for in a Doberman puppy: "energetic, watchful, determined, alert..."

Fran left with her puppy, reassured that her breeding had been sound. Knight was the quality puppy she had thought he was.

As the consultant waved good-by, he thought about what might have gone wrong for Fran, Carl, Josie and Knight.

Did The Breeder Do Her Job?

The steps Fran took in breeding and nurturing produced good Doberman puppies. She knew what kind of Doberman she wanted to produce and studied historical health and temperament data. The healthy, sound puppies fit her vision and the Doberman standard. The puppies had been well mothered and received the best of care, handling and environment. But even though she produced an excellent litter, Fran's job did not end here. There are additional steps which every breeder must take to insure the best prospects for the buyers and the puppy.

A responsible breeder will discuss the reality of living with a particular dog with prospective buyers. After a calm Mastiff, a Doberman could be like a splash of cold water. Wanting a particular breed is easy. Living with the traits of that breed may not be easy.

A concerned breeder will also make it clear what to expect from a dog bred for working drives. Dogs within a breed vary. One breeder's Dobermans are not the same as another breeder's. Fran's puppies were not going to be the easiest puppies to live with because of their stronger drives. Prospective owners need to know what type of puppies

As they grow into adults, puppies go through the same insecurities and testing for power that human children do. Any puppy can be difficult.

the breeder has bred. Then they can discuss whether the dogs are too strong or too mild for their needs and experience.

A thoughtful breeder will consider the buyer's previous experience with dogs. Living with an old dog with long established routines is much easier than living with a puppy which comes with no routine at all. Puppies can be vigorous with tremendous excitement and an assertive interest in everything. An older dog may have been better for Carl and Josie.

A good breeder will emphasize that a puppy needs his education started the moment he's brought home. A puppy needs to be taught household routines. A breeder may make enrollment in a puppy class and one or two obedience classes a condition of sale. Nothing is more painful to a breeder than to find that the perfect puppy she has reared has been given a raw deal by well-meaning owners who neglected to follow through on its education and then blame the puppy.

A thorough breeder will discuss what to expect when the puppy enters canine adolescence. As they grow into adults, puppies go through the same insecurities and testing for power that human children do. Any puppy can be difficult. A male Doberman can be a real juvenile delinquent if there is a lack of reliable leadership, structure and purpose in his life.

An experienced breeder will know her puppies well enough to show prospective buyers just the puppies that fit their situation. Puppies within a litter vary in temperament and personality. The mildest female might fit where the boldest male would not. A wise breeder has learned that a lost sale is better than a poor match.

A considerate breeder will provide a list of books that will support their buyers in understanding, raising and educating the new addition to the family.

The best breeders consider all these steps an essential part of their job. Many breeders don't. Why not?

It takes time, integrity, knowledge and a great deal of experience to be a good breeder and place puppies successfully. Many people who breed simply don't know enough. A successful breeder of show dogs may know little about temperament. A casual breeder may know nothing about training or health problems. Many people who breed don't know enough about breed traits, the significance of canine drives or the importance of individual differences in puppies. Many breeders do not have the facilities to keep puppies beyond 12 weeks and so need every sale. Some people who breed never expect to hear from the buyer again so they give little thought to the matches that are made.

Many prospective owners make it hard for all but the strongest breeders to do it right. They don't "hear" the breeder if she tries to tell them something they don't want to hear. They dismiss it as being irrelevant or fussy or snooty. And, they can say all the right things. With a beautiful puppy in their arms, they make promises and assurances, telling the breeder what they think she wants to hear — and what they would like to be true.

The sad part is that the breeders and owners usually have the best of intentions. In this case, Fran raised the perfect puppy. Carl and Josie wanted the perfect dog. And Knight got caught in the middle.

We wish we could report that when Carl and Josie realized that Knight was a good Doberman they decided to do whatever was necessary to educate themselves and their dog. That didn't happen.

The family didn't have time for the vigorous mental and physical exercise Knight needed. Although he was unruly, Knight was smart and trainable. But, he needed someone with the time and dedication to train him. No one in this busy household stepped forward. To ensure Knight's well being, Fran took him back. The family agreed to accept one half the price Fran received if he was resold.

The last time the consultant spoke with Fran, Knight was still with her, sharing house time with her breeding stock. He had been neutered and had some basic training. Fran was still hopeful that someone would come along who was willing to take on the challenge of a "reject."

Fran told the consultant she had a message on her answering machine, someone looking for an older dog. They were calling back at six. Maybe this phone call would be for Knight.

THE SANDOZ-JEFF'S COMPANION ANIMAL SHELTER AWARD

SPONSORED BY: SANDOZ PHARMACEUTICALS CORPORATION AND JEFF'S COMPANION ANIMAL SHELTER

To the best published work celebrating
the human/animal bond.

DOG PEOPLE
Michael J. Rosen, Editor

Illustrations by Amy & David Butler

INCLUDES WORKS BY:

Michael J. Rosen
Edward Albee
Christine Herman Merrill
Frederick Busch
Brian Hagiwara
Will Shively
Susan Conant
Robert Andrew Parker
Ann Beattie
Merrill Markoe
William Wegman
Dierdre McNamer
Franz Lidz
Jamie Wyeth
Daniel Pinkwater
Dan Yaccarino
Nancy Friday

... and others

ARTISAN - A DIVISION OF WORKMAN PUBLISHING CO.; NEW YORK

A TASTE OF *DOG PEOPLE*...

HARRY SIGHING *by Edward Albee*

Those of us who have lived with Irish Wolfhounds—and I have shared lives with seven, once three of them with me at the same time, more often two—know that the nonsense about we humans being sole possessors of consciousness is exactly that. All seven of my Irish friends possessed a consciousness—awareness of self, awareness of selflessness, awareness of mortality—far more persuasive than that of many people I have known.

Interesting books have been appearing recently about the lives of dogs—their minds, their habits, their needs. These books range from the rather rudely clinical to the mawkishly anthropomorphic, but they all are interesting, at least to those of us who feel incomplete without the company of a dog or two, or more.

When I was a child, my family kept Dalmatians (at the stable where they also kept saddle horses), Pekingese (distaff family here, the asthmatic dogs kept either in upstairs sitting rooms or in the crook of arms), and an unhappy Saint Bernard, who became fat and lazy, for he didn't get to run much or sink deep in snow, or rescue anybody, or anything.

So... I grew up with dogs. There were cats, too, as I recall, but my family did not let them in the house, rather as if they were raccoons, or opossums. I have tried, over the years, to make it up to cats by having them everywhere -- inside, outside, in my lady's chamber -- discovering that dogs and cats coexist splendidly, especially if they are eating from the same bowl, so to speak.

It was not until my (theoretical) adulthood, however, that the Irish Wolfhound and I met across that crowded room, our eyes locking.

There are problems with Irish Wolfhounds, and I would not deny them. They are very large animals and they take up a good deal of space; they are fond of beds and couches, but if they can be persuaded not to usurp these, they will settle for floors, if the floor areas they settle for are close to human feet. Their deeply friendly nature expresses itself in great, swathing tail wags that can clear a table of bibelots in a second—a perfect argument against bibelots, of course. They have,

as well, a great fondness for human food, and their height makes setting a buffet table hazardous. They will not put their paws up on the table and lean in, but if they are walking by and food is within reach, they assume it is there for them—and who is to say it is not? They are very fond of fruit, by the way; one of my dogs sat by pots of wild strawberries, waiting for the fruit to ripen; then he would nose in, carefully, and eat away. The greatest problem with Irish Wolfhounds, though, is that they don't live very long: their great hearts give out. A good deal of this is genetic, of course, but I think it is in part that they worry so for us, care so much.

And then there is the matter of the sighing. Dogs bark; they whimper; they groan; they growl. But Harry sighed... a lot. Harry was the first Irish Wolfhound I shared my life with, and he lived the longest of them all, dying finally at twelve—very, very old for an Irish Wolfhound.

He was terribly arthritic toward the end and clearly in considerable discomfort, and the unhappy sounds he made—standing up, for example—were not the sighs that distinguished him; these were real groans: "Oh, God, not another day with bones like this!" And I am not certain of the sound he made when I told him Hubert Humphrey had died (Harry was a liberal Democrat); perhaps a combination of groan and sigh.

No, I mean the real sigh sounds he made—when we would be sitting together looking out at the ocean and I would say, "Aren't those great waves!?" and he would lean against me a little and just... sigh; or, when he would be stretched out (after a meal?), all thirty-seven yards of him, and I would say, "Happy?" and a great rumbling sound would escape his throat, a deeper, less ruminative sound, but a sigh nonetheless.

I was sitting reading one afternoon by my pool, and Harry was nearby—say, five feet away—and I happened to look over at him; he was staring off into some middle distance, prone, front paws crossed, and he just... sighed. This sigh was not a reply; it was Harry sighing to himself over something.

I miss him a great deal.

THE SULFODENE/SCRATCHEX AWARD
FOR JOURNALISTIC EXCELLENCE IN DOG GROOMING AND SKIN CARE

For excellence in writing on the topics of dog grooming and skin care within the context of the responsible care of dogs.

TAMING THE HAIRY BEAST
by Toni Lett

(DOGS IN CANADA 1995 ANNUAL)

To suggest that grooming is merely brushing a dog would be akin to calling the Boston Marathon a nice little foot race. Grooming encompasses a broad array of practices, all of which are essential to the good health and well-being of your pet.

Consider grooming when considering breed choice. While there are certainly a number of low-maintenance breeds, in all of dogdom there is no such thing as a grooming-free species. Every dog requires regular care of feet, nails, ears, teeth, eyes and skin. And every dog, except hairless breeds, demands regular brushing.

The extent and frequency of brushing and bathing are directly determined by a breed's coat type. Generally speaking, the more coat a breed carries, the more intensive the grooming required. But there are always exceptions to the rule. For instance, many of the terrier breeds, like Airedales, and trimmed breeds, like Poodles, appear - in the finished picture - to have short to moderate length coats. Don't be misled; constant attention is required to keep them looking neat and tailored. The length of a dog's coat does not always correlate with the length of grooming time required; coat density and texture are also major factors. Take the Labrador Retriever, with his dense, double coat unless you prefer your couches and cuffs fur trimmed, you'll have to do regular, thorough grooming to remove dead coat and minimize shedding fallout.

A breed's maintenance requirements are as significant as other factors, like temperament and exercise needs, when choosing a pet. The best way to evaluate the amount of grooming required for a breed is to talk to several breeders. They should also be your num-

> Every dog requires regular care of feet, nails, ears, teeth, eyes and skin. And every dog, except hairless breeds, demands regular brushing.

ber-one source when it comes to learning how to care for your pet.

Most importantly, don't try to fool yourself because you have your heart set on a particular breed. Be ruthlessly honest when it comes to assessing the practicality of the breed vis-a-vis your lifestyle. Understand and accept that you are taking on a commitment that will last for the next 10 to 15 years.

If you do have a hankering for one of the more work-intensive breeds, breeders are a good source for handy tips and short cuts to cut down grooming time. While show dogs need a purist's approach, often pet dogs can benefit from tricks of the trade. For example, the neat jacket on a show terrier, which must be plucked and hand stripped into condition, can easily be shaved to give your pet a similar appearance. The hair on the inside of the back legs and belly of longer coated breeds can be removed to cut down on matting without detriment to the dog's appearance. Your own dog's breeder will have specific suggestions to help you in your grooming efforts.

Another consideration in your choice of breed is the cost related to grooming. Usually, the hairier the breed, the more equipment required. This should be taken into account when budgeting for the purchase of a dog. Since grooming of any puppy begins on day one, the purchase of puppy and equipment must coincide. To get an idea of how much you'll need to spend on your pet's grooming articles, talk to several breeders. Many furnish their puppy buyers with a shopping and source list for these products.

It might also be prudent, before you settle on the dog of your dreams, to ask several professional groomers their rates for your breed. No matter how well-intentioned and prepared you may be, situations do arise where you may have to seek outside help. Just as it's important to know how much you should anticipate paying for food and vet bills, it is also advisable to budget for the occasional trip to the groomer.

The Right Stuff

Grooming table - This is perhaps the most important piece of grooming equipment you may ever own. The basic functions of a grooming table are to elevate your dog to a height comfortable for the groomer (that's you) and to provide the dog with a nonslip surface. A clamp-on grooming arm with noose holds a fidgety dog still, allowing you free use of both hands.

All dogs are easier to control when elevated on a table, and your aching back will thank you for putting a merciful end to all that bending. Also, just as you would hardly expect your hairdresser to do your hair while you were lying on the floor, proper grooming demands that you deal with your subject at waist level for brushing and eye level for finishing.

As a safety precaution, never leave your dog on a grooming table unattended. He may accidently slip or step off, pulling the table down with him or, worse, hanging himself. Even if the dog is not secured, smaller breeds can break a leg jumping from this height.

Buying a grooming table doesn't have to involve a large expenditure. You can buy the convenient stock version, with its folding legs, for about $85 but, if you're handy, you can always build your own. A secure table will also work well, provided that it's not overly large and you cover the top with a nonslip surface. Rickety card tables defeat the purpose, as the dog will be anxious and insecure, making the grooming sessions stressful, if not downright unsafe.

Pin brush - A good pin brush, one with metal pins coming out of a rubber pad, is the fundamental tool for any long-to medium-coated breed. Avoid all-in-one versions that have a pin brush on one side and a bristle brush on the other. Not only do very few dogs require this combination, but such a brush is clunky and awkward to use.

Bristle brush - This is used primarily for short to medium-length coats. While, to some degree, it will remove tangles and dead coat, its chief function is to clean the coat and bring out the shine.

Slicker brush - This often-indispensable tool consists of fine wire pins bent at an angle approximately halfway down their length. These pins are anchored on a flat base. Like the pin brush, slickers come in various sizes and degrees of stiffness. The rule of thumb is that the stiffer the pins, the greater the amount of coat removed.

Gloves and rubber brushes - Surprisingly, many of the short-haired breeds can present the greatest shedding problems. Unlike the hairs of a woolly dog like the Old English Sheepdog, which can be rolled off, shorter coats tend to have needlelike hairs that penetrate fabric, making them much more difficult to remove. One of the easiest ways to stay on top of the shedding situation is with the frequent use of rubber brushes or hound gloves.

> Don't forget the details: Big dogs, small dogs, hairy dogs and sleek dogs all need regular attention to grooming of the feet, ears, eyes and teeth.

Two types of gloves are popular. The first is a two-sided mitt with one side covered in short, rough bristles and the opposing side surfaced with pins similar to those found on a slicker brush. The second version is the rubber hound mitt which, with its small knobs, is designed to drag loose hair out of the coat.

Combs - These are available in a wide variety of sizes, depending upon the breed and coat type. You'll probably want a fine comb for small jobs (around eyes and whiskers), as well as an all-purpose (or 'greyhound') comb, with finely-spaced tines at one end and wider-spaced tines at the other.

Mat combs - If you own one of the hairier breeds, you're bound to encounter mats from time to time. Occasionally, mats may become so thick and solid they are virtually impossible to pull apart by hand. This is when you'll want a mat splitter or mat comb. These devices look like combs, but have sharp tines designed to cut through mats, thus making them easier to pull apart and brush out.

Stripping knives - Primarily the equipment of terrier owners, stripping knives are used to pull out and reduce body coat and shape the longer coat. As there are a wide variety of knives available, each designed for a specific purpose or coat type, consult a reputable breeder with show-ring experience for guidance.

Clippers - While not a necessity, and indeed one of the most expensive grooming tools available, depending on your breed you may find a set of clippers to be a good investment. For keeping pet terrier coats looking tidy, clippers can offer a marvellous short cut around the work of hand stripping. Those with hairy breeds who plan to shear their dogs once or twice a year may find that, over time, clippers, compared to the cost of a professional groomer, will wind up saving you money.

The key word when purchasing clippers is quality. Cheap, nonprofessional grade clippers can't do the heavy-duty work involved in shaving dog coats, so go for the best you can afford. You will also need to purchase clipper blades. Seek the advice of experts, like breeders and groomers, as to which are most appropriate for your breed.

The majority of dogs hate having their feet touched and will fight anyone pawing their paws.

Grooming spray - The primary purpose of grooming spray is to reduce static in the coat during brushing. Today's grooming sprays have gone beyond this simple mandate. You will find sprays that clean the coat, reduce matting, and condition—some even offer a sunscreen. No matter which spray you find best for your dog, all have one common feature -they moisturize the coat, and thereby infuse the hair with greater elasticity. As a result, there is less coat breakage.

Don't forget the details: Big dogs, small dogs, hairy dogs and sleek dogs all need regular attention to grooming of the feet, ears, eyes and teeth.

Foot Care

Basic equipment: Nail clippers, nail files, cauterizing powder.

Method: Too often I see dogs, pampered a and well cared for, with feet, particularly nails, in atrocious condition. While I may sound like a zealot for reflexology, I firmly believe that the happiness and well-being of an animal starts with its feet. Imagine, if you will, how upbeat you would be if you had to function all day in ill-fitting shoes enclosing overgrown toenails. The same is obviously true of a dog.

The initial problem owners face, however, is that the majority of dogs hate having their feet touched and will fight anyone pawing their paws. Naturally, the more often the dog wins this battle, the more the owner caves in and the worse the problem becomes.

The process of trimming nails can also make some owners a bit squeamish. As anyone who has trimmed nails knows, there are times when, if you cut too close to the quick, the dog's nail will bleed not just a little, but enough to look like some pagan bloodletting.

Don't panic. Despite appearances, it's not that serious. Bleeding can be stopped short by packing the nail end with cauterizing powder; any pain inflicted by cutting too close is generally minimal and only temporary.

The bottom line is that if you are going to own a dog, you're going to have to cut its toenails. If your dog has white or clear nails, the job will be easier; you can see the pink quick and trim just beyond it. If your dog has dark nails, however, the best way to avoid cutting the quick is to trim just a little at a time until you reach the desired length. When trimming, don't forget to do the dewclaws, if your dog has them (the extra claw or fifth toe on the inside of the leg, usually removed when puppies are newborn). If left unattended, they can grow back and imbed themselves in the dog's leg.

If your dog puts up a particularly strong fight about having his nails trimmed, it may be best to have someone hold the dog for you. Also, as silly as it may sound, covering the dog's eyes with your hand so it can't see what's happening may make the process a lot more manageable.

After trimming, file away any rough edges. If you own a hairy dog, trim the hair away from around the centre pad of the dog's paw; it can become matted and uncomfortable for the dog. Stones and debris can also get trapped and tangled in the paw hair and contribute to lameness.

Naturally, the more often the dog wins this battle, the more the owner caves in and the worse the problem becomes.

Ear Care

Basic equipment: Cotton balls, rubbing alcohol or ear cleanser, tweezers.

Method: A dog's ears should be cleaned at least weekly. The best way to do this is to take a cotton ball saturated in a solution of one to three parts rubbing alcohol diluted with water. Thoroughly clean the underside of the ear flap and into the upper portion of the ear canal. Don't worry - you won't damage the ear by penetrating this upper portion.

Next, if you have a coated breed, it is advisable to remove excess hair from the ear canal. To do this, lightly dust the hair with baby powder, then gently pluck the hair out either with tweezers or by hand, a few strands at a time. If done patiently, this process should not be painful and can even be rather pleasing to the animal. Finish off by massaging an ear lotion into the ear canal. There are various types available, from those designed to simply soothe to others that treat specific problems, such as infections or mites.

Dental Care

Basic equipment: Tooth scaler, baking soda, rough cloth or gauze pad.

Method: Sorry, but a few dog biscuits at bedtime will not eliminate the need for regular dental care. In fact, with the high incidence of tooth and gum disease, particularly in older dogs, consistent care of the teeth is essential.

While there are many doggy dental products available, here is the most simple approach. First, check the teeth, front and side, for tartar and calcium buildup. Any chalky covering or brownish discoloured film on the teeth should be scraped away. You can use a dental tooth scaler, or even the edge of a thin coin. Try to get your instrument under the upper edge of the debris and firmly chip the substance off the tooth. Having done this, thoroughly 'brush' your dog's teeth using a rough cloth or gauze pad wrapped around your index finger and dipped into a paste of baking soda, salt and water. Depending upon the breed, and the size of your dog's mouth, a finger cot or child's toothbrush may be useful in carrying out the procedure. Maintenance of your dog's mouth can be done daily, but at the very least should be carried out once a week.

Eye Care

Basic equipment: Soft cloth.

Method: Many believe that the eyes arc the window to the soul and, in the case of canines, they are also a portal to your dog's health and well-being. Often, the onset of an illness can be observed and treated early on simply by noting a dullness in your dog's expression or change in his ordinary demeanour. Beyond this, care and attention to your dog's eyes should be a daily procedure.

Note first whether the eyes are bright, clear and free of discharge. It is normal for a dog to have a little 'sleep' or brownish substance at the inner corner of the eyes, and this should be removed. From time to time, you may also feel that your pet is in need of an eye wash. To do this, saturate a cotton ball with warm water and gently clean round the eye. If your dog has 'tear stains' or brownish discolouration of the coat under the eye, treat this area when bathing the dog, using a toothbrush and mild tearless shampoo to clean the coat.

When to Call for Help

When our schedules and routines are occasionally thrown off-kilter, we can usually take it in stride. But when it comes to your dog's grooming, a period of neglect can result in some very big problems that only the expert attention of a professional groomer can solve. If you do think it's time to call in the pros, you'll first want to do a bit of research to ensure that your pet is being placed in capable hands. Although professional groomers are not licensed like hairdressers, try to find one with 'CMG' after his name - it stands for Certified Master Groomer and means that the person has achieved a level of skill acknowledged by his peers. As well, seek out recommendations from your fellow pet owners, particularly those with the same breed. And finally, try to arrange an advance visit to the grooming shop to observe the general standards of professionalism employed in the operation.

Who to Call for Help

On the other hand, your grooming problems may just require input from those in the know. Most breed clubs can provide new owners with more detailed, step-by-step grooming guides. Another good source of information and hands-on guidance is your dog's breeder.

You can also go to a dog show and observe breeders and exhibitors in the grooming area. While most would be only too happy to help a novice in their own breed, bear in mind that they may be too busy to demonstrate techniques at the show. Accordingly, you may want to book an appointment to talk with them at their convenience. You should be prepared to pay for this consultation, just as you would pay to have someone actually groom your dog.

Toni Lett is a breeder, owner and handler of Old English Sheepdogs.

THE SCRATCHEX PET SAFETY AWARD

SPONSORED BY: SCRATCHEX

For the best article on the importance of pet identification.

SUGGESTIONS ON HOW TO AVOID TRAGEDY OF LOST PETS
by Ann Underwood
(THE BROOKFIELD JOURNAL)

Even in small communities, pet theft can be a problem. The unlawful taking of household pets is on the rise in this country and a few safeguards on the part of a pet owner now can prevent tragedy later.

Prevention is the first step. Know where your dog is at all times. Don't leave your dog tied to a tree outside, in the back of a pick up truck or even unsupervised in the back yard.

Spay or neuter your dog as this will cut down on the chance it will be stolen for breeding or fighting purposes.

Vary your dog's routine. Don't let him out every night at 9 p.m. for 20 minutes while you are inside the house. Have your pet tattooed and register the number (call 1-800 NDR DOGS to register or report found dogs).

If your pet disappears, move quickly before it has time to go far. Note that 90 percent of all dogs are found within two miles of where they were lost.

Mobilize help - family, neighbors, breed club members, and assign tasks to everyone.

Walk and drive through the neighborhood calling the pet. Be cautious when calling the pet near a busy intersection as he may run out into traffic. If the pet is friendly with strangers, check schools and playgrounds. Leave your gate open in case your pet returns home on his own.

Notify all residents in the imme-

> **Prevention is the first step. Know where your dog is at all times.**

> **If your pet disappears, move quickly before it has time to go far. Ninety percent of all dogs are found within two miles of where they were lost.**

diate area to be on the lookout for the dog, leaving a written description, name, vet's name and phone number. Some agencies suggest leaving an identifying mark or detail out of the flyers so that you can avoid being conned by individuals who may claim they have found your pet.

> Contact local animal hospitals, leaving information and stating that you will be responsible for any medical care your pet may need.

Contact local animal hospitals, leaving information and stating that you will be responsible for any medical care your pet may need.

If the animal is not found within a few hours, begin more thorough measures. Notify county animal control officials and all local animal shelters. Notify all law enforcement agencies. Police, highway patrol and sheriffs cover different areas.

Place advertisements in all local newspapers offering a reward for information leading to the pet's recovery.

> Make sure that you have good full body and closeup photos of your pet.

Check with radio and television stations because some broadcast news about missing pets. Contact local dog clubs and print and distribute flyers. Most people use about 2,000 flyers.

If the pet isn't recovered within several days or a week, it might have left the area or whoever found it might want to keep it. Remember, lost pets have been recovered up to 300 miles away from where they disappeared so expand the search to surrounding areas.

Make sure you can identify your dog without a doubt. Recently a police officer found his German Shepherd dog missing from his backyard. He located the dog but the new owner refused to give it back. The police officer took the man to court, but he was not able to prove to the judge's satisfaction that he was the dog's owner and the new owner got to keep the dog.

Make sure that you have good full body and close up shots of your pet. Tattoo animals with identifying numbers. It goes without saying that your pets should wear collars with identifying tags at all times. Animals must wear tags because they can't carry wallets.

Lastly, remember that although you may be angry with your pet for running away, be sure you let them know how happy you are to see him. It's a good idea to have a treat ready when you see your pet again.

Ann Underwood breeds and raises Golden Retrievers.

THE PRESIDENT'S AWARD

SPONSORED BY: RALSTON PURINA

Awarded by the DWAA president to that work deemed to be the best of the first-place winners: the best of the best.

OUR TEACHER, OUR DOG
by Joseph Cerquone

(THE WASHINGTON POST)

This article was also winner of Category 1-C Newpaper Editorial, Opinion Piece, Essay.
(Article on page 26.)

THE DWAA DISTINGUISHED SERVICE COMMUNICATOR'S AWARD

SPONSORED BY: THE UNITED KENNEL CLUB

Awarded to that individual who
through excellence in communication and conduct
promotes the best interests of the sport of dogs.

TOM O'SHEA

The Judges

I. Newspapers:

Beth Adelman	Kim Thornton	Maria Goodavage
William Patterson	Gary Wilkes	Ranny Green
Gerri Cadiz	Elizabeth Patterson	Phyllis Ripley

II. Magazines & Canine Newspapers:

Ellyce Kaluf	Susan Pearce	Sharon Lemon
Mary Warzeeha	Susand Conant	Julie Rach
Josephine Campbell	Paul Glassner	Bob Christiansen
Jane Earhardt	September Morn	Mary Thurston
Joe Fulda	Shirley Thayer	Paulette Cooper
Gary Wilkes	Kent Dannen	Laurien Berenson
Gerri Cadiz	Amy Shojai	Steve Dale
Larry Shook	Marilyn Miller	Lyn Richards
Bette LaGow	Kim Thornton	Gina Spadafori

III. Club Publications:

Lisa Hanks	Jane Earhardt	Christine Maxfield-Stone
Marcia King	Bette LaGow	Mary Warzecha
Phyllis Ripley	Josephine Campbell	Faith Uridel
Vicki Hogue	Joe Fulda	Sharon Lemon
Beth Adelman	Ellyce Kaluf	

IV. Books:

Audrey Pavia	Liz Palika	Kim Thornton
Kathleen Wood	Kathy Diamond Davis	Kent Dannen
Mary Burch	Cheryl Smith	Bob Christiansen
Mary Ellen Tarman	Amy Shojai	Lisa Hanks

V. Graphic Arts, Short Fiction, Pamphlets, Poetry:

Dominique DeVito	Michael Siino	Faith Uridel
Gina Spadafori	Susan Conant	Jacqueline O'Neil
David Blum	Vicki Hogue	Debbie Eldredge, DVM
Jerry Thornton	Marion Lane	Rosemarie Craver
Moira Harris		

VI. Videotapes:

Paulette Cooper
Darlene Arden

***Thank you, judges, for giving so generously of
your time and energy!***

NOTES